DATE DUE

D1548664

Food Goals,
Future Structural Changes,
and Agricultural Policy:
A National Basebook

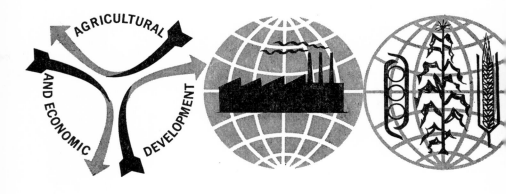

Iowa State University Press,
Ames, Iowa, U.S.A.

Iowa, State University *of Science and Technology, Ames.*
Center for Agricultural
and Economic
Development

Food Goals, Future Structural Changes, and Agricultural Policy: A National Basebook

Organizational Committee: **EARL O. HEADY, LUTHER TWEETEN, JOSEPH ACKERMAN, ELDON WEEKS, W. G. STUCKY, DON KALDOR, WALLACE OGG, LEO V. MAYER, DON WINKELMANN,** and **ROSS TALBOT.**

Volume Editor: **DONALD J. HUNTER**

Other publications of the Center for Agricultural and Economic Adjustment are available from the Iowa State University Press as follows:

Adjustments in Agriculture: A National Basebook, 1961
Food: One Tool in International Economic Development, 1963
Farmers in the Market Economy, 1964
Farm Goals in Conflict, 1964
Our Changing Rural Society, 1964
Economic Development of Agriculture, 1965
Family Mobility in Our Dynamic Society, 1965
Research and Education for Regional and Area Development, 1966
World Food Production and Needs, 1967

The work of the Center is supported in part by a grant from the W. K. Kellogg Foundation.

Composed and printed by
The Iowa State University Press
First edition, 1969

Standard Book Number: 8138–0665–8
Library of Congress Catalog Card Number: 69–17666

Preface

THIS MONOGRAPH was planned and written to provide better bases for evaluating and formulating long-run policies for U.S. agriculture. The problems of agriculture with us today are largely the same as those of three decades back, just as are the policies which we employ. True, some facets of both problems and policies have changed with time, but the core remains the same.

Since our initiation of short-run policies to cope with the problems of surpluses and large production capacity, nearly a whole generation of farmers has entered and left the industry. Hence, both the problems and policies appear to be longer lived than farmers. Yet our policies remain largely short-run in nature. Should we continue this short-run set, or should we admit the permanence of the variables or basic causes underlying the problems and adapt policy accordingly? Since the outset of such programs in the early 1930's we have invested around $60 billion in policies to contain production, dispose of surpluses, and stabilize prices. With current levels of expenditures, we could spend a similar amount over the next fifteen years and still have the problem with us. Should we do so, or should we look to other policy means and broaden the definition of the farm problem?

True, the initiation of a policy or set of policies need not presuppose some terminable data. For example, public choice and policy supporting the availability of free elementary and

v

secondary education to all persons did not presuppose that this policy must be terminated at some future date. It has been continued and obviously will be for the future. But under the changes in the demand for education and the changing productivity of trained persons in different fields and other magnitudes, the policy has been adapted. Much of the change in education relates to economic growth, including both the rising demand for it and the growing awareness of its role and importance in further development.

Similarly, the initiation of agricultural policies need not presuppose a future termination for all policy directed at farmers. Few would argue, for example, that public subsidy and generation of research and extension education should be terminated just because it was started a century back.

It is true, however, that the basic farm problem is both broader and more permanent than was realized when our initial supply control and price supporting legislation was inaugurated. It is more permanent because it is, itself, a product of economic development. The declining real price and growing productivity of modern capital technology are strong incentives to individual farmers. They search them out and adapt them rapidly, even when they are expressing dire concern over production surpluses and low prices. But these capital technologies are equally strong substitutes for both land and labor in the agricultural industry. If the land remains in production, supply is augmented against a more slowly growing domestic demand, and prices and incomes are depressed accordingly. If labor does not migrate as rapidly as it is replaced by capital technology, it suffers a lower real income than is consistent with growing per capita income in a highly developed economy. And the marginal returns from new technology, and support prices as well, become capitalized into land. The capital technology brings high fixed costs which can be spread over a sufficiently large volume to provide a profit margin under competitive conditions only if farms are larger. And farmers respond readily to these stimuli, even though it means larger farms and fewer of them.

These shifts in relative resources, prices, and productivities, and the changing farm structure and supply conditions which attach to them, are "permanent fixtures" of economic growth. They will intensify rather than evaporate under further economic growth. But as they do so, they broaden the problems which surround agriculture. The population decline on farms reduces the opportunities over the entire rural sector, often bringing income pressure on the businesses and families of rural communities. It is no longer possible or useful to separate the problems of the rural community from those of the farm.

Important problems in the equitable distribution of the costs and gains of technical and economic progress impinge broadly over agriculture and the rural community. Without appropriate policies, consumers gain in the form of lower real or absolute prices for food while farmers sacrifice in income. Families of rural towns sacrifice similarly. With some types of policies, farmers can gain along with consumers, but rural towns bear the cost as farms expand and farm families move from the community. One task of policy, then, is to find programs which distribute the gains and costs of technical change and economic development equitably over the whole population, rather than to have all the gains go to some groups while the major costs and sacrifices are the reward of another group. It is unlikely that efficient long-run policies will ever come into being, unless equitable distributions of the cost and benefits of farm technological change are attained over all segments of the rural community.

With this permanence of the forces bringing about structural changes for the future, where should we now go with agricultural policy? Perhaps it is true that the major core of our existing policies is an extension of the past. We thought then that the problem of excess capacity and burdened prices were temporary phenomena. If we could just curtail output and support prices for a short time, things would soon right themselves. Recent concern over the world food situation has renewed this hope—and perhaps the short-run policies which go with it.

Our concentration on short-run policies has been so great that we have too long neglected the rural community, the major recipient of the ongoing structural change in farming. Similarly, we have too long neglected those persons who represent the surplus labor replaced by modern farm technology and changing resource prices. Our city riots may be partly a manifestation of unskilled farm workers fed into a cultural setting to which they are not adjusted.

In any case, a broader and longer view of our farm policy seems in order. What adaptations should be made in it, against the prospects of farm structural changes in the future? Does the world food situation provide a different perspective on possibilities and needs than it did a decade back? How do we adapt policies to those displaced laborers and country merchants with declining business and asset values who bear the deep costs of farming advance? How do we maintain or improve the quality of life and services in the declining rural community? How do we adapt institutions to accommodate these changes and allow a more equitable distribution of the costs and benefits of further change to all relevant groups in farming and the rural community? In short, against our experiences and accumulated costs, what kind of long-run agricultural policies do we need for the future?

The chapters and authors of this book were selected to provide insights and, where possible, answers for these problems. The activity was planned by a committee which included Luther Tweeten, Joe Ackerman, Eldon Weeks, W. G. Stucky, Don Kaldor, Wallace Ogg, Leo Mayer, Don Winkelmann, Ross Talbot, and Earl O. Heady. The chapters were first assigned to individual authors. After early drafts were completed, the authors met in Chicago for three days to evaluate the analyses and provide guidelines for revisions. The chapters which follow are the product of this collective activity.

Donald J. Hunter served as editor of the final drafts.

EARL O. HEADY
Executive Director, Center for
Agricultural and Economic
Development

Contents

ix

Food Goals, Future Structural Changes, and Agricultural Policy: A National Basebook

CHAPTER ONE

The World Food Situation and Its Meaning to the U.S. Agricultural Establishment

H. C. WILLIAMS and R. W. SHERMAN

THE WORLD has always been short of food if the shortage is measured by the amount and quality necessary for adequate dietary standards. Based on what people would like (if income were no more a barrier to food purchases than in the high-income areas of the world), the shortage is almost unbelievable. Malthus thought we would never have more than the barest necessities to sustain life except for relatively short periods and in a few areas of the world. His predictions were based on what he saw in the latter part of the 18th century and on his knowledge of the history of food supplies. At that time, there were about 900 million people in the world. He saw most of them less than well fed except in some of the "newer" areas such as North America.

Today, we know that at least 2 billion people are poorly fed and many of these barely at subsistence levels. This is three or four times as many underfed people as Malthus saw less than two centuries ago. Probably a billion people are better fed now than anyone in Malthus' time. The 2 billion hungry are probably as hungry as the most underfed of his time. Viewed as a world problem, the food situation now is much more serious than in Malthus' time because so many more people are under-nourished. The only solace is that we now have much more advanced technology available to be drawn on when underfed areas are able to take advantage of it.

The hunger problem of the world gets larger as population in the underdeveloped areas increases by about 30 million each year. Per capita shortage in the hunger areas changes little, simply because those people are not able to live below their subsistence levels.

In the past six or seven years, the number of "hungry" people in the world has increased in numbers equal to the present U.S. population. The present shortage must be met and then the problem must be solved further by increasing food production each year sufficient to take care of the needs of the growing world population.

Estimates of future world population as well as that for individual countries or areas differ widely. For example, three authors (3, 4, 16)* looking into world food needs differed by as much as 40 percent in their estimates of probable world population by the year 2000. One used a graphic presentation showing a population well in excess of 6 billion by 2000. Another estimated slightly less than 6 billion, and the third one estimated 4.527 billion. The lowest prediction (by Donald J. Bogue) was accompanied by the prediction that: "It is now technologically possible and operationally plausible that the world population growth will slacken at a pace such that it will equal about 5 billion persons in the year 2000, and when this point is reached, growth rates in all of the major world regions will have declined to zero or so very nearly so that there will be little anxiety about a population crisis."

The ability of the world, and more especially that of the underdeveloped areas, to adequately feed people would be enhanced by slowing down population increase. In recent times, population has increased at a rate which has made it difficult for advancement in food production techniques to do anything at all in increasing food supply per capita. Malthus seems to have been a true prophet. Little doubt exists that a program to raise dietary levels should include some population control measures. Most

---

* Numerals within parentheses indicate the number of the reference cited at the end of each chapter.

areas which have improved their diets in quality and quantity in recent history have done so at the same time that their population growth has slowed significantly.

It is highly improbable that the high rates of population increase in most underdeveloped areas can be sustained over a long period without serious consequences to food supplies. Effects of efforts to slow population growth can only be conjectural, but the chances seem much greater that growth rate will slow rather than continue at present rates. Conscious efforts toward this end will have some effect. Food shortages themselves may become a positive check of an extremely undesirable Malthusian nature.

In the majority of the underdeveloped areas of the world, food production per capita increased a little faster than population during the period 1948 to 1963 (11). However, the last half of the period showed a marked slowing in this increase, and since 1963, we have seen a decreasing crop output per capita in the areas representing a large part of the population of underdeveloped areas. In India and Pakistan—with half the population in such areas of the free world—more than 50 percent of the increased production came from added acres. Such expansion cannot go much further in these areas. In the future, more emphasis on increasing yields per acre will be necessary.

With the increasing demand for food that has come about in some of the developing areas, agricultural production has been unable to supply the demand and this has resulted in an increase in net import of food. Such importation has been especially noticeable in Japan and Israel where industrialization has made trade possible. In other countries where less industrialization exists and where income per capita has made modest gains, import of food has not increased. Increased demand has had to be supplied by indigenous production.

In countries with primarily agrarian economies, population increases must be fed by their own production. Also, most increases in real income in these countries must come from agricultural production until increased industrialization has been accomplished. This means that for short-run progress in real income, they will have to step up agricultural production faster than population increase. Also, there is little historical evidence to indicate that import of food by low-income areas will do much to affect food supplies in those areas.

Predictions placing world population by the year 2000 at 6

billions or over, are based on rates which indicate 84 percent of the increase in the less developed areas or an increase of about 110 percent in areas where food is now inadequate.

The population prediction of less than 5 billion in the year 2000 placed 76 percent of the total increase in the less developed areas with an increase in those areas of 43 percent from 1965 to the year 2000.

Therefore, we find a range of predictions indicating an increase of from a little more than one billion to 2.5 billion in the less developed areas. Increasing food production to feed the population increase in such areas would depend greatly on which of the predictions proved more nearly correct. In either case, the problem is one of major proportions. Those predictions placing population at 6 billion or more by the year 2000 also predict no change in rate of increase even by that time. With such a rate continuing, there is little doubt that world food problems would be insoluble short of dramatic discoveries making synthetic food production possible and at a very low cost. It can be questioned whether or not the higher population predictions for the year 2000 can materialize unless food production of the world is doubled. As a result, the food problem of the world would be more than twice the present magnitude because most of the population increase will be in the deficit areas. It isn't merely a question of how to feed 6 billion people but whether food production will increase enough to allow a population of that magnitude.

What problems of food production are posed by predicted population for the year 2000? Without searching analysis, it seems that a big increase in world population would provide a wonderful opportunity for a market for surplus-producing areas. But as stated in other places in this chapter, world food trade has shown little tendency to increase percentagewise. Unless such trade can be increased much beyond the present 7 percent of world production, the problem of production will have to be solved in the areas where food is needed, not from present surplus-producing areas. Naturally, the potential market will increase but potentials do not constitute a market nor a supply for deficit areas.

If the United States could double its food production by the year 2000, while the population is increasing about 40 percent, it would seem that our exports might be expanded, both on a percentage and value basis, well beyond the present exports. Assuming this doubling in food production ability (without

greatly affecting cost per unit) then the only deterrent to increased exports would be that of a lack of effective demand or a
discontinuation of a costly subsidy for exports. The latter is a
political decision and beyond prediction by economists. What
then can be predicted about effective demand by needy areas?

Since most of the effective demand for food imports has been
by wealthy countries, it becomes almost self evident that, unless
the food shortage areas become much more affluent, no big demand increase will come from less developed areas. Commercial
food exports to any of the needy areas have been so low as to be
of relatively little significance in our agricultural exports—something less than 25 cents per person in those areas in 1965. Our
commercial exports to the 10 best customers for our agricultural
exports amounted to $9.30 per capita. To date then, the really
important buyers for agricultural products of the United States
have been European countries plus Japan and Canada.

There is no denying the tremendous potential demand from
the increase in population in underdeveloped areas. Assuming
that these areas add 1.5 billion to their population by the year
2000, it would take the equivalent of 20 billion bushels of wheat
to furnish 2500 calories per day for these added people—in addition to the protein and fats necessary. It is not idle speculation
to say that very few of these calories can come from U.S. agriculture. With a reasonable amount of purchasing power, the shortage areas could absorb all the potential production of the United
States and still not alleviate their basic problem.

Much more important to U.S. agriculture is the projected
increase in population in European countries where there is
sufficient wealth to pay for their food imports. Most of our
increase in food exports for dollars will go to wealthy areas. The
needy areas will be a market for U.S. agricultural exports, depending almost exclusively on subsidies for many years.

THE FOOD SHORTAGE PROBLEM

"The World Food Budget, 1962 and 1966," published by the
United States Department of Agriculture in 1961, states that
"For most of the 70 less-developed countries in the semi-tropical
and tropical southern areas, diets are nutritionally inadequate
with shortage in proteins, fat and calories." This publication
goes into detail in estimating what it would take to wipe out
these shortages—based on minimal standards of diet. Standards
used in that report are surely so low as to constitute a small pal-

liative to hungry people. Nonetheless, it is an attempt to point up where the needs are and how they might be met.

Protein shortage, according to the publication mentioned above, includes a serious lack of protein from both animal and pulse (such edible leguminous crops as peas, beans, and lentils) sources. (According to minimal standards proposed by the National Research Council, each person should have within his total protein requirements 7 grams from animal sources and a total from animal and pulse sources combined of 17 grams per day.) The shortage of animal and pulse protein could be filled by the use of the dried skim milk from about 50 billion pounds of whole milk. This would be supplemented with about 7 million bushels of dry beans and peas. The remainder of the protein shortage would be supplied from the increase in cereal foods, such as wheat. These would be required to raise calorie intake to a satisfactory level.

In "The World Food Budget, 1962 and 1966," minimal calorie "requirement" or "reference standards" were calculated to "represent physiological requirements for normal activity and health, taking account of regional variations in environmental temperature, body weights, and by age and sex of the national population." Note that "normal activity" was the activity criterion. The standard for the Far East, including Communist Asia, was 2300 calories per day per person.

This standard includes not enough calories—regardless of size of people and the country's climate—for a population which still depends on human energy for so much of their power supply in production. There is no area of the world with an abundance of food where calorie intake is anywhere near this low. In fact 3000 calories are demanded in countries where food is plentiful and only a minimum of physical labor is required in production of goods. Bringing calorie supply up to a reasonable level is by far the biggest problem to be solved. It seems entirely realistic to think of 2500 calories instead of 2300 per day per capita as a reasonable minimum for all areas of the world.

To bring present population of all underfed—or undernourished—areas up to 2500 calories per day per capita would require an additional 4.6 billion bushels of wheat or its equivalent annually in other cereals. This would be lowered slightly when fat shortages were eliminated because calories would be gained from the additional fat consumption.

A summary, then, of major foods required to bring the world

up to a minimal level, including 2500 calories per day per person, would be:

4,250,000,000 bushels of wheat or equivalent
800,000,000 bushels of soybeans or equivalent
50,000,000,000 pounds of milk or equivalent
7,000,000 bushels of peas or beans or other pulses

At present world prices, this total would have a value in excess of $10 billion, exclusive of processing and transportation cost.

These amounts would bring food supplies up to minimal nutritional levels and 2500 calories per person per day (average) if no losses occurred in distribution and each person got the minimum. Probably at least 20 to 25 percent more than these amounts would be necessary to make sure that most of the poorly fed were provided the minimal diet and allow those people in the poorly fed areas who are presently consuming above average diets to continue to do so.

How much of these food products necessary to meet the minimum could the farmers of the United States supply? At present, the United States produces 1.25 billion bushels of wheat, of which about half can be exported. Most or all of this is already being exported. Most of the deficiencies in terms of wheat would have to come from increases above our present production. U.S. wheat production or substitute cereals would have to be quadrupled. At present, we are using 50 million acres for our wheat production. The increase would take at least 150 million acres. Such acreage increase would necessarily come partly at the expense of other crops. At present this would not be possible since there is not much more than 350 million acres of good cropland in the United States. At best, wheat acreage might be doubled, but even this would require considerable readjustment of land use.

Adding 800 million bushels of soybeans to our present production would double our present output. It would require another 30 million acres of good land. This could be done, but would require considerable time and further adjustment in use of land.

The necessary increase in production of beans and peas would be relatively easy to accomplish. Increasing production of milk by 50 to 60 billion pounds or more might be possible, but would require from five to ten years to accomplish. Large shifts in land resources would be necessary to produce required feed-stuffs. This would be in competition with wheat and other cereal production.

Strain on prices of all food products would be very great as a result of increasing production of the beans, peas, soybeans, milk, and even as little as one-third of the added cereal needed to supply the production shown above. The accompanying rise in food production costs would be an extreme burden to U.S. consumers unless technology advanced sharply beyond present expectations.

Some small amount of the shortages might be met from products other than those mentioned, but such amount would be of a minor nature. Those used in the above illustration are probably the most efficient in the United States for production of food to relieve world food shortages.

If we start with the premise that only the free world (excluding Communist China, etc.) will be helped by our production, it would take only about 60 percent as much food. The cost then would be about $6.5 billion at present prices, not including processing and marketing costs. These costs might well be increased by a substantial amount due to added cost of increasing production by such a magnitude.

What chance is there that the world can ever be very well fed? We might look at several levels of nutrition and what it would take in increases of production to supply the diet. Even in the United States with our present consumption, some improvements are needed. Our average of 3100 calories per day per capita is no doubt adequate as an average. The quality of diet of many is not adequate and a small percentage is somewhat deficient in calorie intake. It would be a very difficult task in any country to make sure everyone was well fed.

To supply 3000 calories for each person in the world would require more than 9 billion bushels of wheat or its equivalent in addition to present production. This is well beyond any possibility of production in the United States—but perhaps not for the world if resources were properly used.

To supply everyone in the world with a diet similar to that of the people of the United States would require almost three times the present world crop production. In terms of total cereals to furnish this, it would require about 100 billion bushels increase in production. Present world production of all cereal crops is 34 billion bushels, of which almost half is wheat and rice. The United States produces approximately 7 billion bushels of cereals. We can be sure that the world as a whole will not, at least in the foreseeable future, eat either the quantity and quality of food consumed in the United States or in other well-fed areas.

All calculations were made on the basis of present populations. However, we are adding about 30 million people per year in the underfed countries. This yearly increment in poorly nourished people would require almost 500 million bushels of wheat or its equivalent for 3000 calories per day per capita and a proportionate increase in other products to satisfy protein and fat requirements.

U.S. AGRICULTURAL EXPORTS

The United States is the world's largest exporter of agricultural products. It accounts for one-fifth of all agricultural commodities entering free world trade. The value of exports in fiscal year 1965–66 was $6.7 billion, up 10 percent from the previous year. In the most recent fiscal year—1966–67—exports were expected to rise an additional 6 percent to slightly more than $7 billion. Over the past 12 years, there has been a steady growth in total exports (Table 1.1). Agricultural exports have about doubled since World War II. Since 1951, they have increased at an average annual rate of slightly more than 4 percent.

For an understanding of the reasons for the steady growth in exports, it is essential to go beyond these highly aggregative figures. It is necessary to consider the types of exports, the markets for U.S. agricultural exports, and the commodities exported.

Exports from the United States are of two general types—commercial sales for dollars and concessional sales and donations. A discussion of each follows.

COMMERCIAL SALES

Commercial sales for dollars have more than doubled since 1951. It should be noted that most of this increase came during the 1960's. Actually, there was a decline during most of the 1950's, with exports not surpassing the 1952 level until 1962. During the last four years, commercial exports have accounted for 70 percent or more of the total. Since 1954, they have accounted for 69 percent of the cumulative value of total exports. Over the last six years, increases in total exports have been due to increases in commercial exports. Exports under governmental programs have remained fairly constant.

TABLE 1.1.   U.S. agricultural exports: value of commercial sales for dollars and government programs, years ending June 30, 1951–66*

Year Ended June 30	Total Exports	Commercial Sales for Dollars†	Under Government Programs‡
		(million dollars)	
1951	3,411	2,215	1,196
1952	4,053	3,430	623
1953	2,819	2,369	450
1954	2,936	2,331	605
1955	3,144	2,278	866
1956	3,496	2,129	1,367
1957	4,728	2,771	1,957
1958	4,003	2,752	1,251
1959	3,719	2,465	1,254
1960	4,517	3,207	1,310
1961	4,946	3,374	1,572
1962	5,142	3,482	1,660
1963	5,078	3,539	1,549
1964	6,067	4,481	1,586
1965	6,096	4,426	1,670
1966	6,681	5,066	1,615

* Source: Foreign Agricultural Trade of the U.S., USDA, Nov., 1966, p. 47.
† Commercial sales for dollars include, in addition to unassisted commercial transactions, shipments of some commodities with governmental assistance in the form of (a) credits for relatively short periods; (b) sales of government-owned commodities at less-than-domestic market prices; and (c) export payments in cash or in kind.
‡ Sales for foreign currency, barter, and donations.

This export pattern is associated with developments in Western Europe, Canada, and Japan, our leading market areas. During recovery from World War II in Western Europe and Japan, there existed a need for imported agricultural products to meet deficits in internal production. Recovery initially brought increased productivity which reduced reliance upon imported agricultural products. The rapid growth in income per capita led to substitution in diets of livestock products for cereals which increased the derived demand for cereals. Supporting evidence for this is found in the changing agricultural product mix exported.

Japan is and has been our leading market for commercial sales since 1961. In fiscal year 1966, it was the destination of $900 million of agricultural exports. This value accounted for 13.5 percent of total exports and 17.8 percent of commercial exports. Eight of our other nine best markets are located in Western Europe, five of which are members of the European Economic Community (Table 1.2.).

TABLE 1.2. Leading dollar markets for U.S. agricultural exports, fiscal year 1966*

Country	Sales for Dollars	
	(million dollars)	*(percent)*
Japan	900	17.8
Canada	630†	12.4
Netherlands	513	10.1
West Germany	468	9.3
United Kingdom	417	8.2
Italy—including Trieste	273	5.4
Spain	192	3.8
Belgium-Luxembourg	183	3.6
France	142	2.8
Denmark	85	1.7
Other	1,263	24.9
Total	5,066	100.0

* Source: Foreign Trade of the United States, EFS, USDA, Nov., 1966, p. 35.
† Includes the estimated value of U.S. exports to Canada of grains and soybeans for finishing the loading at Canadian ports of vessels moving through the St. Lawrence Seaway, $148 million.

EXPORTS UNDER GOVERNMENTAL PROGRAMS

The Mutual Security Act of 1951 and the Agricultural Trade and Development Act of 1954, better known as Public Law 480, and their subsequent amendments assisted in maintaining the level of exports experienced during World War II under the Lend-Lease Program. The Mutual Security Program at the outset was a general assistance program to friendly nations for the purpose of increasing their security as well as our own. However, amendments, especially Section 550 of P.L. 118 and Section 402 of P.L. 665, to the Act made possible increased exports of agricultural products.

Exports under governmental programs in 1951 were valued at $1.2 billion. There was a sharp decrease in exports in 1952 from the previous year, a drop associated with the rapid European recovery and the slackening in foreign demand. The Korean conflict did increase foreign demand but the increase was not sufficient to restore exports to the level of 1951.

In the meantime, U.S. farm production began its rapid march ahead of both domestic and foreign demand. This growing imbalance between supply and demand brought on an awareness for the need for corrective measures. The decision reached was one that directed the growing agricultural abundance toward foreign assistance programs. This marked the beginning of increased reliance on these programs for food disposal.

TABLE 13. U.S. exports under specified government financed programs, exports outside specified government-financed programs, and total agricultural exports: value and percent of total, years ending June 30, 1955 through 1966*

Type of Export	1955	1956	1957	1958	1959	1960	1961	1962	1963	1964	1965	1966	1955–1966
						(million dollars)							
Public Law 480													
Title I, sales for foreign currency	73	439	909	659	725	826	952	1,024	1,085	1,064	1,135	864	9,755
Title II, disaster relief	83	91	88	92	56	65	146	176	159	150	72	150	1,328
Title III, donations	135	184	165	173	131	105	144	169	170	189	179	171	1,915
Title III, barter	125	298	401	100	132	149	144	198	60	112	130	227	2,076
Title IV, long-term supply and dollar credit sales	....	....	....	....	....	....	....	19	58	47	151	161	436
Total Public Law 480	416	1,012	1,563	1,024	1,044	1,145	1,386	1,586	1,532	1,562	1,667	1,573	15,510
Mutual Security (AID), Secs. 402 and 550, sales for foreign currency and economic aid†	450	355	394	227	210	167	186	74	14	24	26	42	2,169
Total exports under specified government-financed programs	866	1,367	1,957	1,251	1,254	1,312	1,572	1,660	1,546	1,586	1,693	1,615	17,679
Total exports outside specified government-financed programs‡	2,278	2,129	2,771	2,752	2,465	3,205	3,374	3,482	3,532	4,481	4,404	5,066	39,939
Total agricultural exports	3,144	3,496	4,728	4,003	3,719	4,517	4,946	5,142	5,078	6,064	6,097	6,681	57,618
						(percent of total)							
Public Law 480													
Title I, sales for foreign currency	2	13	19	16	20	18	19	20	21	17	19	13	17
Title II, disaster relief	3	3	2	2	1	2	3	4	3	3	1	2	2
Title III, donations	4	5	4	4	3	2	3	3	4	3	3	3	3

TABLE 1.3 (*Continued*)

Type of Export	1955	1956	1957	1958	1959	1960	1961	1962	1963	1964	1965	1966	1955–1966
Title III, barter	4	8	8	3	4	3	3	4	1	2	2	3	4
Title IV, long-term supply and dollar credit sales	...	...	...	...	...	...	...§	1	1	3	2	1	...
Total Public Law 480	13	29	33	25	28	25	28	31	30	26	28	23	27
Mutual Security (AID), Secs. 402 and 550 sales for foreign currency and economic aid	14	10	8	6	6	4	4	1	§	§	§	1	4
Total exports under specified government financed programs	27	39	41	31	34	29	32	32	30	26	28	24	31
Total exports outside specified government-financed programs	73	61	59	69	66	71	68	68	70	74	72	76	69
Total agricultural exports	100	100	100	100	100	100	100	100	100	100	100	100	100

* Source: Foreign Agricultural Role of the United States, Econ. Res. Ser., USDA, Nov., 1966, p. 23, Table 3.

† Values shown are disbursements for exports.

‡ Exports "outside specified government programs" (sales for dollars) include, in addition to unassisted commercial transactions, shipments of some commodities with governmental assistance in the form of (a) extension of credit and credit guarantees for relatively short periods, (b) sales of government-owned commodities at less than domestic market prices, and (c) export payments in cash or kind.

§ Less than one-half percent.

The Mutual Security Acts of 1953 (Section 550) and 1954 (Section 402) specifically provided for the sales of surplus agricultural commodities. The 1953 Act provided for not less than $100 million and not more than $250 million for the purchase of these commodities. The 1954 Act provided for not less than $350 million. Both of the Acts provided for the sale of these commodities for local currencies, with these proceeds to be used for furthering the objectives of the Mutual Security Program.

Under the program, agricultural products shipped and financed up to 1959 included: wheat, $1.8 billion; cotton, $2.5 billion; fats and oils, $519 million; and corn, $436 million (18). There has been a rather steady decline in exports under this program with more exports moving under P.L. 480.

When P.L. 480 was passed its primary purpose was to use the foreign assistance program for the utilization of domestic agricultural surpluses. In addition to surplus disposal, the act and its amendments provide for many other activities. These include: development of new markets, or the expansion of old markets for U.S. farm products; promoting economic development and trade among friendly nations; international educational exchange and translation of books and periodicals; collecting and disseminating technical information; marketing, utilization, agricultural and other types of research, and others. It should be noted that restrictions were placed on the kinds of research that could be undertaken. The emphasis was on increasing markets for U.S. farm products.

The original act contained three titles. Title I provided for the sale of agricultural commodities in the currency of the recipient country. Title II authorized grants of surplus commodities from CCC stocks for famine and other emergency relief. Title III provided for CCC-owned stocks to be used for domestic and foreign donation programs. Further, it permitted barter for an equivalent value of strategic or other materials. In 1959, Title IV was added which authorized long-term supply and dollar credit sales to friendly governments. In 1962, Title IV was extended to include private trade.

Actual shipments under P.L. 480 did not begin until 1955. In 1956, sales under governmental programs reached the level of 1951. As Table 1.3 indicates, through June, 1966, $15.5 billion or 27 percent of total agricultural exports moved under this program. Title I exports were more important, accounting for 17 percent of total and 63 percent of P.L. 480 exports. Title III

TABLE 1.4. Title I per capita export market value by countries July 1, 1954, through December 31, 1963*

Country	Title I Export Market Value	Population (1960)	Title I Per Capita Market Value†
	(million dollars)	*(million)*	*(dollars)*
Israel	223.9	2.1	106.62
Iceland	14.1	0.2	70.50
Yugoslavia	556.5	18.5	30.08
Egypt	481.5	25.9	18.59
Spain	467.0	30.1	15.51
Poland	439.9	29.7	14.81
Turkey	395.7	27.6	14.34
Korea	338.7	24.7	13.71
Taiwan	143.6	10.6	13.55
Uruguay	34.1	2.8	12.18
Greece	99.8	8.3	12.02
Finland	41.1	4.4	9.34
Chile	64.5	7.3	8.84
Tunisia	30.6	4.2	7.29
Syria	32.6	4.6	7.09
Pakistan	627.3	92.7	6.77
Paraguay	11.0	1.8	6.11
Austria	39.5	7.1	5.56
S. Vietnam	76.9	14.1	5.45
Brazil	350.5	70.8	4.95
Bolivia	16.8	3.5	4.80
Colombia	58.0	14.1	4.11
India	1,701.5	432.6	3.93
Guinea	10.0	3.0	3.33
Peru	31.4	10.8	2.91
Italy	140.0	49.4	2.83
Indonesia	257.8	92.6	2.78
Congo	36.3	14.2	2.56
Ecuador	11.0	4.3	2.56
Ceylon	25.0	9.9	2.53
Burma	45.8	20.7	2.21
Iran	40.2	20.2	1.99
Morocco	19.7	11.6	1.70
Japan	135.0	‡91.7	1.47
Philippines	33.7	27.8	1.21

* Source: Program Operations Division, Foreign Agr. Ser.; and International Monetary Fund, International Financial Statistics. Taken from: Barlow, F. D. and Libbin, S. A., The Role of Agricultural Commodity Assistance in International Aid Programs, Econ. Res. Ser., USDA, March, 1965, ERS-Foreign 118, p. 6.

† Countries where the Title I per capita market value was $1 or less are: Argentina, United Kingdom, France, Portugal, Sudan, Mexico, Thailand, the Netherlands, and West Germany.

‡ 1958 population. This was the last year of Title I shipments to Japan.

TABLE 1.5. U.S. agricultural exports: value by commodity, 1960 to 1965*

Commodity	1960	1961	1962	1963	1964	1965
			(thousand dollars)			
Grains and preparations	1,688,826	1,926,672	2,074,654	2,301,210	2,592,522	2,561,565
Cotton	980,335	874,574	527,866	576,382	681,734	486,169
Tobacco	378,443	390,794	373,390	403,105	412,832	382,686
Vegetable fats and oils	186,280	152,070	204,527	185,317	246,467	282,684
Oilseeds	361,339	366,558	428,354	505,989	609,147	687,117
Protein meal	45,362	47,470	90,996	124,955	144,510	186,673
Fruits and preparations	248,695	271,816	285,536	276,171	278,604	313,123
Vegetables and preparations	139,946	124,409	147,946	172,728	158,016	155,350
Nuts and preparations	21,068	11,770	15,574	21,534	27,160	43,334
Animal products	484,121	534,337	497,923	571,712	741,774	691,962
Other	289,772	329,262	384,637	446,303	454,184	437,974
Total	4,824,187	5,029,732	5,031,403	5,585,406	6,346,950	6,228,637

* Source: Foreign Agricultural Trade of the United States, USDA, Aug., 1966.

accounted for 7 percent of the total and 26 percent of P.L. 480 exports.

Where have these exports gone? Table 1.4 summarizes P.L. 480 Title I sales, by country from July 1, 1954, through December 31, 1963. In terms of total value, India received almost three times as much as the next highest recipient, but ranked 23rd in terms of market value per capita. In contrast, Israel ranked eleventh in total value but first in market value per capita. Its per capita value was 27 times that for India.

India has been the major country recipient of sales under Title I through June 30, 1965. Twenty-nine percent of agreements for Title I sales were made with India. These agreements were valued at $3 billion (10, p. 28). India, Pakistan, and the United Arab Republic accounted for 46 percent of the value of all agreements signed.

COMMODITIES EXPORTED

The principal commodity group exports are shown in Table 1.5. Grains and preparations accounted for 41 percent of total exports in each of the last four years and 35 and 38 percent, respectively, for the first two years. During these six years, there was a steady growth in exports for this group. Protein meal exports which were four times the level of 1960 exhibited the largest increase in 1965. Oilseeds increased 90 percent during this period. Exports of all groups increased between 1960 and 1965, with the exception of cotton, which experienced a 50 percent decline and tobacco exports which were virtually unchanged.

Within the grains and preparation group, the increase in exports was accounted for primarily by feed grains which more than doubled during the 6-year period (Table 1.6). Feed grains

TABLE 1.6. U.S. exports of grains and preparations, calendar years 1960–65*

Year	Wheat and Flour	Milled Rice	Feed Grains
	(million dollars)		
1960	1,026	147	515
1961	1,298	111	517
1962	1,134	153	788
1963	1,331	177	794
1964	1,532	204	856
1965	1,184	243	1,134

* Source: Foreign Trade of the United States, ERS, USDA, Aug., 1966, p. 22.

are now the *number one* dollar earner among all American exports including industrial products.

Table 1.7 shows the share of production exported of selected crops. It can be observed that the more than one-half of the production of wheat, rice, and dry edible peas; two-fifths of nonfat dry milk and soybeans; more than one-fifth of grain sorghum, cotton, and dried prunes were exported during the period, 1962–66. These data indicate the importance of foreign outlets in the distribution of these commodities.

The data of Table 1.8 indicate the relative importance of governmental exports to total exports. These exports account for considerably more than one-half of wheat and wheat flour, nonfat dry milk, and soybean oil exports. The proportion of corn, barley grain, and soybeans moving under government programs decreased indicating increases in dollar sales relative to exports under governmental programs. These data indicate that governmental exports have been effective in moving stocks out of storage and out of the country. In the absence of these exports, stocks would have increased substantially or sharp cut-backs in production would have been necessary for some commodities.

In the future, the continued growth in per capita incomes in our principal commercial markets indicates that agricultural exports will continue to increase. The prospects are bright for feed grains, oilseeds, and protein meal. We will face increasing

TABLE 1.7. Share of physical production exported, fiscal years*

Commodity	Average 1959–61	1962	1963	1964	1965	1966†
			(percent)			
Wheat, incl. flour equivalent	41	58	58	45	55	65
Rice (rolled basis)	52	54	52	64	56	55
Nonfat dry milk	34	40	45	62	44	37
Dried edible peas	58	60	50	49	60	68
Dried whole milk	28	18	43	28	17	22
Grain sorghum	15	18	23	17	26	37
Barley grain	23	21	15	17	15	18
Corn	6	11	11	11	15	16
Tallow	41	41	35	44	40	38
Soybeans‡	39	35	44	41	48	42
Cotton§	41	34	24	32	30	21
Dried prunes	28	30	28	30	27	36

* Sources: Foreign Agricultural Role of the United States, ERS, USDA, Oct., 1964, p. 40; Sept., 1966, p. 58.
† Preliminary.
‡ Includes the beans equivalent of soybean oil for export.
§ Includes the seed equivalent of cottonseed oil for exports.

TABLE 1.8 Government exports as a percentage of total agricultural exports value of selected commodities*

Commodity	1958	1959	1960	1961	1962	1963	1964	1965	1966
					percent				
Wheat and wheat flour	65.6	72.4	73.9	74.8	69.7	75.9	60.1	80.7	68.4
Rice (milled)	47.0	53.7	53.9	40.3	44.2	54.5	38.6	32.5	27.2
Grain sorghums	27.5	23.4	23.3	23.0	30.4	13.8	6.4	8.8	20.7
Barley grain	25.6	47.2	44.1	70.3	26.8	17.0	10.3	10.9	0.4
Corn	28.8	24.9	25.1	18.8	26.2	11.7	11.3	7.2	5.4
Nonfat dry milk	90.9	89.5	79.6	77.7	74.8	77.6	53.5	59.9	58.6
Dried whole milk	3.7	0.6	0.6	1.9	9.1	26.2	36.6	25.8	19.1
Tallow, edible and inedible	8.7	7.3	7.9	7.4	16.2	21.8	18.7	13.6	6.3
Soybeans	5.6	11.3	8.1	5.4	3.2	2.0	0.31	0.37	0.2
Soybean oil	75.4	93.5	66.5	62.3	66.3	45.5	62.0	64.4	76.2
Cotton	34.3	63.2	18.9	24.3	26.5	33.0	20.9	27.0	26.2
Cottonseed oil	46.1	25.7	29.2	28.6	58.6	38.4	26.8	43.4	60.9
Total	31.3	28.8	29.6	31.4	32.1	30.3	25.7	27.4	24.2

* Sources: Foreign Agricultural Trade of the United States, ERS, USDA, Nov.-Dec., 1962, pp. 11–14, Table 7; Sept., 1963, pp. 28–29, Nov.-Dec., 1963, p. 19, Table 7; Nov.-Dec., 1964, p. 42, Table 7; Dec., 1965, p. 25, Table 7; Nov., 1966, p. 38, Table 3; Agr. Stat. 1953, USDA, 1960, p. 597, Table 822; Agr. Stat. 1960, USDA, 1961, p. 599, Table 818; Agr. Stat. 1961, USDA, 1962, p. 589, Table 815.

competition as output increases in the other principal supplier countries, however. For those products that are heavily dependent upon governmental programs, future exports will be largely determined by the success of our efforts in increasing agricultural development in recipient countries as well as the direction and conduct of domestic government programs and of such programs as Food for Freedom.

U.S. CONTRIBUTION TO THE FOOD GAP

The gap between the well fed and the underfed of the world is so great that there is doubt that the farmers of the world will ever be able to see all are well fed. This is true even if incomes would permit a demand for food equal to that existing in well-fed areas today. Here we use the term "well fed" to connote not merely that which will give minimal standards, but what people demand when income permits. This is the case in most of the highly developed areas today. Therefore, the potential demand exists for the complete capacity of resources and technology available. The only question is where the food will be produced as a result of increased demand. Historically, only about 6 or 7 percent of food has moved between countries and almost 90 percent of imports based on dollar value have been by high-income nations and areas, representing about one-third of the world's population.

Table 1.9 is a summarization of food imports and exports in 1963 reported in F.A.O. *Yearbook of Commerce*. The export sum of $21,788,400,000 represents FOB values. If one assumes some for the countries for which data were not available, it can be seen that trade between countries represents only about 8 percent of farm value. Actually, some deduction should be made from the FOB export values to reduce them to farm value and then a figure of something like 7 percent is obtained which represents the proportion of all food going into trade. Almost 15 percent of the food trade is in such items as coffee, tea, and spices which have no bearing on dietary needs. Ninety-three percent of food is consumed in the country where produced. There is little indication that these percentages have varied materially for at least the last 40 years. Trade, then, is relatively unimportant in the world food picture. It is important as exports by a few countries such as Australia, New Zealand, Canada, and the United States and as imports in such countries as the United Kingdom and Japan.

Table 1.10 summarizes the import and export totals by

TABLE 1.9 Value of food exports and imports, 1963*

Continent	Animals and Products	Fruits and Veg.	Cereals and Prep.	Sugar	Coffee, Tea, Cocoa, and Spices	Fish and Prep.	Misc. Foods	Fats and Oils	Total
				Exports					
				(million dollars)					
Europe	$3,059.2	$1,707.7	$1,230.2	$ 559.4	$ 266.9	$ 526.4	$ 164.1	$ 379.6	$7,893.5
North and Central America	489.1	672.6	3,161.1	225.4	362.5	272.6	85.5	920.4	6,189.2
South America	396.5	163.8	312.5	166.8	1,129.9	12.3	1.6	116.7	2,283.1
Asia	54.4	436.5	440.4	104.9	693.2	268.8	11.7	261.1	2,271.0
Africa	66.4	325.2	176.5	67.1	558.2	71.9	9.2	449.6	1,724.1
Oceania	773.5	97.3	330.6	143.7	12.3	18.7	7.9	43.5	1,427.5
Total	4,839.1	3,403.1	5,651.3	1,267.3	3,006.0	1,170.7	280.0	2,170.9	21,788.4
				Imports					
				(million dollars)					
Europe	3,406.0	3,147.3	2,964.2	1,240.8	1,779.9	595.8	143.1	1,698.8	14,975.9
North and Central America	789.3	620.6	186.5	821.5	1,339.2	423.2	29.1	234.2	4,443.6
South America	72.9	65.7	247.2	2.0	332.5	19.7	5.1	55.3	500.4
Asia	329.3	296.0	1,611.2	376.6	159.0	122.5	29.8	514.5	3,488.9
Africa	91.1	58.8	295.8	127.8	117.0	39.1	13.5	79.6	822.7
Oceania	12.4	23.5	22.1	14.8	58.8	24.0	4.7	22.6	182.9
Total	4,701.0	4,211.9	5,327.0	2,583.5	3,486.4	1,224.3	225.3	2,605.0	24,364.4

* Source: Yearbook of Commerce, F.A.O., USDA. (Figures for 1962 were used when 1963 data were not yet available in F.A.O. reports.) Export and import figures were not available from all countries and, therefore, the totals given are not world totals and in some cases (such as for sugar) may be very misleading. Import value for sugar is double the export value because heavy importing countries are included while figures from some important exporting countries were not available.

Countries accounting for well over half the imports vs. c.i.f. values for imports. This means that import value is at least 10 percent higher than export value from countries of origin. For world food trade as a whole, imports would be valued between 5 and 10 percent above FOB values.

TABLE 1.10. Value of food exports and imports by continent, 1963*

Continent	Exports Total	Per Capita	Imports Total	Per Capita	Net Export Per Capita	Net Import Per Capita
Europe	$7,893,500,000	$12.80	$14,975,900,000	$24.30	....	$11.40
North and Central America	6,189,200,000	23.20	4,443,600,000	16.67	$ 6.53	....
South America	2,283,100,000	17.10	500,400,000	3.75	13.35	....
Asia	2,271,000,000	2.46	3,438,900,000	3.73	....	1.27
Africa	1,724,100,000	8.44	822,700,000	4.07	4.37	....
Oceania	1,427,500,000	88.10	182,900,000	11.28	76.82	....
Total	$21,709,000,000	$10.07	$24,364,400,000	$11.30	....	....

Source: Data derived from 1964 F.A.O. Report of Production and U.S. Foreign Agricultural Trade Reports, ERS.
* Total for each continent represents all trade of each country, whether with another country of that continent or or of another continent. Intercontinental trade would be considerably less. 80.4 percent of imports by developed areas (Europe, North and Central America, and Oceania); 71.1 percent of exports by developed areas (Europe, North and Central America, and Oceania).
In underdeveloped areas, exports exceeded imports by $1,516,200,000, 1964–65 fiscal year:

U.S. exports to developed areas,	$3,241,227,000
U.S. exports to underdeveloped areas,	$2,855,736,000
U.S. imports from developed areas,	$1,382,428,000
U.S. imports from underdeveloped areas,	$2,604,780,000

countries under the six continental designations and shows the importance on a per capita basis. If trade were to solve or alleviate food shortage problems, a net import per capita of major proportions would be necessary in areas where shortages now exist. Of the shortage areas, only Asia shows a net import figure and this of only an insignificant amount. For 1960, the net import per capita for Asia was only 17 cents and for 1963 it was $1.27, mostly from subsidized sources. Europe accounts for almost 60 percent of all food imports. Food imports then are largely by well-to-do countries and are for the purpose of enriching quality and pleasurability of diets rather than in supplying any real shortage of dietary requirements. A few countries such as the United Kingdom present historic exceptions to this rule.

It is easy to conclude that the 2 billion underfed people in the underdeveloped areas need more and better food. Where will or should it come from? We like to think that the world benefits by allowing the most efficient producers to trade with others who have a relative advantage in other products with a resultant benefit to all parties. But as far as food is concerned, we have seen very little evidence that such production and trade has increased very much in recent times. Perhaps we have proven that generally food can be produced more efficiently in countries where needed rather than trading for it. We must also realize that in most underfed areas, food production is rather primitive and yields are exceedingly low. These areas probably have more to gain by using their efforts to increase food production rather than by producing other products to trade for food. More trade will be generated when and if these low-income countries are able to raise their income, as evidenced by trade in food between wealthy areas. For example, North America and Europe use many products in quantity which would not be used if per capita income were as low as in Asia or Africa.

There is no lack of prospective demand for all the food the world can produce, providing income were no barrier, nor do trends indicate that the world food gap as measured in quantitative terms will ever be decreased. In the last 30 years, the total food gap has increased by an estimated 45 to 50 percent. As long as population of the underfed areas continues to increase with no per capita change in food production of those areas, the gap continues to widen.

In 1965, our total exports to India furnished them with about 95 calories per day per capita if no losses occurred between export ports and the Indian consumers. Ninety percent of this was from wheat. For Pakistan, U.S. exports furnished 130 calories per day. Eighty-four percent of these calories came from wheat. Studies made in Pakistan in 1963–64 indicated sizeable losses of imported grains, suggesting that considerably less than this quantity was consumed. The three most important exports from the United States in 1965 in terms of caloric content were wheat, soybeans, and rice. Wheat furnished 67 percent of all calories exported and the three commodities together comprised 90 percent of calories exported which were used directly as food. Of these three export commodities, only 56 percent went to food-deficit areas. Food-deficit areas received about 54 percent of the calories from all U.S. exports. Using the rather widely accepted figure of 2 billion people in the food-deficit areas would mean that U.S. exports would have contributed about 55 calories per day per capita to these areas. India and Pakistan received 55 percent of U.S. food export calories going to food-deficit areas of the world.

APPRAISAL OF FOOD AID

Food aid has some measure of appeal to both donor and recipient nations. Initially, the appeal to the United States stemmed largely from the opportunity to reduce governmental stocks and to improve our image abroad at little or zero costs. Food aid also had appeal in that it permitted a postponement of consideration of the politically difficult questions of dealing with the growing domestic imbalance between supply and demand. Over the past decade, food aid has been rationalized to U.S. citizenry largely on the basis of its contribution in filling an appreciable part of the food gap in developing nations. Appeal has been made on the basis of humanitarian motives and moral obligations to use U.S. abundance for improving the welfare of the less fortunate two-thirds of the world population. It has also been argued that food aid contributes to economic development.

Food aid has appeal to recipient nations. It has provided a means for placating political pressures in urban areas that have grown more from a rural over-population push than from an urban economic opportunity pull. Recipient countries have been able to minimize riots and unrest that probably would have developed in the absence of food aid to ward off the effects of famine. It has provided an opportunity for recipient nations to postpone some of the hard decisions that must be made. It has had appeal to some individuals in recipient countries in that it afforded an opportunity for them to aid the United States in solving its major farm production surplus problem.

Undeniably, certain uses of surplus agricultural commodities do contribute to increased welfare and economic development in underdeveloped areas. These uses include famine relief, gifts to the starving, and build-up of national reserves against the fluctuations in an already inadequate supply. In short-run periods, food aid may be the only way calorie intake of a growing but seriously underfed population may be raised (6).

Other short-run benefits are often cited. These include (a) reduction in price instability and/or a prevention or dampening of inflation. Schultz suggests that food aid can be used to reduce price uncertainty facing cultivators and thus providing a more favorable environment for agricultural production (21, p. 1029). In Israel the increase in the price level was less than it would have been in the absence of Title I imports. During the 6-year period of these imports, the domestic price level increased 28 percent which otherwise would have risen $36\frac{1}{2}$ percent (12, p. 145), and (b) increased productivity of workers. The increase in food intake acts as a kind of "producer good" in enhancing the energy and strength and thereby the amount of productive work that is done.

In this connection, the Costa Rican section of the Pan-American Highway No. 1 came to be known as "The Road That Food Built" because of the fivefold increase in workers' output due to improved feeding (5). Further, (c) food provides assistance in development through savings in foreign exchange. In the underdeveloped countries, capital along with managerial skills and public services are likely to be limiting factors. Where capital is a limiting factor, there is likely to be a need for foreign exchange earnings for the importation of tools of development. But if food is short, then food imports compete for limited capital. However, food aid permits the purchase of food items for local currencies and saves funds that would go into food purchases abroad at unfavorable rates of exchange. It was suggested by Witt and Wheeler that in the absence of Title I wheat imports in Colombia, internal pressures probably would have forced the adoption of an aggressive technical assistance program, higher wheat prices, increased resources devoted to an inefficient sector and, in the interim, forced the use of more of its export earnings for commercial wheat purchases (26). Thus the saved capital becomes available for investment within the country. Crawford suggests that food aid can contribute to development if it functions as an addition to foreign exchange, but may be an inefficient way of transferring income from rich to poor countries (6, p. 388). (d) It also will aid internal capital investment through the use of local currency generated under Title I sales. These funds can be used in building up the infrastructure of the economy and for capital investments in ancillary aids for agriculture as well as in other sectors of the economy. Ginor reports that during the period 1955–60, imports of surplus agricultural commodities valued at $152 million permitted additional investment of about $100 million. This made possible a permanent increase of 2 percent in GNP. The program, in 1959, accounted for 11½ percent of the increase in production and generated additional employment by an annual average of 7800, or about 1.2 percent of the total number employed (12, pp. 1–3).

In summary, it might be stated that these are all possible contributions of food aid to underdeveloped countries. Some evidence suggests that food consumption has been increased. Sen points out that in 26 countries where wheat has been supplied under Title I during the 4-year period, 1955–56 through 1958–59, the average per capita consumption increased 7.4 pounds of which 3.4 pounds were attributed to normal increase and 4 pounds to P.L. 480 supplies (22, p. 1035). Stice indicates that U.S. shipments to India from 1956 through 1960 added about 74 calories per capita per day to India's food supplies; that the 474 million bushels of wheat received alone added about 66 calories per capita per day (14, p. 13). However, these are short-run benefits and could inhibit the attainment of increased welfare and economic development which would ultimately finance such programs. One of the dangers in food aid is that dependence on food aid may lead to a neglect in the development of the agricultural industry. Such has been the experience in some countries where agriculture has been looked upon as a "tradition-bound" industry and therefore received zero or low priority in development funding. Another danger is to equate food aid with dollar aid. Food aid can contribute but does not eliminate the need for dollar assistance. If the United States is really concerned with increasing the welfare of people in underdeveloped nations, some evaluation must be made of the productivities of food and dollar aid. The type of aid with the highest expected productivity should be provided. The United States agricultural surplus problem has caused emphasis to be placed on food disposal. Food aid has helped the United States to rid itself of surpluses, but at the same time has provided an opportunity for the creation of a situation in which supply could again begin its rapid march ahead of demand, leading to chronic imbalances similar to those of the recent past. What have been the effects of food aid on economic development?

Food aid can contribute to economic development and to the long-run solution of the food and population problems. However, recipient countries must use concomitant domestic policies suited to individual country conditions. In general, these policies have not been adopted and consequently food aid has contributed little to the long-run solution of food and population problems.

In most of the underdeveloped nations, the majority of the labor force is dependent upon and employed in the agricultural sector characterized by an extreme low level of productivity. This condition places a millstone around the neck of development. Ways and means must be found to increase the physical productivity of these resources. As this is accomplished, the value productivity is diminished but at the same time increased output is experienced. As output continues to increase, surpluses are generated. This permits the siphoning off of resources and more products, and increased capital accumulation which can be tapped for further investment in the agricultural as well as in the industrial sector. Such expansion induces increased demand for goods and services from the industrial sector. With the multiplier effect, economic development proceeds at a vigorous pace. However, for such a process to evolve, there must be incentives to individual producers. In most of these countries, there must be price or profit incentives.

Price incentive does not necessarily mean a higher price, but one that is reasonably certain and gives expectations of adequate returns. There must be rewards, rather than potential disaster, to the progressive farmer who breaks tradition in methods of production. In some cases where the innovation fails, "losing face" appears to be as great a deterrent to new practices as is lack of capital or lack of know-how.

Many of the developing nations have followed a policy of maintaining low farm product prices so as to provide cheap food and a source of cheap labor to facilitate industrialization. Such policy assumes that agricultural output is not responsive to price or if there is a response, the supply curve must be backward sloping. Are producers in underdeveloped areas responsive to price?

Limited empirical research and other observations indicate that producers the world over will, subject to knowledge and managerial restraints, respond to price. Witt and Eicher state, "Farmers in underdeveloped nations appear to respond significantly to relative price changes." (27, p. 30.) Khatkhate presents an opposing viewpoint stating that in an economy where small-scale subsistence production is predominant, there is no response in production to price and hence a fall in price does not lead to a decrease in output (15). Both Beringer and Falcon present empirical evidence to refute Khatkhate's viewpoint. Beringer argues that there is a much more significant response of cash crops than of food crops on above-subsistence farms and that any depression in food prices received by farmers relative to cash crop prices is likely to lead to acreage or input substitution on these farms in favor of cash crops (2).

Falcon presents a similar view arguing that depressed prices due to increased use of surplus commodities could lead to significant changes in the composition of agricultural output in recipient countries, especially as between cash and food crops (8). In the same vein, Witt and Eicher point out the fact, that with a fall in food grain prices, total agricultural output may be relatively unresponsive, but there could be shifts in land use altering the product output-mix (27, p. 30). They also point out that given adverse price effects, "They may shift to a closely competitive crop for which demand is increasing, technology advancing, and for which their land, equipment, and market facilities are adapted." (27, p. 31.)

Have P.L. 480 shipments had adverse effects? The Ginor Report indicates that Title I grain imports had a marked effect on free market grain prices (12, p. 232). Large imports of wheat in Taiwan under U.S. aid programs caused the area planted to wheat to decrease in the early 1950's and production did not surpass the level of 1950 until the support price for local wheat relative to Ponlai rice was set at a ratio of 1:1.31 (23, p. 201). Witt and Eicher state, "The evidence here is equivocal. Additional farm imported products have helped prevent consumer protests and permitted an expansion of industry without necessarily a concomitant, supporting expansion in agricultural and marketed supplies." (27, p. 72.)

Evidence and logical reasoning clearly indicate that imports of food under P.L. 480 have had adverse price effects. However, adverse price effects on food prices need not have the same effect on agricultural producers. It is possible through policy measures to insulate domestic producers from adverse price effects of P.L. 480 imports. Such measures might include subsidies on outputs or inputs, and a purchase and sales program.

POTENTIAL FOR FOOD PRODUCTION
IN THE SOVIET BLOC

Planning and export policy of the United States cannot be formulated and implemented without taking into consideration policies and activities of other exporting countries. The policies and practices of the non-Soviet Bloc countries are much easier to appraise and make adjustments for because they operate within the existing international market framework. Those of the Soviet Bloc, on the other hand, are more difficult to deal with, primarily for two reasons: first, extreme variability in production due to weather fluctuations and the concomitant policy of administratively determining the quantity that will be made available for domestic consumption, especially in the Soviet Union; second, this disruptive practice of participation in international trade outside of the existing market framework, whether exporting or importing.

The Soviet Bloc is a major producer of cereals, accounting for slightly more than one-fifth of world production. It also accounts for about one-half of the world production of potatoes and sugar beets.

Russia alone is the world's largest producer of wheat. However, its production is more a function of area under production than of yield. The area devoted to wheat is more than two-and-one-half times that for the United States. Official average yield for the period 1958–62 was only 16.1 bushels per acre, while during the same period U.S. average yield was 24.9 bushels. In interpreting these data and in analyzing the Soviet grain situation, caution must be exercised because of the unreliability of crop statistics and the paucity of utilization data. For example, Soviet official grain output is reported in terms of "bunker weight"—the weight of grain as it comes from the combine. This weight is known to include excessively large amounts of moisture and trash. Actual grain weights would have to be adjusted downward for these; however, the adjustment factor would vary from year to year, region to region, and by type of grain. These would suggest that the official average yield cited above is considerably overestimated.

The Soviet Union has been a major importer of wheat since

the disastrous crop harvest of 1963. In fiscal year 1963–64 it imported almost 11 million metric tons, with about one-half of it coming from Canada. Prior to that year, it was a major exporter of wheat, principally to Communist countries. The wheat crop of 1966 estimated at 73.5 million tons, exceeding the record 1958 crop by 11 million tons could mean that production has recovered and the Soviet Union will once again become a major exporter. However, whether the Soviet Union will continue imports, become self-sufficient, or a major exporter depends upon the ability of Soviet agriculture to raise its low per acre yield. No further large expansion of acreage is possible and requirements will increase as population continues to increase at a rate of about 3 million a year. The reduction in meat supplies will also contribute to increased demand for bread grains.

It is likely that output will increase in the years ahead. Plans under Khruschev and his successors have been directed toward increasing crop yields. Increased inputs of fertilizer, herbicides, and machinery, improved grain varieties, and greater economic incentives to farm workers and managers have been included in government programs. These, along with favorable weather, contributed to the record output in 1966.

It is probable that production will increase further due to yield increases in the future. An estimated wheat yield increase of 4.3 bushels and a rye yield increase of 6.6 bushels over 1958 yields would provide a bread grain supply of 79 million tons in 1970. Estimated requirement for 1970 is 71 million tons for internal use and exports (3 million tons) to Communist countries. This would leave a residual of 8 million tons which could be exported or used for livestock feeding. If this residual entered the export market, it could have a significant effect on world prices and market shares (25).

TECHNICAL ASSISTANCE

The United States nonfood aid is extended for the purpose of economic, social, and political growth and development in the underdeveloped countries. This aid takes the form of loans, grants, training, and capital and technical assistance. All of these forms can play strategic roles in economic development. However, the effectiveness is conditioned by the timing, amount, form, aid, mix, and capacity of the recipient country to absorb and fully implement their use. While all of these forms of aid are important, the following discussion is limited largely to technical assistance.

Technical assistance makes possible the transfer of knowledge, skills, and techniques from the developed countries to the underdeveloped to improve human skills and attitudes and create and support institutions necessary for growth and development. One might raise the question, is technical assistance necessary? To answer this question, one must consider the conditions necessary for growth and development and the vital role of the human resource and technology in the process.

Economic development has as its objective the increase in welfare of a people over time, measured largely in terms of the quantity of goods and services available. The increase in welfare is reflected in gains in real income of the population. The population of a nation, as the human resource, plays a vital role in increasing welfare and at the same time reaps the gains of economic development through increased per capita income. Numerous writers have suggested the importance of people educated in technical and administrative skills and with an understanding of the requirements of a society based on the philosophy of specialization and exchange. Further, they suggest that lack of education, technology, and experience adapted to development needs are likely to be major obstacles to development. In addition, there is also the need for an understanding of the basic organization of a society, how it functions, and the need for change or modification to improve its functioning to meet the needs of society. Education plays a vital role in meeting this need.

We would hasten to point out that while education, measured in terms of literacy, is important and is associated with growth and development, other factors under given sets of circumstances might be as important as education. Aziz points out that in Malaysia there are many Malay and Chinese farmers, both producers of rubber and rice. The literacy rate among Malay farmers is quite high, while it is quite low among Chinese farmers. Yet, by and large, Chinese farmers' incomes are twice that for Malay farmers (1, p. 216).

A country can develop the needed pool of trained manpower through expenditures for education. However, in the underdeveloped countries, capital is likely to be an extremely limiting resource while the avenues and demands for investment capital are likely to far exceed quantities available. Hence, education must compete with other, perhaps high pay-off, high priority investment opportunities for funds. The cost of education is likely to be high. Dalisay indicates that the Philippines has been spending about 25 percent of its yearly government budget on education. Dalisay also indicates that public expenditure for education in the Philippines has varied from 2.11 to 3.22 percent of GNP from 1952–53 to 1961–62. In India and Pakistan about 3 percent of GNP and in Ceylon 10 percent of GNP were spent for education and social services (7, pp. 184–85).

Another short-run alternative is available to the underdeveloped countries for acquiring the needed skilled manpower. They can tap the skilled resources of the developed nations. Presumably technical assistance makes this possible.

AGRICULTURAL DEVELOPMENT

No underdeveloped country can afford to neglect its agriculture in development; not withstanding this fact, many of them have. Increasing productivity and output are not only essential in meeting the growing demand for food and fiber in domestic markets, but in providing additional output to aid in development through trade and the release of resources for employment in other sectors. The agricultural sector is also potentially a major market for the output from the industrial sector.

Many countries, in their effort to make the great leap forward to emulate the developed countries of the mid-twentieth century, have not only placed high priorities on industrial investment, but in many cases have generated negative incentives to agricultural development. Many of these countries have come to the full realization that for over-all economic growth and development, a necessary condition is increased agricultural output. It is evident that the United States has also come to realize that these must be given higher priority by assisted countries. The amended Food For Freedom Program makes these explicit.

A number of yardsticks attest to the importance of increasing agricultural output in over-all growth and development. First, in the underdeveloped countries a majority of the population (50 to 80 percent or even higher) is engaged in agriculture often with near zero alternative employment opportunity. The large labor supply and its low elasticity means that marginal costs are low or close to zero. Consequently, it can be used in quantities causing marginal productivity to be low. Second, population growth rates are higher in rural areas than in urban areas. As a result, an already large, underemployed, inelastic labor supply with a marginal productivity close to zero is continually increased; and, third, exports markets needed to generate foreign exchange for the importation of the tools for development for agricultural products are more accessible. These markets can be tapped without resort to special sales techniques and promotion. On the other hand, attempts to industrialize and export are dubious in the face of fierce competition from the developed nations and relatively low quality of product offered.

These conditions give agriculture a short-run advantage over durable and producer goods industries in development in that high payoffs are probable in a shorter time span. The payoffs from investments in capital complementary to labor—fertilizer, improved seeds, knowledge, insecticides, etc.—in the agricultural sector are likely to be higher than for comparable investments in the industrial sector in the early stages of development. Heady suggests that returns on these investments might be as high as those from research and education in U.S. agriculture (13, p. 657). Yet, these returns have not been realized. These countries are producing less than their full potential. They could reach their potential if the vast and valuable stock of scientific and technical knowledge pertinent to their situations were made available to them and fully implemented. This is based upon the fact that the real difference between the developed and underdeveloped countries is found in the stock and use of available technology. Along this same line, Schultz suggests that the endowment of natural resources is not likely to be a limitational factor to large increases in agricultural production in most countries (20, p. 7). Much of this productivity-increasing technology can be made available through technical assistance programs. Let us examine the U.S. commitment to these programs.

MAGNITUDE OF PROGRAM

Technical assistance has constituted a relatively small part of U.S. aid programs, accounting for slightly more than one out of every 10 dollars. Table 1.11 indicates that between 1962 and 1965, U.S. disbursements increased 28 percent. Expenditures in 1965 increased 12.5 percent over those for 1964 and accounted for about one-half of the total increase in technical assistance of Development Assistance Committee (DAC) members (Australia, Austria, Belgium, Canada, Denmark, France, F.R. Germany, Italy, Japan, Netherlands, Norway, Portugal, Sweden, United Kingdom, United States). Between 1961 and 1965, the technical assistance component for all DAC members increased from 10 percent in the former year to 18 percent in the latter (19, p. 88).

It is difficult to determine the proportion of technical assistance which went to agriculture. From AID information on

TABLE 1.11.   U.S. technical cooperation, 1962 to 1965*

Year	Commitments	Disbursements	Technical Cooperation as a Percent of Official Bilateral Net Contributions
		(million dollars)	
1962	413.00	331.28	9.7
1963	424.00	368.00	10.3
1964	433.00	377.00	11.8
1965	466.00	424.13	12.2

* Source: OECD, Development Assistance Efforts and Policies, 1966 Review, Sept., 1966, p. 163.

operations, about 12 percent went to food and agricultural projects in both the 1964 and 1965 fiscal years. For the first nine months of fiscal 1966, 11.3 percent was spent for these projects. Education was the only major category with a larger expenditure. The benefits to agriculture are probably underestimated as it is probable that expenditures in other categories such as education provided benefits to the agricultural sector.

The number of personnel engaged in technical assistance programs has increased over the years. Personnel is provided through publicly financed, private, and volunteer sources. Publicly financed technicians include those under direct hire by AID, employees of other federal agencies paid by AID (PASA), and contract employees. In March of 1966, there were 2822 direct hire, 656 employees of other federal agencies, and 2596 contract employees. Of the 6074 technicians overseas, slightly more than one-half of them were employed by AID. There were about 1300 agricultural technicians overseas.

There is no reliable estimate of the number of personnel in technical assistance provided by private enterprise. Limited evidence indicates that activity has been increased in technical and administrative training in less developed countries. It is likely that private enterprise will do even more in the formation of industrial skills. This is especially true if more of the countries follow the current practice of Brazil and Mexico. These countries insist that new foreign investment make firm commitments to train local people with a view to replacing foreign staff at the earliest opportunity. Some companies have gone beyond their immediate interests, establishing and running schools, building hospitals and training necessary staff, and launching community projects. Included in private source also are charitable foundations, religious and secular organizations, cooperatives, professional organizations, and the like.

The number of volunteers has been increasing more rapidly than the number of publicly financed personnel. OECD reports an increase from 8100 in 1964 to 11,800 in 1965 (19, p. 163). There is a degree of complementarity between volunteer efforts and those of publicly financed personnel. The latter normally works with official and semiofficial employees such as civil servants and teachers, while volunteers work at the grass roots or lower levels than do government-to-government programs. Also, they are not subject to the same constraints and pressures as governments. They have often been allowed to continue to operate in situations where official aid has been stopped by the local government.

American land-grant colleges and universities have provided technical assistance under contract. Between 1952 and 1965, 35 of them had 65 AID University Contracts for rural development projects in 38 countries. Twenty-three of these contracts had expired as of June 30, 1965. In terms of all American universities and colleges, 126 were participating either overseas or in the training of foreign participants in the United States in 1966. Seventy-one of these were participating overseas. The amended Food for Freedom Programs will increase the involvement of U.S. universities and colleges in technical assistance programs.

The other side of the coin in technical assistance programs involves training for indigenous people of underdeveloped countries in other countries. From 1959 through 1964, training was received by 51,694 foreign technicians under AID educational assistance. Of this number 39,661 came to the United States and 12,038 went to other countries for advanced education or training. Agriculture has accounted for the largest number of foreign technicians coming to the United States. In both 1959 and 1960, there were about 1800 of them. From 1961 through 1964, there was a steady decline with 1423 in the latter year. Yet there still was a larger number in agriculture than in any other area. In 1964, education ranked second with 1309 technicians. The areas of public safety and public administration exhibited sharp upswings in the number of participants (24, p. 15).

From the foregoing, it becomes evident that technical assistance has been extended in a variety of forms and involved a variety of people. The logical question that might be raised is, how effective has it been in helping underdeveloped countries in solving their food problems?

APPRAISAL OF TECHNICAL ASSISTANCE

Technical assistance is an area where payoffs can be extremely high over the intermediate or long-run period. On the other hand, it is an area in which scarce resources can be ill used and wasted if there is not careful planning and resources are used to their best advantage. The practice of extending technical assistance through grants has not contributed to basic planning and the establishment of priorities for its use. The grant system has also aided and abetted the acceptance of programs often unrelated to needs. This has led to misdirection, wastefulness in the use of scarce resources, and often resulted in more harm than benefit to efforts of recipient countries to move ahead in development and bring to bear the "best set" of forces for solution of the food problems faced.

Our net appraisal of technical assistance programs is that, on balance, they have been less than successful. This lack of success or only modest success can be attributed to factors on the donor side, the recipient side, and their interaction. Before discussing these, it would be well to point out the difficulty in measuring effectiveness, or the lack of standard criteria for the measurement of effectiveness. There is a multiplicity of complex forces and factors which might impinge upon effectiveness. These include stage of development in recipient country, cruciality of need and relevance of assistance extended, length of run, timing, method of injection, absorptive capacity of recipient countries, and the degree of complementarity among specific technical assistance aids provided as well as between those provided and those available within recipient countries. When all of these factors and others are taken into account, but inadequate provision is made for interaction, the conclusions drawn are likely to be misleading. When any subset of these factors are considered, the conclusions drawn are necessarily a function of the particular subset chosen. When comparative country studies are made, conclusions are likely to rest upon the quantitative and qualitative differences incorporated into the analyses. In spite of these difficulties, appraisals of effectiveness have been made and will continue to be made. The following discussion is certainly not free of the possible pitfalls enumerated above.

United States technical assistance is not new. The first mission was sent to Hokkaido Island in Japan in 1871. However, the big push came during the last quarter century. Assistance programs are based on the assumption that modern technology can be readily transferred. The experience in Western Europe and Japan following World War II was consistent with this assumption. But, as Moseman points out, these areas had similar industrial and technological bases as well as similar temperate zone environments (17). This led many to believe that U.S. modern technology could be transferred to the underdeveloped areas as well. But these people failed to take into consideration the differences. In Western Europe and Japan, the major component missing was the physical plant necessary for the production of agricultural inputs (machinery, fertilizer, insecticides, improved seeds, etc.) and ancillary capital aids (transportation, processing facilities, etc.) needed for agricultural productivity. These countries possessed high levels of literacy, technology, skilled manpower, managerial capability, viable institutions, incentives, and the will for increasing agricultural productivity. We discovered through long experience that these characteristics were totally or almost totally lacking in the underdeveloped countries.

We also learned through experience that different climatic environments placed restraints on the direct transferability of U.S. know-how. But we could have learned this at home if a careful scrutiny had been made of our own development. For example, the use of hybrid seed corn in the Midwest was widespread in a few years after its introduction. But a number of years elapsed before its use became widespread in the South. Why? The early varieties developed were not adapted to the climatic conditions of the South. It was only after adaptable varieties were introduced that hybrid seed corn use become widespread there.

We were quite successful in transferring hybrid seed corn to Western Europe in the early years of our cooperation, but unsuccessful in our efforts to transfer its use to Asia. Why? Moseman states, "The lack of adaptation of U.S. inbreds to the high temperatures and otherwise vastly different growing seasons in Asia, and the lack of acceptance of the gain type of the U.S. hybrids, actually built up prejudices against hybrid corns that are yet to be overcome even though well adapted hybrids with suitable grain type are now available for many areas of Asia." (17, p. 3.) There have been similar experiences in attempts to transfer other U.S. know-how.

Schultz argues that on the assumption that usable and profitable new technology and other agricultural inputs are available in the underdeveloped countries we have launched extension programs only to discover that the assumption was contradictory of the fact. What is needed, he argues, is a transformation of existing knowledge, through organized agricultural research, so that it will be economically useful in the underdeveloped countries. Has the encouragement of such effort been undertaken in our assistance programs? Schultz's answer is no; that inadequate attention has been given to the development of viable agricultural research centers (20, p. 19).

Moseman in a similar vein makes a plea for a "prompt acceleration of research in developing countries to adapt scientific and technological advances from countries with progressive agriculture." (17, p. 1.) This is an area where publicly financed technical assistance has been most inadequate. A part of this has been due to U.S. policy which has placed restraints on the types of research that could be undertaken. Our efforts have been influenced by a congressional desire to rid America of "embarrassing surpluses." A part might also be attributed to other foreign policy objectives which have conflicted with the goals of economic development in recipient countries in the short run.

This neglected area has been the one in which the private foundations, notably the Rockefeller Foundation, have been extremely successful in contributing to economic development. The Foundation began cooperative research in 1943 in Mexico with the Ministry of Agriculture. This adaptive research produced wheat varieties that were disease resistant, possessed the strength of straw, the capability to utilize high levels of nitrogen fertilizer, and other characteristics that together increased yields from about 11 bushels in 1939 to more than 39 bushels in 1964 (17, p. 4). It is reported today that many farmers are producing as much as 65 bushels per acre. This occurred in a country that once depended upon imports for about one-half of its wheat. Now, Mexico is able to consume more wheat without imports.

These varieties developed in Mexico are also well adapted to other countries in Latin America, in some parts of Africa, in the Near and Middle East, and in Pakistan and India.

A similar story can be written for corn. The development of adapted hybrids in Mexico by the Rockefeller Foundation increased yields from about 10 bushels per acre.

The International Rice Research Institute in the Philippines was established as a cooperative effort between the Government of the Philippines, the Ford Foundation, and the Rockefeller Foundation. Research efforts are beginning to pay off through identification of productive varieties and determining effective means for disease and pest control. Varieties have been identified which are capable of producing several times the average yields common in the rice bowl area. Some of these varieties will mature in about 100 days, making possible two or three crops a year.

Within recipient countries many factors have decreased the effectiveness of technical assistance. These factors include: the building of an infrastructure to meet the growing political pressures from urban populations, yet one that is inadequate to serve the purpose of increasing farm output; excessive controls; uneconomic price support programs; the pricing of farm products, farm purchased inputs in production, and consumption at levels that stifle incentives; inappropriate forms of taxation; inadequate farm credit, transportation, marketing and storage facilities; and a lack of or poorly conceived measures of agrarian reform. Our own agricultural development tells us that under these conditions, output will either not expand or do so at a very low rate. These countries must institute agricultural reforms which will provide incentives to producers; adequate supplies of improved factor inputs at prices that will encourage their use; new technology; and will reduce uncertainty faced by producers. There must be a change in attitude toward the relative status and low prestige associated with agriculture. As these changes are implemented, effective utilization can be made of assistance, and agricultural productivity and output will increase. However, this increased output will not insure increased welfare unless these countries institute measures to control population increases.

Even though our net appraisal of assistance programs indicates a lack of success, there are some country cases that suggest success. The most notable are Israel, Mexico, and Taiwan. However, the success cannot be attributed to U.S. assistance alone. At best, assistance can have only a catalyzing effect; but there must be something to catalyze. The assistance must be complementary to recipient country efforts. For example, in Israel, it was not U.S. aid per se, but rather to the efforts of the Israeli and the way in which it was incorporated in the total effort. The USDA study of 26 developing nations indicates top ratings for Israel with respect to literacy rate, technological features, tenure features, marketing facilities, availability of production requisites, and fertilizer prices (11, p. 15). The inflow of unrestricted external aid and effective public administration also contributed to the Israeli development.

In Mexico, success can be attributed largely to the adaptive research efforts of the Rockefeller Foundation and agricultural reforms instituted by the government. Agricultural reforms have facilitated increased use of improved seeds, fertilizer, pesticides, and irrigation; they have increased mechanization; and have increased the availability and use of credit through supervised agricultural programs and risk insurance for private banks extending loans to farmers.

In Taiwan, success can be attributed largely to the agricultural reforms implemented by Taiwanese which provided incentives for producers to increase agricultural productivity and output. It should be noted that the base for Taiwan's development had been established under Japanese rule.

An examination of agricultural development over the world suggests the hypothesis that there is a direct relationship between progress in these efforts and the extent to which countries have instituted measures to more effectively adapt modern technology, make available production requisites, and establish price relationships that provide incentives. In countries where these changes occur, assistance can accelerate development.

Private enterprise can help the developing nations in the solution to their food problems. They can make a substantial contribution in the provision of production requisites. In the case of fertilizer, they can help through the production, distribution, and in the development of technological innovations. They can do the same for the other chemicals useful in production. They can contribute in the development of processing, storage, and other facilities which could lead to higher producer returns without any increase in consumer prices. They could provide useful managerial aids that would improve the decision-making process. In U.S. agriculture, many of these organizations have had a significant impact in channeling improved materials and techniques into practice. They can perform similar services in the underdeveloped nations. To bring out this participation, recipient countries must make those facilitating changes that will give reasonable guarantees that an effective demand exists for the product or services; that the venture will produce reasonable profits for both the indigenous producer and the private firm; that the venture can be viewed as a long-term investment; and that the venture is capable of growth. Specific and extended risk guaranties under the AID Investment Guaranties Program are helpful but are not sufficient. Recipient countries must establish an environment which gives reasonable guaranties of success in their own right. Such an environment would promote increased participation by private enterprise in the solution to food problems faced by developing countries.

LITERATURE CITED

1. Aziz, U. A. Investment in agricultural and community development. Proceedings of the Twelfth International Conference of Agricultural Economists, Lyon, France. Pp. 216–17. 1964.
2. Beringer, C. Real effects of foreign surplus disposal in underdeveloped economies. A comment. Q. J. Econ. 77:317–23. 1963.
3. Bogue, D. J. The prospects for world population control. In: Alternatives for Balancing World Food Production and Needs. Ames: Iowa State Univ. Press. 1967.
4. Brown, L. R. The world food problem situation: an overview. In: Alternatives for Balancing World Food Production and Needs. Ames: Iowa State Univ. Press. 1967.
5. Cepede, M. Food consumption as a production factor. Indian J. Agr. Econ. 14:87–90. 1959.
6. Crawford, Sir John. Using surpluses for economic development. Proceedings of the Eleventh International Conference of Agricultural Economists, Cuernavaca, Moreles, Mexico. Pp. 377–95. 1961.
7. Dalisay, A. M. Assessing the contribution of investment in human resources to agricultural and community development. Proceedings of the Twelfth International Conference of Agricultural Economists, Lyon, France. Pp. 182–209. 1964.
8. Falcon, W. P. Real effects of foreign surplus disposal in underdeveloped economies. Further comment. Q. J. Econ. 77:323–26. 1963.
9. Food and Agricultural Organization of the United Nations. Food aid and other forms of utilization of agricultural surpluses. Rome. 1964.
10. Food For Peace. 1965 Ann. Rpt. on Public Law 480. U.S. Dept. of State. June, 1966.
11. Foreign Development and Trade Division, Changes in Agriculture in 26 Developing Nations, 1948 to 1963. USDA, ERS, Foreign Agr. Econ. Rpt. 27. Nov., 1965.
12. Ginor, F. Uses of agricultural surpluses. Analysis and Assessment of the Economic Effect of the Public Law 480 Title I Program in Israel. Bank of Israel, Jerusalem. 1963.
13. Heady, E. O. Agricultural Policy Under Economic Development. Ames: Iowa State Univ. Press. 1962.
14. India: Future Prospects for U.S. Farm Products, Cooperative Ext. Ser., Dept. Agr. Econ. AE 3933, Univ. of Ill., Urbana: July, 1963.
15. Khatkhate, D. R. Some notes on the real effects of foreign surplus disposal in underdeveloped economies. Q. J. Econ. 76:186–96. 1962.
16. Kirk, D. and G. Jones. World population: causes and consequences of growth differentials. In: Alternatives for Balancing World Food Production and Needs. Ames: Iowa State Univ. Press. 1967.
17. Moseman, A. H. Dimensions of agriculture in international development. A paper presented before the annual meeting of the Assoc. of Universities and Land-grant Colleges, Minneapolis. Nov., 1965.

18. The Mutual Security Program Fiscal Year, 1960: A Summary Presentation. Departments of State and Defense and Internat. Cooperation Adminis. U.S., GPO. March, 1959.

19. Organization For Economic Cooperation and Development. Development Assistance Efforts and Policies. 1966 Review, Paris. Sept., 1966.

20. Schultz, T. R. U.S. malinvestments in food for the world. In: Alternatives for Balancing World Food Production and Needs. Ames: Iowa State Univ. Press. 1967.

21. Schultz, T. W. Value of U.S. farm surpluses to underdeveloped countries. J. Farm Econ. 42:1019–30. Dec., 1960.

22. Sen, S. R. Impact and implications of foreign surplus disposal on underdeveloped economies. The Indian perspective. J. Farm Econ. 42:1031–41. 1960.

23. Shen, T. H. Agricultural Development on Taiwan Since World War II. Ithaca, New York: Comstock Publ. Assoc. 1964.

24. U.S. Agency For International Development, Operation Report. U.S. Dept. of State. 1964.

25. Volin, L. and H. Walters. Soviet Grain Imports. Econ. Res. Serv. USDA, ERS-For. 135. 1965.

26. Witt, L. and R. Wheeler. Effects of Public Law 480 Programs in Colombia: 1955–62. Dept. of Agr. Econ., Mich. State Univ., East Lansing. 1962.

27. ——— and C. Eicher. The Effects of United States Agricultural Surplus Disposal Programs on Recipient Countries. Res. Bul. 2, Dept. Agr. Econ., Mich. State Univ., East Lansing. 1964.

CHAPTER TWO

Agricultural Growth, Structural Change, and Resource Organization

REX F. DALY

WORLD HUNGER and its associated problems have moved to center stage in U.S. farm policy discussion. Indeed, the purpose of this book is to evaluate agriculture's role in economic growth and the impacts on agriculture of alternative developments in exports. The chapter on the world food situation and its meaning outlines the different points of view regarding world population growth, food deficits, the costs of filling these gaps, and some of the economic and political problems of determining the meaning of the world food situation to U.S. agriculture. In view of the range of possible developments, it is felt the purpose of this appraisal will best be served by considering some plausible alternative export assumptions and examining possible impacts on growth and structural change in commercial agriculture.

In many respects, agriculture may be moving into a new era in the latter half of the 1960's. During the past 6 years, under

---

Views expressed in this paper are those of the author. They do not necessarily represent an official USDA position on the future of U.S. agriculture.

voluntary production control incentives and rapid advances in exports, the supply-demand balance in agriculture has changed from burdensome stocks to a situation in which stocks approach minimum desirable levels, except for cotton.

Despite its similarity to previous legislation, the Agricultural Act of 1965 embodies some important changes which shift program emphasis toward greater flexibility. Pricing provisions for grains and cotton provide for pricing around world market levels with farm incomes maintained by direct payments to cooperators. Such pricing practices move the government a big step toward ". . . a role of referee in the marketplace rather than an active participant."

The new Food For Peace legislation also emphasizes some important changes which will influence the course of U.S. exports in coming years. It explicitly recognizes that the United States cannot feed the world and emphasizes the need for self-help in the recipient nation. With grain surpluses gone, the new legislation requires positive action to gear domestic production to "aid" as well as commercial export prospects, rather than simply exporting surpluses. Farm product exports and the growth of U.S. agriculture will depend to a considerable extent on the administration of this legislation and how rapidly self-help provisions can bring about increased production in the hungry nations.

In this general problem setting, let us look at the role to be played by U.S. agriculture—the prospective demand-supply-price balance under various alternatives, and probable changes in farm numbers, resource requirements, and the general organization and structure of agriculture.

TRENDS IN DEMAND, OUTPUT, AND RESOURCE USE

Dramatic changes have taken place in agriculture in the postwar years, particularly in the resource organization and structure of agriculture. Domestic use of farm products in 1964–66 was nearly 30 percent above the 1949–51 average. Population growth accounted for most of this increase with a gain of around 1 percent in per capita use. Although over-all per capita use was very stable, food use of crops declined 10 percent from the 1949–51 average, reflecting downtrends in per capita use of wheat and in fresh uses of most fruits and vegetables. Per capita use of livestock products increased about a tenth over the period, as big gains in consumption of beef and poultry more than offset declines in per capita use of milk, pork, eggs, and animal fats (Fig. 2.1).

Although the domestic market grew only slightly more than population from 1950 to 1965, the volume of exports more than doubled, increasing about 5 percent per year. In 1949–51, crop exports were equivalent in volume at the farm level to less than 14 percent of crop output. By 1964–66 this ratio had risen to 22 percent. Exports take more than half of the wheat and rice crops and a very substantial share of other grains, fats, oils, oilseeds, tobacco, and cotton.

Farm output increases met the expansion in domestic use and exports without strain (Fig. 2.2). The increase in productivity in agriculture—output per unit of input—was rapid enough that total resource inputs in 1964–66 were about the same as in 1949–51. But this stability reflected some big changes in the composition of resources. The input of labor was down nearly 50 percent, and cropland used for crops declined about 13 percent. The volume of production assets increased about a tenth. Inputs of mechanical power and machinery increased 17 percent, miscellaneous inputs increased 41 percent, and use of fertilizer materials more than doubled. These changes reflected the rapid advance of technology in agriculture as well as shifts in the relative cost of major inputs. Output per man-hour increased about 2.5 times over the period, rising nearly 6.5 percent per year. Crop output per acre averaged in 1964–66 some 41 percent above 1949–51. Accompanying these changes, the number of farms declined by about 2.25 million from 1950 to about 3.4 million in 1965. The larger sized classes were the only farms that increased in number. In 1965 there were an estimated million farms—30 percent of the total—with sales above $10,000 per farm. These accounted for more than 80 percent of total cash receipts.

GENERAL ECONOMIC GROWTH AND AGRICULTURE

Developments in agriculture are importantly interrelated with those in the general economy. Growth in domestic markets depends largely on growth in population and consumer buying power. A growing prosperous nonfarm economy provides off-farm employment alternatives for farm people and greatly influences the cost of labor, land, capital, and many other inputs.

The population growth rate, the major determinant of domestic demand, is expected to hold around 1.3 percent per year in

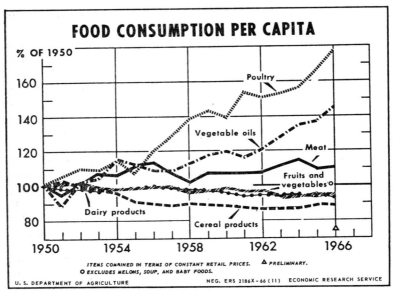

Fig. 2.1. Graphs showing trends in per capita consumption of food products.

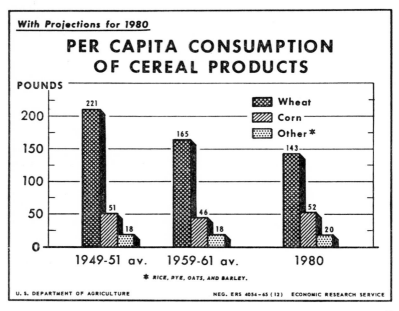

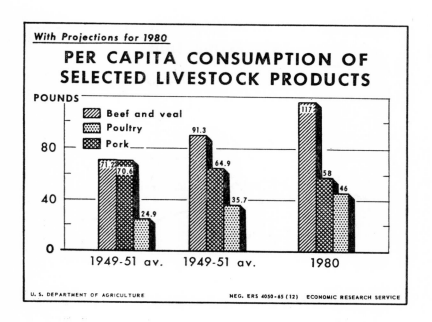

With Projections for 1980

PER CAPITA CONSUMPTION OF SELECTED LIVESTOCK PRODUCTS

POUNDS

Beef and veal
Poultry
Pork

80

40

0

71.2 70.6 24.9   91.3 64.9 35.7   117 58 46

1949-51 av.   1949-51 av.   1980

U. S. DEPARTMENT OF AGRICULTURE   NEG. ERS 4050-65 (12)   ECONOMIC RESEARCH SERVICE

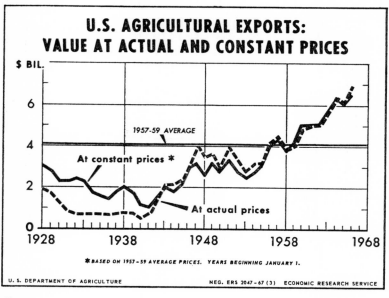

U.S. AGRICULTURAL EXPORTS: VALUE AT ACTUAL AND CONSTANT PRICES

$ BIL.

6

4

2

0

1957-59 AVERAGE

At constant prices *

At actual prices

1928   1938   1948   1958   1968

★ BASED ON 1957-59 AVERAGE PRICES. YEARS BEGINNING JANUARY 1.

U. S. DEPARTMENT OF AGRICULTURE   NEG. ERS 2047-67 (3)   ECONOMIC RESEARCH SERVICE

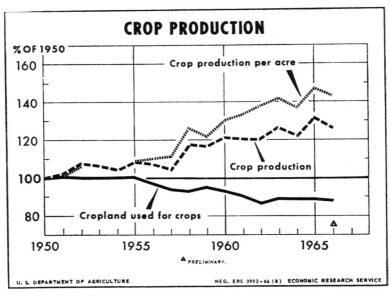

CROP PRODUCTION

% OF 1950

Crop production per acre

Crop production

Cropland used for crops

1950   1955   1960   1965

△ PRELIMINARY.

U. S. DEPARTMENT OF AGRICULTURE   NEG. ERS 3992-66 (8)   ECONOMIC RESEARCH SERVICE

Fig. 2.2. Graphs showing trends in farm input and output.

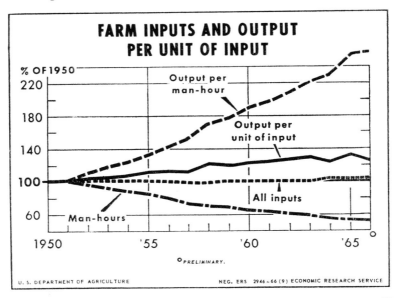

FARM INPUTS AND OUTPUT PER UNIT OF INPUT

% OF 1950

Output per man-hour

Output per unit of input

All inputs

Man-hours

1950   '55   '60   '65

○ PRELIMINARY.

U. S. DEPARTMENT OF AGRICULTURE   NEG. ERS 2946-66 (9) ECONOMIC RESEARCH SERVICE

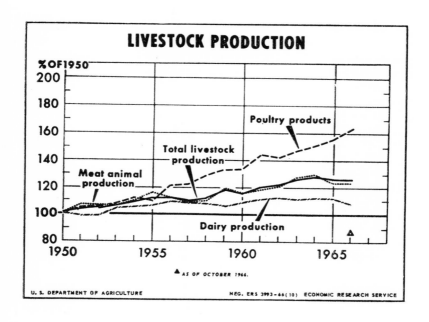

LIVESTOCK PRODUCTION

% OF 1950

Poultry products

Total livestock production

Meat animal production

Dairy production

1950   1955   1960   1965

▲ AS OF OCTOBER 1966.

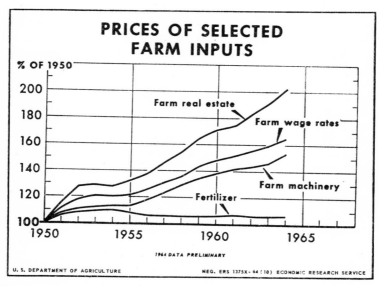

PRICES OF SELECTED FARM INPUTS

% OF 1950

Farm real estate

Farm wage rates

Farm machinery

Fertilizer

1950   1955   1960   1965

1964 DATA PRELIMINARY

the next decade or so, although the projection for 1980 assumes a growth rate of about 1.5 percent for the period. This compares with growth of 1.5 percent per year from 1960 to 1965 and 1.8 percent from 1950 to 1960 (Table 2.1).

Although population growth is slowing, increases in age groups 20 to 34 will be rapid in the next decade. Accordingly, the labor force is projected to grow about 1.9 percent per year for the next several years. This rapid growth presents an opportunity as well as a challenge if the economy is to assure jobs, schools, and housing for the growing labor force. If economic conditions bring forth adequate investment, labor force growth and trends in productivity suggest an economic output potential of perhaps 4 to 4.5 percent per year extending into the 1970 decade. The real gross national product projected for 1980 is about 85 percent above the 1964–66 average—a growth in real output of over 4 percent per year. A similar increase in real disposable income results in an annual gain in per capita income of 2.5 percent, or an increase of 45 to 50 percent in real consumer buying power per person from 1965 to 1980.

PROSPECTIVE GROWTH IN AGRICULTURE

Agriculture will continue to change in coming years. Technological advances and adjustment possibilities suggest that changes in the organization and structure of agriculture may be more rapid in the next 10 to 15 years than in the past. Unfortunately, appraisals of the future seldom yield specific conclusions that stand out in bold relief. However, it is fairly certain that domestic markets will continue to grow, perhaps a bit more rapidly than projected population growth. Even at high income levels, further advances in income and changes in relative prices will continue to modify our diet toward more beef and poultry, more prepared foods, and more convenience foods. Such changes will likely result in more resources being used for food production per person, but most of the increased use will be in nonfarm goods and services.

Domestic use of livestock products and feed use of crops will likely increase more rapidly than food uses of crops. But growth in demand, as in the past, will depend heavily on exports of farm products. The general uptrend in crop exports is expected to continue. How rapidly they rise will depend on U.S. availabilities and relatives prices, the operation of food aid programs, and a host of economic and institutional forces. In view of the difficulties of anticipating such unknowns as the impact of self-

TABLE 2.1. General economic growth and agriculture, selected periods, 1940 to 1966, and projections for 1980

Period	Population (mil.)	Labor Force (mil.)	Employment*		Output Per Man-hour†		Gross National Product†		Disposable Income†	
			Total (mil.)	Farm (mil.)	Total (dol.)	Farm (dol.)	Total (bil. dol.)	Farm (bil. dol.)	Total (bil. dol.)	Per capita (dol.)
1940	132.0	56.2	48.1	9.5	2.08	0.72	227.0	17.5	166.3	1,259.0
1950	152.0	64.7	61.8	7.5	2.72	1.03	355.0	19.4	249.6	1,646.0
1959–61 average	181.0	73.1	68.7	5.4	3.51	1.79	487.0	21.7	341.3	1,891.0
1964–66 average	195.0	78.5	75.0	4.4	4.07	2.24	614.0	22.7	429.6	2,208.0
Change from 1950 (%)	28.3	21.3	21.4	−42.9	49.6	117.5	73.0	17.0	72.1	34.1
Annual rate	1.7	1.3	1.3	−3.6	2.7	5.3	3.7	1.1	3.7	2.0
Projected:										
1970										
Export I‡	207.0	86.0	82.7	3.8	4.65	3.05	757.0	25.3	530.0	2,560.0
Change from 1964–66 (%)	6.2	9.6	10.3	−13.6	14.3	36.1	23.3	11.5	23.4	15.9
Annual rate	1.3	1.9	2.0	−2.6	2.7	6.3	4.3	2.2	4.3	3.0
1975										
Export I‡	223.0	93.5	90.0	3.3	5.30	3.95	920.0	27.4	650.0	2,900.0
Change from 1964–66 (%)	14.4	19.1	20.0	−25.0	30.2	76.3	49.8	20.7	51.3	31.3
Annual rate	1.4	1.8	1.8	−2.3	2.7	5.8	4.1	1.9	4.2	2.8
1980										
Export I‡	242.0	101.0	97.5	2.8	6.10	5.10	1,126.0	30.0	790.0	3,250.0
Change from 1964–66 (%)	24.1	29.3	30.0	−36.4	49.9	127.7	83.4	32.2	83.9	47.2
Annual rate	1.5	1.7	1.8	−2.1	2.8	5.6	4.1	1.9	4.1	2.6

* Bureau of Labor Statistics series.

† Gross national product, productivity and disposable income in constant 1958 dollars.

‡ Export I—Crop export volume rises at about 4.5 percent per year.

help programs, population control, worldwide participation in food aid, etc., this analysis explores the impacts of three assumed alternatives for crop exports ranging from a growth of 3 percent to 6 percent per year. This range is plausible relative to the appraisal of probable exports outlined in the opening chapter (Table 2.2).

Total farm output projected for 1980 ranges from about 40 percent above the 1964–66 average for the low-export assumption to about 50 percent above for the high-export assumption. These increases and productivity trends imply small increases in resource requirements. Labor use in agriculture continues to decline, perhaps to around 3 to 3.5 million workers by 1980. This compares with 5.7 million in 1964–66 (SRS concept). Rising output and resource shifts would suggest a continued rise in capital inputs (Table 2.3). Total inputs will be concentrated on fewer and fewer farms. By 1980, if recent trends continue, farm numbers could be down to around 2 million compared with 3.4 million in 1965. Approximately half these farms may account for about 95 percent of total cash receipts, 90 percent of total production assets, and 75 to 80 percent of total labor inputs. The remaining farms would be small, part-time, and part-retirement farms—many of which would be largely rural residences.

This appraisal points up the importance of export markets to the growth and prosperity of commercial agriculture in the United States. A rapid or slow growth in exports of farm products can materially influence farm prices and incomes as well as the ease or difficulty of adjusting the output potential of agriculture to growth in demand. The appraisal also illustrates the sensitivity of farm prices and incomes to variations in demand. This sensitivity greatly complicates the problems of gearing the output potential of agriculture to expanding domestic and export markets.

Continued expansion in foreign markets is not likely to come about without some positive efforts to facilitate growth in exports. Food goals, policy implications, and cost of continued expansion in exports are explored in other chapters.

METHODOLOGY, DATA, AND SOME CRITICAL ASSUMPTIONS

Analytical techniques used in this study appraise simultaneously projected increases in aggregate output and demand for crops and livestock. The domestic demand functions reflect the rela-

TABLE 2.2 Demand for farm products: Domestic use and exports, selected periods, 1950 to 1966, projections to 1980, and per cent of change (1957–59 dollars)

Period	Livestock Products — Other			Crops — Other			Net Domestic		
	Feed and seed	Total	Per capita	Feed and seed	Total	Per capita	Total	Per capita	Export
	(bil. dol.)		*(dol.)*	*(bil. dol.)*		*(dol.)*	*(bil. dol.)*	*(dol.)*	*(bil. dol.)*
1949–51 average	1.2	14.2	93.3	7.6	10.1	66.8	24.3	160.1	2.7
1959–61 average	0.6	18.0	100.0	8.5	10.9	60.4	28.9	160.4	4.3
1964–66 average	0.5	19.8	102.0	8.8	11.7	60.0	31.5	162.0	5.6
Change from 1949–51 (%)	−58.0	39.4	9.3	15.8	15.8	−10.2	29.6	1.2	107.4
Projected:									
1970									
Export I*	0.5	21.8	105.0	10.0	12.5	60.0	34.3	166.0	6.9
Change from 1964–66 (%)	0	10.1	2.9	13.6	6.8	0	8.9	2.5	23.2
1975									
Export I*	0.5	23.9	107.0	11.4	13.4	60.0	37.3	167.0	8.6
Change from 1964–66 (%)	0	20.7	4.9	29.5	14.5	0	18.4	3.1	53.6
Export II†	0.5	23.6	106.0	11.1	13.2	59.0	36.8	165.0	9.7
Change from 1964–66 (%)	0	19.2	3.9	26.1	12.8	−1.7	16.8	1.9	73.2
Export III‡	0.5	24.3	109.0	11.6	13.5	61.0	37.8	170.0	7.3
Change from 1964–66 (%)	0	22.7	6.9	31.8	15.4	1.7	20.0	4.9	30.4
1980									
Export I*	0.5	26.4	109.0	12.9	14.5	60.0	41.0	169.0	10.5
Change from 1964–66 (%)	0	33.3	6.9	46.6	23.9	0	30.2	4.3	87.5
Export II†	0.5	26.0	108.0	12.6	14.3	59.0	40.3	167.0	12.5
Change from 1964–66 (%)	0	31.3	5.9	43.2	22.2	−1.7	27.9	3.1	123.2
Export III‡	0.5	26.9	111.0	13.2	14.8	61.0	41.7	172.0	8.3
Change from 1964–66 (%)	0	35.9	8.8	50.0	26.5	1.7	32.4	6.2	48.2

* Export I–Crop export volume rises at 4.5 percent per year.
† Export II–Crop export volume rises at 6 percent per year.
‡ Export III–Crop export volume rises at 3 percent per year.

TABLE 2.3. Farm output, productivity, and resource use, selected periods, 1950 to 1966 and projections to 1980

	Farm Output		Productivity			Resource Inputs			
Period	Crop	Livestock products	Output per acre	Output per man-hour	Output per input	Total inputs	Labor	Cropland*	Production assets†
	(1957–59 = 100)		(1957–59 = 100)			(1957–59 = 100)		(mil. acres)	(bil.)
1949–51 average	91.0	88.0	85.0	60.0	86.0	102.0	146.0	382.0	194.0
1959–61 average	106.0	105.0	108.0	114.0	104.0	101.0	93.0	351.0	212.0
1964–66 average	113.0	112.0	120.0	152.0	112.0	103.0	75.0	334.0	212.0
Change from 1949–51 (%)	24.4	28.4	41.2	153.4	30.2	1.0	–48.6	–12.6	9.3
Projected:									
1970									
Export I‡	132.0	124.0	131.0	200.0	125.0	104.0	65.0	360.0	218.0
Change from 1964–66 (%)	16.8	10.7	9.2	31.6	11.6	1.0	–13.3	7.8	2.8
1975									
Export I‡	151.0	136.0	142.0	270.0	137.0	106.0	54.0	380.0	224.0
Change from 1964–66 (%)	33.6	21.4	18.3	77.6	22.3	2.9	–28.0	13.8	5.7
Export II§	154.0	134.0	145.0	270.0	137.0	107.0	55.0	380.0	...
Change from 1964–66 (%)	36.3	19.6	20.8	77.6	22.3	3.9	–26.7	13.8	...
Export III‖	145.0	138.0	144.0	270.0	137.0	104.0	53.0	360.0	...
Change from 1964–66 (%)	28.3	23.2	20.0	77.6	22.3	1.0	–29.3	7.8	...
1980									
Export I‡	172.0	151.0	162.0	360.0	152.0	107.0	45.0	380.0	242.0
Change from 1964–66 (%)	52.2	34.8	35.0	136.8	35.7	3.9	–40.0	13.8	14.2
Export II§	180.0	148.0	169.0	360.0	152.0	110.0	47.0	380.0	...
Change from 1964–66 (%)	59.3	32.1	40.8	136.8	35.7	6.8	–37.3	13.8	...
Export III‖	164.0	153.0	162.0	360.0	152.0	104.0	44.0	360.0	...
Change from 1964–66 (%)	45.1	36.6	35.0	136.8	35.7	1.0	–41.3	7.8	...

* Cropland used for crops including fallow.
† Farm Production assets estimated in 1965 dollars.
‡ Export I–Crop export volume rises at 4.5 percent per year.
§ Export II–Crop export volume rises at 6 percent per year.
‖ Export III–Crop export volume rises at 3 percent per year.

tively inelastic response of consumption to changes in prices and consumer income.

The output functions illustrate the tendency for output to increase in response to increases in relative prices—a small short-run response and a larger long-term response. Technological advance, which is also to some extent a proxy variable for the uptrend in inputs, is the major determinant of output. Accordingly, the crop output function and projections into the future assume a continuation of past trends in technology in agriculture. The output function for livestock products reflects prices and feed costs as well as the uptrend in technology which has been comparatively slow for major livestock, other than poultry. Obviously a technological breakthrough affecting production costs and feeding efficiency for cattle and hogs could accelerate output and affect relative prices for livestock and products.

The simple framework used for this appraisal projects crops and livestock output, domestic food and nonfood use, prices, incomes, crop output per acre, labor use, and other major resource requirements. For this exercise, concerned mainly with possible impacts of food exports, projections are examined under three assumed crop export alternatives. However, the impacts of other assumptions—technology, population growth, and acreage levels—may be even larger than for exports. Price projections assume constant dollar incomes and no general inflation in the price level.

No attempt is made to specify the capacity of U.S. agriculture. Output potential is not some fixed quantity, except under very specific conditions. It varies with changes in technology and the relative cost of inputs; and it varies with demand pressures and returns to producers. The land input does not rigidly limit crop output. Increases in crop output in recent decades have resulted from technological advances and increased use of fertilizer and other inputs. In addition to these inputs, there is a substantial acreage of land which might be brought into cultivation if demand pressures and returns to farmers warrant. The last inventory of land capability and use reported more than 250 million acres of land in capability classes I, II, and III, ". . . suited for regular cultivation and other uses," in addition to some 450 million acres now used as cropland (1).

The conditions under which new lands would come into production are difficult to specify. Small changes, both into and out of production, are continuously underway. If demand increased and prices rose up under rapid demand expansion, some of the additional land resources as well as nonfarm inputs would expand the output potential of U.S. agriculture. Land use levels were specified for the appraisals in this report. However, indicated prices and incomes, under the highest demand projection in this study, could be moderated if additional land came into production and stepped up the output potential of agriculture. Moreover, the low-demand projection implies a continuation of programs designed to limit resource use in agriculture.

PROJECTED DEMAND AND OUTPUT BALANCES

Prospective demand expansion and the output potential of U.S. farms point to little pressure on resources during the next decade or so. Following the planned reduction in carry-over stocks of grains, some cropland is coming back into production in 1967. The projected demand-output balance for the years beyond the mid-1970's, in the framework and assumptions of this appraisal, points to some upward pressure on prices assuming crop export volume increases by about 6 percent per year. Over a period of years high prices and income would likely attract new land and other resources into production and moderate somewhat the price advances indicated under the high demand alternative. If crop exports were to increase around 3 percent per year, projected demand and output, with cropland use at about the 1967 level, would imply some downward pressure on prices and incomes. Although the low-demand projection does not assume full use of land resources, indicated prices for crops are below the 1964–66 average.

The domestic use of farm products projected for 1980 ranges about 28 to 33 percent above the 1964–66 average. This range in output reflects primarily the effect of variations in projected prices under the three assumed crop export alternatives. These increases compare with a projected increase in population of 20 to 25 percent. Livestock and products would account for the small gain in per capita domestic use. Among the crops, increased feed concentrate use for an expanding livestock industry and exports will account for growth in demand. These were the expanding sectors in past years (Table 2.4). Crop export volume increased about 5 percent per year between 1959–61 and 1964–66, and Q. M. West's published projections extend this rate of gain to 1970 (2). The range in crop export increases assumed for this appraisal—3 percent, 4.5 percent, and 6 percent—were chosen to illustrate possible impacts on agriculture.

TABLE 2.4. Total farm output, utilization, prices and income, averages 1949 to 1951, 1964 to 1966, and projections to 1980

Item	1949–51 Average	1964–66 Average	1970 Exp. I	1975 Exp. I	1975 Exp. II	1975 Exp. III	1980 Exp. I	1980 Exp. II	1980 Exp. III
SUPPLIES:									
Farm output (bil. 1957–59 dol.)	...	32.5	36.8	41.2	41.8	40.3	46.3	47.7	44.9
Farm output (1957–59 = 100)	88.0	113.0	129.6	145.0	147.2	141.9	163.0	168.0	158.1
Livestock (1957–59 = 100)	86.0	113.0	124.3	136.2	134.5	138.3	150.6	148.3	153.1
Crops (1957–59 = 100)	90.0	113.0	132.2	150.6	154.2	145.0	172.3	179.8	163.5
Imports (bil. 1957–59 dol.)	3.3	4.0	4.4	4.6	4.7	4.8	5.1	5.1	5.1
UTILIZATION:									
Domestic, excluding feed and seed (bil. 1957–59 dol.)	24.4	31.5	34.3	37.3	36.8	37.8	41.0	40.3	41.7
Per capita (1957–59 dol.)	160.8	162.0	166.0	167.0	165.0	170.0	169.0	167.0	172.0
Livestock (1957–59 dol.)	93.6	102.0	105.5	107.0	106.0	109.0	109.0	108.0	111.0
Crops (1957–59 dol.)	67.2	60.0	60.5	60.0	59.0	61.0	60.0	59.0	61.0
Feed and seed (bil. 1957–59 dol.)	8.8	9.3	10.5	11.9	11.6	12.1	13.4	13.1	13.7
Exports (bil. 1957–59 dol.)	2.7	5.6	6.9	8.6	9.7	7.3	10.5	12.5	8.3
Total net use†	27.1	37.1	41.2	45.8	46.5	45.1	51.4	52.8	50.0
Inventory change	0	−0.6	0	0	0	0	0	0	0
PRICES RECEIVED (1910–14 = 100):‡	270.0	250.0	258.0	264.0	284.0	246.0	276.0	307.0	252.0
Livestock (Pa)	296.0	263.0	277.0	287.0	305.0	266.0	297.0	319.0	276.0
Crops (Pc)	241.0	235.0	235.0	238.0	259.0	226.0	252.0	297.0	226.0
CASH RECEIPTS (bil. dol.):	29.7	39.7	45.9	52.6	56.7	48.3	61.7	69.4	55.1
Livestock	17.0	22.1	25.6	29.1	30.5	27.3	33.3	35.2	31.5
Crops	12.7	17.6	20.3	23.5	26.2	21.0	28.4	34.2	23.6

* Export I assumes crop exports increase at 4.5 percent per year; Export II assumes crop exports increase at 6 percent per year; and Export III assumes crop exports increase at 3 percent per year.

† Feed and seed are subtracted from total production in order to avoid double counting in the total.

‡ Projected prices reflect real income growth and a relatively stable general price level.

Farm output projected for 1980 ranges some 40 to 50 percent above 1964–66. With crop exports increasing at 4.5 percent per year (alternative I), domestic use (excluding feed and seed) increases around 30 percent and feed uses increase about 45 percent. The combined volume of exports under this assumption rises almost 90 percent from the 1964–66 average. This would be nearly as large as the export increase over the past 15 years. A farm output increase of about 45 percent would match this demand projection at prices averaging around 1966 levels. These comparisons make no allowance for big changes in the general level of prices. Under the slower crop-export assumption (III)— 3 percent per year—an output increase of about 40 percent from 1960–64 would meet projected demand, with about 20 million fewer acres than for export alternative I, at prices received around the 1964–66 average.

CROPS

Crop output projected for 1980 varies from 45 to 60 percent above the 1964–66 average. This relatively wide range reflects the three assumed increases in crop exports, and the major variable element is demand. Under the high-export assumption, the increase in domestic use is the smallest and prices are the highest of either alternative. But domestic demand is very inelastic relative to price and accordingly varies little under the three export assumptions (Table 2.5). Combined domestic use of crops, assuming an annual increase in exports of 4.5 percent (alternative I), is projected to increase a third from the 1964–66 average; the assumed increase in exports would nearly double crop exports by 1980. With such an increase, exports would rise to about 29 percent of crop output compared with 22 percent in 1964–66. To match these demand increases, under this demand alternative, output increases around 55 percent and projected prices average around 5 percent above the 1964–66 average. Such a small price increase could hardly be considered significant in the simple analytical framework used for these projections.

Price levels implied from the projected demand-output balances for crops average about a fourth lower for the low than for the high export growth assumption. Similar projections for 1970 and 1975 show approximate impacts of alternative export levels assumed and illustrate the very inelastic demand for crops. The output increase projected for crops assumes cropland use at 380 million acres for the two high export assumptions and 360 million acres for the lower export alternative. Projected crop

TABLE 2.5. Crop output, utilization, prices and cash receipts, averages 1949 to 1951, and 1964 to 1966, and projections to 1980

Item	1949-51 Average	1964-66 Average	1970 Exp. I	1975 Exp. I	1975 Exp. II	1975 Exp. III	1980 Exp. I	1980 Exp. II	1980 Exp. III
SUPPLIES:									
Production (1957-59 = 100)	90.0	113.0	132.2	150.6	154.2	145.0	172.3	179.8	163.5
Production (bil. 1957-59 dol.)	17.4	21.7	25.4	28.9	29.6	27.9	33.1	34.6	31.5
Imports (bil. 1957-59 dol.)	2.8	3.1	3.3	3.5	3.5	3.6	3.9	3.9	3.9
Total (bil. 1957-59 dol.)	20.2	24.8	28.7	32.4	33.1	31.5	37.0	38.5	35.4
UTILIZATION:									
Domestic (bil. 1957-59 dol.)	17.8	20.5	22.6	24.7	24.3	25.1	27.4	26.9	28.0
Feed & seed (bil. 1957-59 dol.)	7.6	8.8	10.0	11.4	11.1	11.6	12.9	12.6	13.2
Other, total (bil. 1957-59 dol.)	10.2	11.7	12.5	13.4	13.2	13.5	14.5	14.3	14.8
Per capita (dol.)	67.2	60.1	60.0	60.0	59.0	60.56	60.0	58.7	60.97
Exports (bil. 1957-59 dol.)	2.4	4.9	6.1	7.7	8.8	6.4	9.6	11.6	7.4
Total (bil. 1957-59 dol.)	20.2	25.5	28.7	32.4	33.1	31.5	37.0	38.5	35.4
Net stock change	0	-0.7	0	0	0	0	0	0	0
Cropland used† (million acres)	382.0	334.0	360.0	380.0	380.0	360.0	380.0	380.0	360.0
Yield per acre (1957-59 = 100)	85.0	120.0	131.0	142.0	145.0	144.0	162.0	169.0	162.0
Prices received (1919-14 = 100)‡	241.0	235.0	235.0	238.0	259.0	226.0	252.0	297.0	226.0
Cash receipts (bil. dol.)	12.7	17.6	20.3	23.5	26.2	21.0	28.4	34.2	23.6

* Export I assumes crop exports increase at 4.5 percent per year—about 95 percent from 1964-66 to 1980; Export II assumes crop exports increase at 6 percent per year—140 percent from 1964-66 to 1980, and Export III assumes crop exports increase at 3 percent per year—56 percent from 1964-66 to 1980.

† Cropland used for crops which includes fallow and crop failure.

‡ Projected prices reflect real income growth and a relatively stable general price level.

output per acre for 1980 ranges from 35 to 40 percent above the 1964–66 average under the three alternatives.

LIVESTOCK

Increases in per capita use of livestock products account for the projected rise in per capita demand for farm products. Per capita use projected for 1980 is 6 to 8 percent above 1964–66. Rising consumer buying power generates a gradual rise in per capita use of livestock products. With output geared primarily to growth in the domestic market, projected demand increases balance with production increases at levels ranging some 30 to 35 percent above 1964–66. But, unlike for crops, the higher livestock production comes under the low-export assumption and the corresponding low crop price alternative. Livestock product prices, under the high export and high grain price assumptions, run around 15 percent higher than under the low-export assumption. These variations in production and prices reflect primarily differences in feed costs and in domestic demand for livestock products under the 3 export assumptions (Table 2.6).

Output of livestock products projected for 1980 implicitly reflect continued rapid technological advances in feed production with feed costs declining some, relative to livestock product prices. Major technological breakthroughs in the production and feeding of livestock could materially change output-price balances projected for the next 10 to 15 years.

Feed concentrate use is projected to increase 45 to 50 percent under the low-export assumption and 40 to 45 percent under the high-export alternative. The rise reflects the projected gain in production of livestock products as well as some further rise in the feeding rate, particularly under the low-crop price alternative. Similar comparisons of differential impacts are shown also for 1975.

PRICES AND INCOMES

Output and demand projections for the next decade or so, assuming an annual increase of 4.5 percent in the volume of crop exports, point to average prices received around the range of recent years. Because of the very low price elasticity of demand for crops, there is a rather large price range—around 25 percent—from the high- to the low-export assumption. This variation influences feed costs, livestock production, and prices of livestock

TABLE 2.6. Livestock production, feed use, utilization, price and cash receipts, averages 1949 to 1951 and 1964 to 1966, and projections to 1980

				Projected*					
	1949–51	1964–66	1970	1975			1980		
Item	Average	Average	Exp. I	Exp.I	Exp. II	Exp. III	Exp. I	Exp. II	Exp. III
SUPPLIES:									
Production (1957–59 = 100)	86.0	113.0	124.3	136.2	134.5	138.3	150.6	148.3	153.1
Production (bil. 1957–59 dol.)	15.2	20.1	22.0	24.1	23.8	24.5	26.6	26.2	27.1
Imports (bil. 1957–59 dol.)	0.5	0.9	1.1	1.2	1.2	1.2	1.2	1.2	1.2
Total (bil. 1957–59 dol.)	15.7	21.0	23.1	25.3	25.0	25.7	27.8	27.4	28.3
UTILIZATION:									
Domestic (bil. 1957–59 dol.)	15.4	20.3	22.2	24.4	24.1	24.8	26.9	26.5	27.4
Feed & seed (bil. 1957–59 dol.)	1.2	0.5	0.5	0.5	0.5	0.5	0.5	0.5	0.5
Other, total (bil. 1957–59 dol.)	14.2	19.8	21.8	23.9	23.6	24.3	26.4	26.0	26.9
Per capita (dol.)	93.6	102.0	105.0	107.0	106.0	109.0	109.0	108.0	111.0
Exports (bil. 1957–59 dol.)	0.3	0.7	0.8	0.9	0.9	0.9	0.9	0.9	0.9
Total (bil. 1957–59 dol.)	15.7	21.0	23.1	25.2	24.9	25.7	27.8	27.4	28.3
Production units (million)	175.4	212.0	233.0	254.0	251.0	258.0	279.0	275.0	284.0
Concentrates fed (mil. ton)	122.9	157.0	176.0	200.0	195.0	205.0	228.0	223.0	235.0
Feed use per unit (ton)†	.70	.74	.75	.79	.78	.80	.82	.81	.83
Prices received†									
Livestock and products (1910–14 = 100)	296.0	263.0	277.0	287.0	305.0	266.0	297.0	319.0	276.0
Feed grain and hay (1910–14 = 100)	199.0	173.0	165.0	150.0	165.0	135.0	135.0	150.0	120.0
Ratio Pa/Pf‡	1.49	1.52	1.68	1.91	1.85	1.97	2.20	2.13	2.30
Cash receipts (bil. dol.)	17.0	22.1	25.6	29.1	30.5	27.3	33.3	35.2	31.5

* Export I assumes crop exports increase at 4.5 percent per year—95 percent per year from 1964–66 to 1980; Export II assumes crop exports increase at 6 percent per year—140 percent from 1964–66 to 1980; and Export III assumes crop exports increase at 3 percent per year—56 percent from 1964–66 to 1980.
† Projected prices reflect real income growth and a relatively stable general price level.
‡ Ratio of livestock product prices to prices for feed grains and hay.

products, though the price range projected for 1980 is only about half as large as that for crops.

The high-price projections for crops are associated with the high-export assumption and the larger output projection. Since the effect of high prices on domestic use is relatively small, projected crop receipts under the high-export assumption (II) are 45 percent above those for the low-export assumption (III). The level of cropland use was assumed at 380 million acres, but returns under the high alternative could well attract additional land for crop production. This would narrow the projected difference in prices and cash receipts between the high and low alternatives. The projected range in market receipts for livestock products is much narrower than for crops—around a tenth from the low alternative (III) to the high alternative (II)—reflecting mainly the impact of variations in crop exports on the cost of feed.

Under the assumption that crop exports increase about 4.5 percent per year, projected livestock receipts increase about 50 percent above the 1964–66 average. Combined receipts for both crops and livestock products, under this assumption (I), are projected for 1980 at a level 50 to 60 percent above the 1964–66 average. With declining farm numbers, cash receipts per farm rise much more sharply than total cash receipts (Table 2.4).

During 1960 to 1965, a period of rapid rise in farm income, realized net income per farm in real terms (adjusted for price level increase) rose more than 6 percent per year. Median income per family for the nonfarm population, similarly adjusted, rose in this period by around 2.5 percent per year. Although the farm-nonfarm income gap was substantially narrowed, per capita farm incomes still averaged only about two-thirds nonfarm incomes.

The output-demand balance projected under the middle export assumption (alternative I) would push net income per farm up by possibly 3.5 to 4 percent per year in the next 10 to 15 years, well above the increase projected for real income of nonfarm families. If these rates continued, it would take about two decades to close the income gap.

FARM ORGANIZATION AND RESOURCE INPUTS

The most rapid changes in agriculture have been in resource adjustment and associated changes in numbers of farms, the farm population, and advances in average productivity of resources in farming. The shifts in resource use associated with technological advances and changes in relative cost of inputs have in general resulted in the replacement of labor, and to some extent land, with inputs such as machinery and equipment, fertilizer, and other capital inputs. Many of these adjustments are expected to continue at a rapid rate and could accelerate in the foreseeable future. They will bring further declines in the number of farms and extensive shifts in the labor-capital resource mix which will likely be accompanied by rapid advances in the productivity of agriculture.

Farm consolidation and the sharp decline in farm numbers have been associated with some big changes in the resource structure of agriculture. There were about 3.4 million farms in 1965 compared with 5.6 million in 1950. The downtrend in farm numbers reflects sharp declines in the smaller sized classes and a continued increase in the number of larger farms. If trends of recent years continue, farm numbers could easily be down to around 2 million by 1980. About half of these would be the larger, commercial family farms with sales above $10,000 per farm. The remaining half of the farms would include part-time and part-retirement farms and a sizable number of units with sales per farm below $10,000. Under the current definition of a farm, many people will live in rural areas on places considered farms which, in fact, may be rural residences.

Technical possibilities exist for an even more rapid decline in farm numbers than in the past. It would not be unreasonable to visualize an organization of agriculture in which a half million farms could carry out the production job. If all farms were in general organized like those with sales of more than $40,000 per farm, projected requirements might be supplied by around a half million commercial farms. These farms would have average sales around $110,000 per farm with average net incomes of about $25,000 and production assets around $400,000 per farm. A commercial agriculture made up of fewer and more specialized units probably would be more responsive to economic forces and possibly would be a stronger influence in the market.

LABOR INPUT

The downtrend in labor requirements is projected to continue in coming years. This decline assumes that output per man-hour will continue to rise much as in the past with further extensive shifts in resource use. A continued uptrend in output per man-hour of 5.5 to 6 percent per year and the output-demand balance projected for 1980 would suggest a decline of around 40 percent from 1964–65. This compares with a drop in use of labor of nearly 50 percent in the past 15 years (Table 2.3).

Labor requirements suggest 3 to 3.5 million workers (SRS concept) compared with 5.7 million in 1964–66. The comparable census concept implies fewer than 3 million workers. These declines reflect the downtrend in farm numbers as well as projected output and productivity trends. Labor inputs project for 1980 a little decline in use of labor per farm, though the average size of farms as well as capital inputs per farm and average labor productivity rise rapidly.

Labor requirements and projected farm numbers, assuming no big changes in the definition of a farm, imply a farm population by 1980 of around 7.5 million. This compares with about 12.4 million in 1965. The decline would represent a slower drop than that during the past 15 years. But the farm population would decline from around 6.5 percent of total population in 1965 to around 3 percent of the total projected for 1980.

CAPITAL REQUIREMENTS

Total resource inputs have changed little in the past decade or so and may increase only slightly in the next 10 to 15 years. This projection assumes no big acceleration from the recent relatively rapid growth in domestic and export demand for farm products. Projected demands and productivity trends do not point to great pressure on land resources. Projections make no allowance for any significant change in the land base.

There are around 1150 million acres of land in farms. Around 450 million acres are classified as cropland and some 300 million acres have been harvested in recent years. The remaining acreage of cropland in farms was either pasture, fallow, idle, or diverted under government programs. An inventory of land capability and use taken in 1962 reported, in addition to the cropland above, more than 250 million acres of land in capability classes (I to III) suitable for regular cultivation. Undoubtedly, much of this land would come into production if demand expansion, prices, or public investment provided the inducement.

Crop output per acre is projected to trend upward much as in the past. However, the increase may be a little slower than in the past decade if additional acreage of cropland is brought into production.

Production assets used in agriculture, after adjustment for price level change, have increased around a tenth in the past 15 years. However, capital of nonfarm origin and inputs of inter-mediate nonfarm products used in farm production increased around 50 percent. The latter include big increases in the use of fertilizer and other chemicals, fuels, services, and many other operating inputs.

The uptrend in use of many nonfarm operating inputs will continue and may accelerate in coming years. Total capital use in agriculture is also expected to rise further and possibly more rapidly than in the past. Trends and shifts in the mix of capital, land, and labor in agriculture are not easy to anticipate even under simplifying assumptions about technological advances, relative productivity, and costs. A continuation of past growth in capital inputs appears conservative and implies some accelera-tion in the advance in technology. A slower but still plausible technological advance would require an increase in productive assets of perhaps as much as 50 percent from 1965 to 1980. But such an increase seems unreasonably large. In any event, capital likely will play an even more strategic role in determining farm output and the output potential of U.S. agriculture than will land and labor.

NUMBER AND SIZE STRUCTURE OF FARMS

As indicated above, farm numbers are projected to decline to around 2 million farms by 1980, but the adjustment surely could be more rapid and it may be slower. Around a million of these farms would fall into sales classes with more than $10,000 per farm; about 350–400 thousand would be in the $2,500 to $10,000 per farm sales groups; and about 700 thousand farms with sales under $2,500 per farm. More than two-thirds of the latter would be part-time and retirement farms.

The reasonableness of the projected distribution was checked by using distributions projected for 1970, 1975, and 1980 to compute total cash receipts and land in farms, i.e., the product of number of farms and average receipts in each size class, etc. Pro-jected distributions of farm numbers yield aggregate cash receipts equal to those projected as well as total land in farms without straining the top open-end size class (Table 2.7). Receipts based on the projected demand-output balance are expressed in 1965 prices and income-expense relationships rest heavily on estimates for 1959 and 1965. These distributions yield some interesting im-plications about productivity gains and the labor-land-capital mix. Some of these questions can be at least partially explored.

For the projected distributions to yield the labor input pro-

TABLE 2.7. Income and resources of farms by economic class, estimated 1965, and projections to 1980

Farm Sales Class and Year	Number of Farms	Land in Farms		Cash Receipts*		Production Assets		Labor Used	
		Total	Per farm	Total	Per farm	Total	Per farm	Total	Per farm
	(1,000)	(mil. acres)	(acres)	(mil. dol.)	(dol.)	(mil. dol.)	(dol.)	(mil. hours)	(hours)
1965 Estimated									
$40,000 and over	170	385	2,265	17,369	102,171	64,272	378,070	1,565	9,206
$20,000 to $39,999	300	209	697	9,000	30,000	44,235	147,450	1,201	4,004
$10,000 and over	990	798	806	34,169	34,514	149,783	151,245	4,220	4,263
$50 to $9,999	1,360	245	180	6,252	4,597	40,865	30,048	2,660	1,956
Other†	1,025	108	105	1,218	1,188	19,562	19,085	1,096	1,069
All farms	3,375	1,151	341	41,639	12,337	210,160	62,270	7,976	2,363
1970 Projected									
$40,000 and over	215	478	2,223	23,784	110,623	88,022	409,405	1,958	9,107
$20,000 to $39,999	325	227	697	9,750	30,000	47,920	147,406	1,189	3,658
$10,000 and over	1,000	885	885	40,434	40,434	172,394	172,394	4,322	4,322
$50 to $9,999	1,025	182	177	4,626	4,513	30,123	29,388	1,825	1,780
Other†	785	84	107	940	1,197	15,096	19,231	771	982
All farms	2,810	1,151	410	46,000	16,370	217,613	77,442	6,918	2,462
1975 Projected									
$40,000 and over	270	550	2,037	28,838	106,807	106,696	395,170	2,052	7,600
$20,000 to $39,999	340	237	697	10,200	30,000	50,132	147,447	1,075	3,162
$10,000 and over	1,020	948	929	45,188	44,302	189,333	185,621	4,034	3,955
$50 to $9,999	780	137	175	3,478	4,459	22,656	29,046	1,199	1,537
Other†	610	66	109	734	1,203	11,776	19,305	517	848
All farms	2,410	1,151	477	49,400	20,498	223,765	92,849	5,750	2,386
1980 Projected									
$40,000 and over	335	602	1,796	36,023	107,531	133,287	397,872	2,100	6,269
$20,000 to $39,999	355	247	697	10,650	30,000	52,344	147,448	920	2,592
$10,000 and over	1,060	994	938	52,223	49,267	214,964	202,796	3,690	3,481
$50 to $9,999	590	103	174	2,621	4,442	17,063	28,920	750	1,271
Other†	490	54	110	591	1,206	9,481	19,349	340	694
All farms	2,140	1,151	538	55,435	25,904	241,508	112,854	4,780	2,234

* Cash receipts plus government payments in 1965 and 1970.
† "Other" is mostly part-time and part-retirement farms.

jected for 1980, based on output and a continued uptrend in the productivity, it is necessary to assume that some 60 to 70 percent of the rise in labor productivity is due simply to a change in the number and size distribution of farms. The larger farms have higher output per man-hour. The combining of smaller, less efficient units into fewer, larger, more efficient farms can materially increase output per man-hour in agriculture over time even if productivity on individual farm units changes little. Accordingly, projected increases in labor productivity for agriculture as a whole rise about twice as rapidly as productivity gains projected for the major size groupings.

If prices are held constant, as assumed, average sales and the value of output per farm must hold around the midpoint of the size classes. But with yields increasing, this assumption requires some decline in average acreage per farm in these classes, or some other change in the resource mix. Are average yields for agriculture as a whole increasing more rapidly than those on individual farms? What do projections for labor productivity and yield imply for capital requirements, in total and by size of farm? These are not easy questions to answer conceptually or empirically. One alternative is suggested by the apparent tendency in the past for a relatively constant capital-output ratio for agriculture, in total and, insofar as it can be approximated, by economic class. From a relatively constant capital-output ratio (K/O), projected output per man-hour (O/L), we can approximate the capital-labor ratio (K/L). With projected labor requirements, capital requirements are determined. Under this high productivity alternative, productive assets are projected to increase about 15 percent by 1980 (Table 2.7).

Exploring the implications of productivity advances and changes in resource mix by economic class are interesting, but the investigation does not yield solid and unequivocal conclusions. It is quite apparent that much of the rapid increase in average output per man-hour and possibly in other measures of productivity for agriculture is due directly to changes in number and size distribution of farms. Although these observations are not new, differences in trends on individual farms and the average for all farms may be greater than generally realized.

LITERATURE CITED

1. Soil and Water Conservation Needs. Stat. Bull. 317, USDA. Aug., 1962.
2. West, Q. M. Foreign supply and demand projections: outlook for U.S. exports. J. Farm Econ. 48:1359. 1966.

CHAPTER THREE

Major Price and Income Consequences From Policies Over the Past Thirty-Five Years

WALTER W. WILCOX

PROFESSOR MURRAY BENEDICT of the University of California, in his 500-page book *Can We Solve the Farm Problem,* published in 1955, has a final chapter entitled "Two Decades of Experience —What Conclusions Are Warranted." In fifty pages the record is summarized and interpreted in great detail, but no sweeping conclusions are presented. The final paragraphs include these statements:

> In the early 1920's, agriculture was depressed and out of step with other parts of the economy. . . . The more severe and general depression of the 1930's created a willingness on the part of farmers, and of the public as well, to go much farther in the direction of government control over economic relationships than would have been acceptable in earlier periods. . . . Agriculture was to be given some aid in exercising the kinds of control that had become common in other types of business.
>
> There was little public opposition to official guarantees that prices would be supported at relatively high levels for a reasonable period following cessation of [World War II] hostilities. . . . Since [the Korean

War] weaknesses in the current program have reappeared and new policies are being widely and actively discussed. Adjustments will apparently have to be made (1, p. 480).

Professor Don Paarlberg, nine years later, published a 375-page book entitled *Farm Policy*. He takes the unusual course of stating his over-all conclusions in the preface:

> . . . government price supports and production controls did improve economic conditions during the disastrous days of the Great Depression, improvement then desperately needed. . . . Continuation of price supports . . . during World War II [was] not needed.
> . . . .
> Government regulation of farm prices and production during the postwar period was harmful in that incentive prices provided more stimulation to the agricultural plant than the weak controls could overcome. Hence, to some degree, the excess capacity, the surplus, the disposal problem, the cost, and the political wrangling (2, pp. viii–ix).

Many other agricultural economists and a number of popular writers have evaluated our agricultural polices, or specific aspects of them, during the past thirty-five years. Their evaluations have been favorable or unfavorable, depending on the particular aspects discussed—and to a large extent depending on the value judgments of the writers.

This essay attempts to present, in more or less summary form, information and evidence that have accumulated from these many studies.

VARIATIONS IN ECONOMIC CONDITIONS IN THIRTY-FIVE YEARS

The thirty-five years under review naturally divide themselves into four periods from the standpoint of basic economic conditions affecting farmers. The first eleven years, 1930 to 1941, were dominated by the Great Depression. Widespread unemployment continued throughout the period. Largely because of the drop in nonfarm purchasing power, farm prices fell more than 50 percent from 1929 to 1932 and did not return to predepression levels until 1942 when the country was at war.

The second period, 1942 to 1945, was dominated by wartime needs for all the food that could be produced.

The third period, 1946 to 1952, began immediately after World War II when maximum farm production was needed to meet pressing world food needs. Two years later, production was far greater than needed. Farm prices fell, and the Commodity Credit Corporation made price-supporting loans totaling $2 billion per year in 1948 and 1949, mostly on wheat, cotton, and corn. Three years of military action in Korea followed, and stocks which had been accumulated in 1948 and 1949 were drawn down by the increased demands associated with the war.

The fourth period, 1953 to 1965, although beginning eight years after the end of World War II, is in fact the only period in the past thirty-five years in which the U.S. economy has been characterized by relatively high-level, peaceful business activity.

Each of these periods will be treated separately in the evaluation of the price and income consequences of past farm policies.

THE YEARS OF THE GREAT DEPRESSION, 1930 TO 1941

What were the major price and income consequences of the farm program of the 1930's?

Farmers' realized gross farm income dropped from $13.9 billion in 1929 to $6.4 billion in 1932. From that low point, it increased to $11.4 billion in 1937, dropped back to $10.1 billion in 1938, and then again increased each year to reach the 1929 level again in 1941. This record of farm income during the Great Depression includes the benefits of the government's agricultural adjustment, surplus disposal, and market order programs.

Operators' net farm incomes in 1932 dropped to less than one-third their 1929 level and gradually improved in the succeeding years, finally reachieving the 1929 level in 1941 (Fig. 3.1).

By far the most important government programs for agriculture during this period were the adjustment and price support programs for cotton, corn, wheat, tobacco, rice, and peanuts. These programs were supplemented, however, by surplus removal purchases of perishable fruits and vegetables and by marketing agreement and market order programs, administered by the Secretary of Agriculture, covering the marketing of a number of fruits and vegetables and fluid milk.

Although all analysts agree that these programs resulted in substantial improvements in producers' incomes during this period, no one has attempted a quantitative estimate of their benefits. Harold Rowe, of the Brookings Institution, prepared an appendix to *Three Years of the Agricultural Adjustment Administration,* published by the Brookings Institution in 1937. It was entitled "Ascertaining the Benefits and Burdens of Adjustment Programs," was forty pages of small type, and illustrated

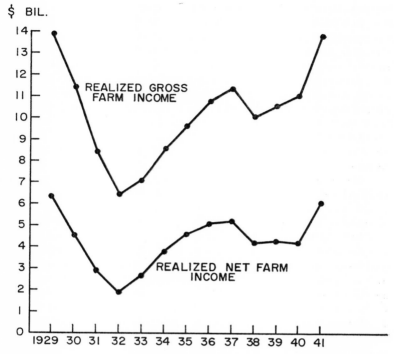

Fig. 3.1. Realized gross and net farm income, 1929–1941.

with 17 diagrams. Yet in the author's words, "it does not in itself furnish a basis for sweeping conclusions."

The well-known economist of the Stanford Food Institute, Joe Davis, in an earlier footnote in the Brookings publication, probably accurately summarized the effectiveness of the first three years of the AAA and related programs. He said the AAA was fortunate to operate in a period of economic recovery and though it contributed to agricultural recovery, it claimed and received more credit than if it had been operating in a period of declining economic activity.

The present writer, in an article published in the *Journal of Farm Economics* in 1958, concluded that in the absence of government price support, adjustment, and marketing programs, farmers' realized net farm income would have been as much as up to 55 percent lower than it was in each of the years 1937 to 1941. In 1938, for example, large crops and lessened business activity caused gross farm income to decline $1.3 billion and net farm income to decline $1 billion as compared to 1937. Commodity Credit Corporation loans and surplus removal purchases removed $725 million worth of farm products from commercial markets in their price and income stabilization activities and prevented farm income from falling even further. Because of the inelastic demand for farm products, these loans and purchases kept farmers' incomes from falling an estimated $1.8 billion further. In addition, government payments to farmers totaled $482 million. Without the government programs the decline in net farm income might well have been $3.3 instead of $1 billion.

Because of the difficulties in estimating the effect of price changes on subsequent production and market supplies, no definitive studies have been made of the price and income effects of these early programs.

Official statistics indicate that crop yields and total farm output were 12 percent higher in 1939–40 than 10 years earlier, and that Commodity Credit Corporation price-supporting loans and inventories totaled $1.3 billion in early 1941. One can only speculate as to what would have happened to crop yields and farm output in the absence of the farm programs in the 1930's. It is highly probably, however, that much lower prices and incomes would have been realized in the absence of farm programs, and the lower income would have prevented much of the increase in mechanization which took place during this period.

In part, because of the farm programs, the number of tractors on farms increased from 920,000 in 1930 to 1,665,000 in 1941, an increase of 80 percent. Also, the inventory value of machinery and motor vehicles on farms which declined to $2.2 billion in 1935, increased to $3.3 billion in 1941. Associated with the increase in farm mechanization was a decline in hired farm workers of almost 18 percent—from 3,190,000 in 1930 to 2,652,000 in 1941.

THE WAR YEARS, 1942 TO 1945

As mentioned earlier, the Commodity Credit Corporation had under price support control some $1.3 billion of farm products in 1941 when the United States became directly involved in World War II. Farmers also had many relatively new tractors and other farm machines in their machine sheds as a result of the previous farm programs.

As early as April, 1941, the Secretary of Agriculture announced that he would support hog prices at $9 per 100 pounds to encourage increased hog production. This was followed by legislative action and other price-supporting announcements until in 1945 government price support guarantees had been extended to some 166 farm products.

The wartime demand for all farm products was so great, however, that prices dropped to support levels only in exceptional situations. Egg prices dropped to and below support levels in the springs of 1944 and 1945. Poultry dropped to support levels in the fall and winter of 1945–46. Potato prices dropped to support levels in the summer of 1943 and each fall thereafter for several years. Prices of several other vegetable and truck crops fell to support levels for short periods when temporary seasonal gluts occurred.

Hog prices also required governmental support action in the winter of 1943–44. But, with these exceptions, the government was not required to make good on its price support guarantees. Rather, it was more active in maintaining price ceilings on the processed farm products as they moved through retail stores.

Living costs continued to rise during the war in spite of retail price ceilings. In the spring of 1943, labor unrest became so widespread that the Office of Price Administration "rolled back" retail meat and butter prices and introduced consumer subsidies to avoid reducing prices to producers. By the end of the war in 1945, consumer subsidies were being paid at the rate of $1.6 billion a year on eighteen different food and agricultural products.

Undoubtedly, farm prices would have gone even higher during the war if the government had not established retail price ceilings. Also, the release of the Commodity Credit Corporation stocks accumulated in the prewar years moderated the farm price increases.

In spite of these influences, farm prices doubled between 1940 and 1945, and cash receipts from farm marketings increased two-and-one-half times. Farmers' net income increased almost three times between 1940 and 1945 (Fig. 3.2).

Agricultural economists are generally agreed that the soil conservation activities and adjustment programs in the late 1930's, together with the new farm machinery purchased in those years, made it possible for farmers to increase their output, with fewer workers in the war years, than otherwise would have been possible. Farm output increased some 15 percent during these years.

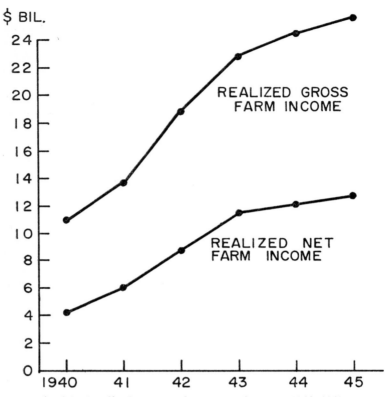

Fig. 3.2. Realized gross and net farm income, 1940–1945.

No comprehensive studies are available on the effects of the government wartime price support announcements. Although Don Paarlberg may be correct in concluding that they were not needed, it is more probable that they had at least a small positive effect on production without having important adverse effects on the use of resources.

Reviewing the price and income consequences of farm programs for these first two periods, one concludes that the effects of the prewar programs carried over into the war years and contributed substantially to the production and income realized in those years—a period when both farm equipment and hired farm labor were in inadequate supply.

THE IMMEDIATE POSTWAR YEARS, 1946 TO 1952

In 1945 the war came to an end with $480 million of cotton in the loans and inventories held by the Commodity Credit Corporation. Other commodities held by the CCC brought loans and inventories to a total of $1.1 billion. But 1946 and 1947 were years of worldwide food shortages rather than surpluses. Unfavorable grain yields in 1945, combined with widespread disruption of food production during the war and immediate postwar years, resulted in famine and near famine conditions in India and other parts of Asia and Europe in 1946 and 1947.

The worldwide need for food and fiber for relief and rehabilitation, together with the removal of retail price ceilings in the United States, resulted in an increase of 15 percent in farm prices in 1946 over 1945, and a further increase of 16 percent in 1947. Wheat and meat animal prices increased 50 percent. Although the wartime price guarantees were still in effect, few if any products sold at or near government price support levels in 1946 and 1947.

By 1948 and 1949, however, world production had recovered somewhat, and U.S. crop yields were considerably higher than in previous years. Prices dropped sharply and CCC inventories and loans outstanding increased from $294 million in 1948, to $2.372 billion one year later and 3.538 billion two years later.

The Korean hostilities which broke out in the summer of 1950 caused a sharp reversal in CCC stocks. Loans and inventories dropped a half in the following 12 months and another fifth in the 1951 crop year. Wartime price ceilings and mandatory price supports which had expired in 1948 were renewed. But market prices remained at relatively favorable levels, over one-third higher than when hostilities ceased in 1945. As fighting drew to a close, however, farm prices weakened. Favorable crop yields in 1952 lowered market prices, and the Commodity Credit Corporation made price-supporting loans totaling $2.9 billion on the 1952 crops. Clearly, the immediate postwar, worldwide shortage of food was at an end.

Again, it is impossible to draw sweeping conclusions as to the price and income consequences of the farm programs operating during these immediate postwar years. The substantial price supports extended in 1948 and 1949 not only kept farm income from dropping even further, but resulted in carrying forward stocks which were utilized during the Korean War period. Farm prices which had declined 12 to 15 percent in the calendar years

1949 and 1950, increased 18 percent in 1951 and probably would have moved even higher in the absence of retail price ceilings and the accumulated stocks carried forward from the 1948 and 1949 crops.

Without doubt, the price support programs stabilized farm prices and income somewhat during this period and kept farm income from falling even further in 1949 and 1950, when farmers' net income fell one-fourth from the $17 billion record established in 1947 (Fig. 3.3).

THE POSTWAR ADJUSTMENT PERIOD, 1953 TO 1965

Most early postwar discussions of farm policies stressed the importance of high-level business activity to farmers. If the nation's workers were fully employed, the demand for food and fiber would be relatively high and nonfarm job opportunities would attract underemployed farm workers into better paying jobs. Many agricultural economists believed that if high-level business activity were maintained at home and abroad, farmers would be

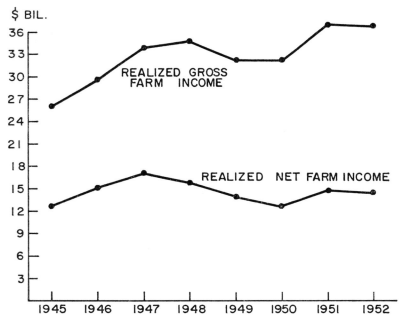

Fig. 3.3. Realized gross and net farm income, 1945–1952.

able to adjust to peacetime conditions without continued government price support and adjustment programs. They looked forward to the gradual lowering of government price supports and to the liquidation of the prewar adjustment programs.

In 1954 Professor Benedict said, "New policies are being actively discussed. Adjustments will apparently have to be made." A new administration took over the executive branch of the government in January, 1953. The new Secretary of Agriculture, in an early statement on agricultural policy, said:

The supreme test of any government policy, agricultural or other, should be, "how will it affect the character, morals, and well-being of our people. . . ." It is doubtful if any man can be politically free who depends upon the State for sustenance.

This emphasis on freedom from government direction and regulations as perhaps the most important goal of farm policy also was vigorously advanced by the American Farm Bureau Federation, the largest general farm organization, in all farm policy discussions.

The active discussion of alternative policies continued throughout the Eisenhower Administration, much of it turning on how farmers might regain their "freedom." Much of the discussion implied that with "freedom," marginal producers would be eliminated and the more efficient larger farmers would not experience lower incomes if price supports were lowered and adjustment programs were phased out. The implication was that market forces, if permitted, would soon bring about an adjustment in supplies and prices resulting in improved net income for each remaining farm family.

Net farm income drifted lower each year, however, from 1951 to 1957, recovered somewhat in 1958, and dropped back again in 1959 and 1960. Viewing this trend, the majority in Congress could not be convinced of the desirability of liquidating the government programs. The Congress refused either to lower price supports to market levels or to adopt sufficiently restrictive measures to bring supplies into balance with market outlets at the support price levels. In 1954, it did, however, approve the Agricultural Trade Development and Assistance Act (P.L. 480). Under this legislation, in addition to modest acreage diversion, Congress authorized surplus disposal or concessional sales to foreign countries outside commercial market channels and the distribution of surpluses to people on relief rolls. Rather than lower price supports further, or adopt more restrictive programs, it permitted the accumulation of the remaining surplus stocks in government inventories.

President Eisenhower and his advisers were so unhappy with the program which Congress insisted on continuing, that Congress was sent a special message in January, 1959, which said:

Three of the twelve mandatory products (wheat, corn, and cotton) account for about 85 percent of the Federal inventory of price-supported commodities, though they produce only 20 percent of the total cash farm income.

The price-support and production control program has not worked.

1. Most of the dollars are spent on the production of a relatively few large producers.

Nearly a million and a half farms produce wheat. Ninety percent of the expenditures for price support on wheat result from production of about half of these farms—the largest ones.

Nearly a million farms produce cotton. Seventy-five percent of the expenditures for cotton price support result from production of about one-fourth of these farms—the largest ones.

For other supported crops, a similarly disproportionate share of the expenditure goes to the large producers.

For wheat, cotton, and rice producers who have allotments of 100 acres or more, the net budgetary expenditures per farm for the present fiscal year are approximately as follows: wheat, $7,000 per farm; cotton, $10,000 per farm; rice, $10,000 per farm.

Though some presently unknown share of these expenditures will eventually be recovered through surplus disposal, the final cost of the operation will undoubtedly be impressively large.

Clearly, the existing price support program channels most of the dollars to those who store the surpluses and to relatively few producers of a few crops. It does little to help the farmers in greatest difficulty. . . .

2. The control program does not control.

Mandatory supports are at a level which so stimulates new technology and the flow of capital into production as to offset, in large part, the control effort.

Despite acreage allotments and marketing quotas, despite a large soil bank program, and despite massive surplus disposal, Government investment in farm commodities will soon be at a new record high (3).

Congress was unable to discover any better alternatives, however, and refused to make major changes in the program.

Under Presidents Kennedy and Johnson, price support levels were lowered, but government payments for acreage diversion and for surplus disposal were increased sharply. Supplies were brought into better balance with market outlets. Farm income increased a little in 1961 and remained at that level until 1964 when it increased again slightly, continuing to increase in 1965 (Fig. 3.4). These later increases were due in part to the military activities in Viet Nam and in part to the increased shipments of food under P.L. 480 (surplus disposal abroad).

Studies evaluating the farm programs during the period 1953–65 conclude that 5 to 10 percent of potential farm production was diverted from commercial markets in those years. A part of the diversion was achieved by acreage adjustment programs, a part by surplus disposal programs outside commercial markets at home and abroad, and, prior to 1961, a part was added to government storage stocks.

Official budget estimates for 1955–64 indicate that the government cost of these programs approximated $31 billion, or 9 percent of the value of the farm products marketed.

Because of the inelastic demand for farm products, the di-

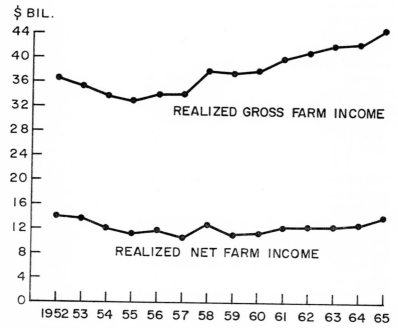

Fig. 3.4. *Realized gross and net farm income, 1952–1965.*

version of 5 to 10 percent of potential commercial supplies permitted farm income to remain substantially higher than if the potential production were marketed.

A number of studies made in 1959 and later years by Pennsylvania State University, Iowa State University, and congressional committees indicated that if the price support and production adjustments programs were dropped, even though the P.L. 480, or surplus disposal, program were continued at the recent levels, gross farm income would decline 20 percent or more, and net farm income would fall by almost one-half. It was noted in the opening paragraphs that Don Paarlberg, writing in 1964, although aware of these studies, concluded that "Government regulation of farm prices and production during the postwar period was harmful in that incentive prices provided more stimulation to the agricultural plant than weak controls could overcome."

Many farm and nonfarm economists agree with Paarlberg. They believe that if wheat, cotton, and feed grain prices had been allowed to drop to world levels, new technology would not have been adopted as rapidly as it was, hence supplies would have been smaller and prices higher, in the absence of government programs, than these studies indicate. Without question, new technology and industrial supplies such as pesticides, chemical fertilizers, and improved farm machinery increased farm output more rapidly than commercial markets expanded during those years. Farm output increased 10 percent in the 5-year period 1954 to 1959, in spite of the acreage adjustment programs, and it increased another 9 percent in the next 5 years, in spite of even more extensive acreage diversion programs. How much would it have expanded in the absence of the government programs?

A review of the evidence suggests that the production control or acreage diversion programs were more effective than is generally assumed on the basis of a superficial review of production trends. It also suggests that the new technology, farm pesticides, fertilizers, and new farm equipment would have been acquired by farmers at record rates for several years, even though farm prices had fallen to much lower levels.

Raymond Christensen and Ronald Aines, of the Economic Research Service, made an exhaustive study of the acreage control programs of the 1950's. They concluded that yields per acre of the nonquota crops increased about as much as for the quota crops and that acreage diversion programs were effective in reducing the output of the crops to which they were applied (4).

On the basis of all the evidence available, it appears probable that if the price support, acreage diversion, food distribution, and storage programs had been discontinued at any time after 1953, market supplies of farm products would have been 5 to 10 percent larger. Grain and cotton prices in the United States would have fallen 20 to 40 percent, and within a few years, livestock prices would have declined sharply. Commercial exports of both grains and cotton would have been substantially higher, and world prices would have been depressed. This situation would have continued for several years.

Eventually, the adoption of improved technology would have slowed down under sharply lower prices, as lack of capital limited the replacement of worn-out farm equipment. But agriculture would have been financially impoverished at that point.

Opponents of the farm price support programs attribute the overrapid adoption of yield-increasing practices during these years primarily to the price levels maintained by the programs. It is noteworthy, however, that congressional appropriations for federal and state agricultural research and extension programs were more than doubled between 1950 and 1960. The mistaken view that farming could be returned to prosperous conditions by lowering production costs through the use of improved production practices was widespread. Individual farmers were aided and encouraged to adopt improved production practices, both by government institutions and by farm supply industries, on a scale never achieved in earlier years. And since the improved practices lowered production costs, the level of prices was not a deciding factor as long as the farmer was financially able to purchase the additional supplies and equipment.

President Eisenhower's 1959 farm message was somewhat misleading in stating that the three crops, cotton, corn, and wheat, account for only 20 percent of cash farm income. Actually cotton, feed grains, and wheat account for about two-thirds of the acres of cropland harvested, and these crops, together with the livestock products produced largely from feed grains, account for three-fourths of the income from all crop and livestock sales.

Clearly, the programs in the 1950's stabilized the market supplies and prices of the major farm products during a period when new technology and improved practices were increasing farm output more rapidly than markets were expanding.

In addition to the price support and acreage control programs, federally administered marketing agreements and orders were utilized to improve and stabilize prices and incomes for fluid milk producers in many urban market areas and for producers of fruits, vegetables, and nuts in a number of producing areas.

Although the income gains attributable to the farm programs have been of great benefit to the larger commercial farms, they have also been of real help to the families on smaller-sized farms. They have probably maintained the net farm income of these families 25 percent or more above what it would otherwise have been; while those who wished to sell out and enter a nonfarm occupation have benefited from a higher value of their farm assets stemming from the income effects of the programs. The higher level and increased stability of farm income resulting from the farm programs also has permitted the operators of small farms to make a greater use of credit than otherwise would have been possible. In this sense, the programs have been of special benefit to the more aggressive and beginning operators on small farms.

The increased income resulting from the farm programs also has had an important influence on farm land prices, contributing to their substantial rise over the past 35 years. This has been of great benefit to farm owner-operator families who wished to shift to other occupations and has reduced the number of new entrants into farming.

The increased value of land having allotments of price-supported crops such as tobacco has operated to prevent new producers from benefiting as much as established producers from the continuing programs.

However, the effects of the program go far beyond income benefits to specific groups of farmers. The stabilization of market supplies and prices of the major farm products has stimulated farmers to adopt new technologies and improved practices.

The welfare aspects of farm programs must be appraised in terms of their effect on the industry, on its efficiency, and on its contribution to the other sectors of the economy, rather than on direct income benefits to specific groups of farmers. Agriculture's performance in this period is most impressive.

Sufficient workers were released from the agricultural labor force to provide one-fourth the growth in civilian nonagricultural employment. Farm output increased almost one-third in spite of the reduction in workers and the acreage diversion programs.

The value at farm prices of the farm food purchased by Americans as a percentage of their disposable income dropped from 7.6 percent in 1953 to 5.3 percent in 1965. These percentages highlight the efficiency of American farmers. Farmers in no other country in the world today produce such a high proportion of its citizens' food and receive such a small fraction of the consumers' income for their products.

Many agricultural economists, reviewing the economic developments in the period 1953–65, conclude that although the farm programs might have been improved in important details, the results would have been financially disastrous to many farmers had the programs been discontinued.

While the year-to-year costs were relatively high—10 percent of the value of farm product sales—and farm prices were maintained 20 percent or more higher than in the absence of the programs, the long-run results were a 3 percent decline in farm prices from 1953 to 1965, at a time when: wholesale prices for finished goods increased 12 percent, consumer prices for all items purchased increased 18 percent, retail food prices increased 14 percent, food processing and marketing charges for a market basket of food increased 20 percent, and hourly earnings in manufacturing employment increased 50 percent.

After reviewing the published studies of farm policies and the alternatives proposed by a large number of individuals and interest groups, it appears that in the past 35 years the farm programs have kept the agricultural industry sufficiently prosperous to permit continued rapid technological advance—a rate of technological advance not equalled by other sectors of the economy characterized by large corporations and national labor unions. In their absence or in the absence of roughly similar supply-adjustment and price-stabilization programs in the 1930's and again in the period 1953–65, farm prices and incomes would have been sharply lower for protracted periods. While the agricultural industry might have recovered from its depression losses in the immediate postwar years, without the 1953–65 programs agriculture almost surely would be relatively less prosperous than it is today.

LITERATURE CITED

1. Benedict, M. Can We Solve the Farm Problem? New York: The Twentieth Century Fund. 1955.
2. Paarlberg, D. Farm Policy. New York: Wiley and Sons, Inc. 1964.
3. Support Prices for Agricultural Commodities. Message from the President (H. Doc. No. 59, p. 1312). Congressional Record. Jan. 29, 1959.
4. USDA. Agr. Econ. Rpt. 18. 1962.

CHAPTER FOUR

Impacts of Noncommodity Programs on the Structure of Agriculture

JAMES G. MADDOX

FOR DECADES before the depression of the 1930's agricultural policy in the United States was characterized mainly by programs aimed at enlarging the quantity and improving the quality of resources used in agricultural production. Emphasis was on maintaining low prices of productive inputs, as contrasted with several of the depression-born programs which were aimed at raising farm product prices. The earliest expression of a low price policy for an important productive input was in the disposition of public land through sales at low prices or as gifts to squatters and homesteaders. Early land policies were, however, only one manifestation of numerous public programs aimed at enhancing agriculture's productive resources and at keeping their prices low to farmers. The basic goal of these programs was not to bring about low food and fiber prices to consumers, but to enhance the productivity and incomes of farmers.

My colleague, Dale M. Hoover, read an early draft of this chapter and his comments helped me in clarifying several points.

In this century, the most important of the nationwide programs of this nature have been: (a) the research and extension activities of the USDA and the Colleges of Agriculture, and the teaching of vocational agriculture in secondary schools; (b) the lending programs of federally sponsored credit agencies which serve agriculture; and (c) publicly supported soil conservation activities.

In this chapter attention is centered on the ways in which these programs have affected farm output, the incomes of farmers, and the structure of agriculture.

THE FRAME OF REFERENCE

Programs which improve the quality, expand the supply, and lower the prices of inputs used in farming tend to increase farm output. The effect which increased output has on total farm income is dependent on the characteristics of the demand for farm products. It is further dependent on the level and rate of growth of employment in nonfarm industries. Public policies aimed at maintaining low prices for such inputs as technical knowledge and farm capital tend to benefit both farmers and consumers and to increase the rate of growth of the entire economy when the demand for farm commodities is expanding, the income elasticity of demand for food and fiber is well above zero, and nonfarm jobs which require relatively unskilled laborers are expanding so that excess workers in agriculture can readily find employment in other industries. When these conditions do not prevail, programs which increase agricultural output tend to lower total farm income by lowering the prices of farm products, and the benefits of such programs accrue to consumers and to some marketing and processing firms, rather than to farmers. This tendency can, of course, be offset by government actions to prevent farm commodity prices and farm income from declining. Such actions, however, involve costs to both consumers and taxpayers.

In analyzing the impacts of output-increasing programs on the structure of agriculture, their effects on changes in the distribution of income among farmers must be taken into consideration. Neither land nor other farm inputs such as managerial ability, production techniques, and capital are distributed equally among all farmers. Consequently, changes in total farm income have differing effects on the various groups and classes of farmers. Even in a period of declining total farm income, some farmers will make a profit because of superior land, greater managerial ability, improved production technology, or ready availability of capital. During this same period, other farmers will lose money and either be forced out of farming or voluntarily choose to move into nonfarm jobs. Programs affecting the quality and prices of farm inputs have their major impacts on the structure of agriculture through the differential impact on the various classes of farmers. Thus, in analyzing the impacts of the educational, credit, and conservation programs, four questions are relevant. First, how have such programs affected farm output? Second, how has the change in output affected total farm income? Third, how has the change in total farm income been distributed among different classes of farmers in various regions of the country? Fourth, how has the differential distribution of income affected the number, size, and tenure of farms?

In studying this interrelated train of effects between 1930 and 1965, it is necessary to recognize differences in prevailing demand and employment conditions in three different periods. They are: (a) the 11 years of depression from 1931 through 1941; (b) the 12-year period, 1942 through 1953; and (c) the 12 years from 1954 through 1965.

In the early 1930's, both foreign and domestic demand for farm products drastically declined and remained at unusually low levels for almost a full decade. National unemployment was high throughout the decade—15 to 25 percent of the labor force during the midthirties. Consequently, the prices of farm products reached their lowest levels in many years, and total net farm income in 1932, excluding government payments, was less than one-half of its 1910–14 average. Many farmers were unable to carry the heavy load of debts which they had accumulated in earlier years, and were faced with bankruptcy. The decade from 1931 to 1941 was clearly a period in which any increase in farm output either lowered farm income or increased government costs in supporting farm prices.

The period from 1942 through 1953 presented a different situation. The demand for food expanded rapidly. Unemployment disappeared and manpower shortages developed throughout the economy. Farm product prices and farmers' incomes were rising. Food rationing and price controls became necessary. Not since the first world war had there been such a strong demand for increased and improved inputs to raise farm production. Because of the worldwide shortages of food in the years between the end of World War II and the outbreak of the Korean conflict, this situation continued through 1953 with minor exceptions in 1948 and 1949. Thus, during most of the 12-year period from early 1942 through 1953, employment and demand conditions were virtually the reverse of those which prevailed during the 1930's. This was a period during which both farmers and consumers benefited from output-increasing and laborsaving inputs to increase farm output.

From the end of the Korean conflict through 1965, demand and employment conditions again reverted to a situation in which increased farm output tended to decrease farm product prices and farmers' incomes. The production capacity of the agricultural industry had expanded enormously during the 1940's and early 1950's, and consumers' incomes had risen greatly. However, the majority of Americans were so well fed that the income elasticity of unprocessed food products was extremely low. The domestic demand for food was expanding only slightly faster than the increase in population, which was higher than in former years but still too slow to keep pace with the increase in farm production. In addition, unemployment exceeded 5 percent of the civilian labor force during 8 of the 12 years from 1954 through 1965, and skill requirements for many of the available jobs were so high they could not be met by poorly educated, unskilled workers from farms. Therefore, this was a period in which increased farm output tended to result in lower prices for farm products. Government price support programs were again necessary to prevent severe declines in farm income.

THE PERIOD OF DEPRESSION, 1931 TO 1941

Although demand and employment conditions of the 1930's might have resulted in deemphasizing those input programs which tended to increase farm production, such was not the case. In fact, greater emphasis was placed on research and education, existing farm credit programs were expanded and new ones were added, soil conservation subsidies were inaugurated, and other steps were taken to enhance both the quantity and quality of inputs used in farming.

RESEARCH AND EDUCATION

By the beginning of the depression of the 1930's, research and educational activities of the USDA, state experiment stations, and the Extension Service already had a long and respected history of creating and supplying farmers with up-to-date technical knowledge. Their main focus of emphasis had been on discovering and disseminating information by which individual producers could increase the output of their farms. These programs were expanded during the depressed 1930's. For example, the number of research workers employed by state agricultural experiment stations increased from almost 3,600 in 1932 to over 4,700 in 1941, and the number of personnel of the Extension Service rose from about 6,500 to 9,100 during the same decade. Expenditures from federal, state, and local sources for agricultural research and extension activities and the teaching of vocational agriculture in high schools rose from approximately $69 million to $93 million between 1932 and 1941.

During the depression, the research and extension agencies placed greater emphasis than in earlier years on assisting farmers to reduce cash farm operating and living costs, assisted in the educational and administrative activities of the acreage allotment programs, and generally devoted more resources to some of the broad economic and social problems facing farm people. Nevertheless, their aims, their methods, and most of their accumulated knowledge continued to be focused on increasing the efficiency of individual farms. As a result, their activities tended to increase the total volume of agricultural output at a time when the main efforts of the USDA were aimed at reducing agricultural production.

CREDIT PROGRAMS

The farm financial situation at the depths of the depression was extremely serious. Thousands of farmers were overburdened with debt and faced with foreclosure. Many farm lending agencies could not collect their loans and were in financial difficulties.

To cope with this situation, the federal government took several steps to ease the financial strains of farmers and their creditors. It created three new agricultural credit agencies—the Farm Credit Administration, the Resettlement Administration (which later became the Farm Security Administration and still later the Farmers Home Administration), and the Rural Electrification Administration. Each agency had different aims and authorities. Nevertheless, all were significant suppliers of credit to farmers or farmer-owned cooperatives. Directly, or indirectly, they added to the stock of farm capital.

Farm Credit Administration

The Farm Credit Administration which came into being in 1933 had been preceded by the establishment of 12 regional Federal

Land Banks in 1917, which provided long-term, farm mortgage loans to farmers, and by 12 Federal Intermediate Credit Banks, organized in 1923, which discounted notes of local agencies that supplied short-term credit to farmers. These institutions were unable, however, to supply the credit needs of farmers during the 1930's (Table 4.1).

The government, therefore, expanded the resources of the institutions and established a nationwide network of several hundred local Production Credit Associations (PCA's) which made short-term and intermediate loans to farmers by discounting their notes with the Federal Intermediate Credit Banks. PCA's, established as local cooperatives of borrowers, were organized, capitalized, and supervised by 12 regional Production Credit Corporations. The government also established a Central Bank for cooperatives and 12 Regional Banks for cooperatives. In addition, it increased the capital stock of the 12 Federal Land Banks; authorized them to issue bonds on which both interest and principal were guaranteed by the federal government; and reduced the interest rates on both old and new Federal Land Bank loans to 4.5 percent.

Legislation in 1933 made farm mortgage funds available through Commissioner Loans. These were usually secured by a second mortgage on real estate owned by farmers who received loans from a Federal Land Bank which held the first mortgage. A nationwide farm debt adjustment program was also put into operation, through which local farm debt adjustment committees induced lenders to scale down loans of farmers to levels that could be refinanced by the government lending agencies.

During the depressed 1930's, few private banks, insurance companies, or individuals were able or willing to renew outstanding loans to farmers or to make new loans. Thus the work of the local farm debt adjustment committees and the refinancing of loans by the Farm Credit Administration agencies were extremely important in bringing order into a chaotic credit situation. According to the 1941 annual report of the administrator of the Farm Security Administration, approximately 163,000 farmers had their debts reduced from $493 million to $374 million, or 24 percent, between September, 1935, and July, 1941, through the actions of the farm debt adjustment committees. Between May, 1933, and June, 1941, more than 951,800 Federal Land Bank and Commissioner Loans totaling approximately $2,550 million were made to farmers. During the same period, the newly organized Production Credit Associations made short-

TABLE 4.1. Expenditures and loans by publicly sponsored agencies for agricultural education, conservation, and credit, 1932 to 1965[*],[a]

Agency and Program	Expenditures and Loans (millions of dollars)						
	Depression Period 1932–1941	War Period 1942–1953		Postwar Period 1954–1965		Total 1932–1965	
	(current dollars)	(current dollars)	(constant dollars)[b]	(current dollars)	(constant dollars)[b]	(current dollars)	(constant dollars)[c]
I. Expenditures							
A. Research and Education							
1. Research and experiment stations	346.2	915.5	529.8	2,821.9	1,380.8	4,083.6	2,256.8
2. Extension services	282.5	703.7	410.5	1,767.2	866.7	2,753.4	1,559.7
3. Vocational agriculture	123.1	358.4	208.2	713.7	352.6	1,195.2	683.9
4. Subtotal	751.8	1,977.6	1,148.5	5,302.8	2,600.1	8,032.2	4,500.4
B. Soil Conservation							
1. Soil Conservation Service	109.6	476.6	276.8	900.6[p]	444.0	1,486.8	830.4
2. Agricultural Conservation Program payments	2,523.6[d]	3,149.4[m]	2,061.2	2,321.9[q]	1,149.3	7,994.9	5,734.1
C. Total Expenditures	3,385.0	5,603.6	3,486.5	8,525.3	4,193.4	17,513.9	11,064.9
II. Credit programs							
A. Farm Credit Administration							
1. Federal Land Bank and Land Bank Commissioner loans	2,549.8[e]	1,899.0	1,106.5	7,065.8	3,457.3	11,514.6	7,113.6
2. Production Credit Associations	1,994.0[f]	9,869.5	5,692.4	29,194.9	14,256.8	41,058.4	21,943.2
3. Banks for Cooperatives	653.9[g]	4,964.6	2,948.9	8,881.8	4,348.1	14,500.3	7,950.9
4. Federal Intermediate Credit Banks[h]	1,679.2	1,766.9	1,034.0	2,635.8	1,293.9	6,081.9	4,007.1
5. Net total	6,876.9[e]	18,500.0	10,781.8	47,778.3	23,356.1	73,155.2	41,014.8
B. Farmers Home Administration							
1. Loans[i],[j]	820.7[k]	2,155.7[m]	1,350.2	5,846.5[r]	2,854.1	8,822.9	5,025.0
2. Grants	131.9[g]	15.2[n]	13.1	….	….	147.1	145.0
3. Subtotal	952.6[g]	2,170.9[o]	1,363.3	5,846.5[r]	2,854.1	8,970.0	5,170.0
C. Rural Electrification Administration	296.4[k]	1,965.7	1,071.7	2,489.3	1,222.8	4,751.4	2,590.9
D. Total Loans[l]	8,125.9[e]	22,636.6	13,216.8	56,114.1	27,433.0	86,876.6	48,775.7
III. Total expenditures and loans	11,510.9	28,240.2	16,703.3	64,639.4	31,626.4	104,390.5	59,840.6

TABLE 4.1. (Continued)

* Sources: I. A, 1. Report on the Agricultural Experiment Stations, yearly issues 1932–1959, Agr. Res. Ser., USDA (ARS-23 series); Funds for Research at State Agricultural Experiment Stations and Other State Institutions, yearly issues 1960–65, Cooperative State Res. Ser., USDA (CSRS-23 series); and unpublished USDA tabulations, B & FR-2321 and B & FR-2322, Office of Budget and Finance, USDA, Oct. 12, 1964.

2. Report of Cooperative Extension Work in Agriculture and Home Economics, yearly issues 1932–53, and unpublished data for years 1954–65, USDA; Office of Budget and Finance tabulations, B & FR-2321 and B & FR-2322, op. cit.

3. Digest of Annual Reports of State Boards for Vocational Education, yearly issues, Office of Education, U.S. Dept. of Health, Education and Welfare. (OE-80008 and predecessor series.)

B, 1, 2. Office of Budget and Finance tabulations, B & FR-2321 and B & FR-2322, op. cit., and Agricultural Conservation Program, Summary by States, 1964, Agr. Stab. and Conserv. Ser., USDA, Dec., 1965, p. 71.

II. A, 1–5. 32nd Ann. Rept. of the Farm Credit Administration on the Work of the Cooperative Farm Credit System, 1964–65, FCA, Feb. 10, 1966, pp. 67, 82, 92, and 106.

B. Ann. Rept. of the Farm Security Administration, 1937–41, 1943, 1945, and 1946 issues; Annual Report of the Farmers Home Administration, 1948–53; and Agricultural Statistics, 1966, USDA, pp. 521 and 523.

C. Ann. Rept. of the Rural Electrification Administration, USDA, 1941, 1953, and 1965 issues.

This table was prepared by Edward Yu-Yen Long, Dept. of Econ., N.C. State Univ., Raleigh. Data are for fiscal years except where otherwise noted.

[a] This table was prepared by Edward Yu-Yen Long, Dept. of Econ., N.C. State Univ., Raleigh. Data are for fiscal years except where otherwise noted.

[b] Current dollars deflated by the index of prices paid by farmers for all commodities bought for use in production (1941 = 100).

[c] Total of current dollars 1932–41 and constant dollars for subsequent periods.

[d] Calendar years, 1936–41 inclusive.

[e] May 1, 1933–June 30, 1941.

[f] June 16, 1933–June 30, 1941.

[g] Fiscal years, 1934–41 inclusive.

[h] Excluding Federal Intermediate Credit Bank loans to and discounts for Production Credit Associations and Banks for Cooperatives.

[i] Including funds expended for migratory labor camps and resettlement projects for farm families for the Depression Period.

[j] For both real estate and non-real estate loans, including loans to associations.

[k] May, 1935–June 30, 1941.

[l] Including $147.1 million in grants for the period 1934–46.

[m] Calendar years, 1942–53 inclusive.

[n] July 1, 1941–Dec. 31, 1946.

[o] July 1, 1941–Dec. 31, 1953.

[p] Fiscal years, 1954–64 inclusive.

[q] Calendar years, 1954–64 inclusive.

[r] Calendar years, 1954–65 inclusive.

term loans totaling approximately $1.994 billion, and the Banks for Cooperatives loaned about $654 million (4).

Much of the money loaned by the Farm Credit Administration agencies during the 1930's was to refinance existing debts held by private lenders, and thus did not represent new additions to farm capital. However, a rather large percentage of the short-term farm production loans must have been utilized by farmers for the purchase of farm machinery, fertilizer, and other forms of capital inputs. Moreover, all of the Farm Credit Administration agencies liberalized the terms and conditions on which commercial farmers with reasonably adequate security could obtain credit, and reduced uncertainty with respect to the availability of loan funds. Their total effect, therefore, was to expand and strengthen the productive potential of the agricultural industry and to expand farm output.

Resettlement Administration

During the middle 1930's, a large number of farm families were on some form of public relief, and in many rural areas there were no jobs, acreage allotments, or credit available to farm laborers, sharecroppers, and tenants. The Resettlement Administration was established to aid the thousands of low-income farm families who could not obtain credit from the Farm Credit Administration agencies or private lenders, and who received few, if any, benefits from the production control and price support programs of the Department of Agriculture.

The most important programs administered by the Resettlement Administration and its successor, the Farm Security Administration, were: (a) a nationwide system of rural rehabilitation loans to low-income farmers who could not obtain credit from other sources; (b) short-term emergency loans and subsistence grants to farm families who could not immediately qualify for rural rehabilitation loans; (c) a series of resettlement projects, through which selected families who were on public relief were given an opportunity to purchase small subsistence homesteads or family-sized farms in planned communities; (d) camps and clinics for migratory farm laborers (mostly in the Pacific Coast states) to improve the housing and health facilities of families who moved from place to place in search of jobs during harvest periods; and (e) long-term farm mortgage loans, after the passage of the Bankhead-Jones Tenant Act in 1937, to enable selected farm tenants to become owners of family farms.

Most of the early activities of the Resettlement Administration and Farm Security Administration were aimed at aiding farm families to remain on the land, where they could produce most of their food plus a few products for sale. Otherwise, many of them would have been on some form of direct relief or would have had intermittent employment on publicly financed "make-work" projects as ways of preventing severe human suffering. To some extent, therefore, several of the early activities of the Resettlement Administration and the Farm Security Administration were basically income transfer programs similar to those of welfare or relief agencies.

From the beginning of the programs through June 30, 1941, approximately $953 million were utilized by these agencies for purposes directly related to improving living conditions and raising incomes of farm families. The major items in millions of dollars were as follows (12).

	Amount	Percent
1. Rural rehabilitation and emergency loans	$586.4	61.6
2. Rehabilitation and subsistence grants	131.9	13.9
3. Farm ownership loans (1938–1941)	117.2	12.3
4. Resettlement projects for farm families	102.4	10.7
5. Migratory labor camps	14.7	1.5
Total	$952.6	100.0

There is no way of determining the proportion of these funds which represented additions to farm capital, as distinct from funds for refinancing existing debts, for land purchase, and for consumption goods and services. However, it is not unreasonable to estimate that about one-half of the rural rehabilitation and farm ownership loans and an equal proportion of the funds expended on resettlement projects—a total of slightly more than $400 million—represented additions to farm capital.

An annual farm and home plan was prepared for each rural rehabilitation and farm ownership borrower by local farm and home supervisors. Through periodic farm and home visits and rather strict control over borrower bank accounts, the supervisors assisted the family in carrying out its plan and in managing its financial affairs. These plans aided the borrower families in raising the efficiency of their farming operations. They also resulted in the amount of each loan being based on careful estimates of funds needed for family living and farm operating expenses. Thus, the combination of planning, supervision, and credit were mutually interdependent elements in a total process of raising family income and insuring the government against heavy losses from loans to families who had little, if any, equity in marketable assets.

The loans, farm plans, and supervisory assistance provided by the Resettlement Administration and the Farm Security Administration added to the productiveness of the agricultural industry, and had some effect on raising farm output. In this respect they were similar to the research and education programs, and to the lending activities of the Farm Credit Administration agencies. The families served, however, were low-output farmers, and the amount of funds loaned was relatively small.

Rural Electrification Administration

The Rural Electrification Administration came into being by executive order in 1935. The Rural Electrification Act of 1936 made it exclusively a lending agency, and authorized a 10-year electrification loan program, which was extended indefinitely by amendment in 1944.

At the time REA was established, only about 10.9 percent of the farms in the United States were receiving central station electricity. During the next five years, both the number and proportion of farms with electric service increased rapidly. Between 1935 and 1941, REA made loans totaling approximately $296 million. During this period, the proportion of farms in the nation which received central station electricity rose from a little over 10 percent to 25 percent. Some of the increase came from an extension of service into rural areas by privately owned power companies as well as from agencies financed by REA.

The REA made most of its loans to newly organized cooperatives, and a high percentage of its early loan funds were used for the construction of transmission lines and related distribution facilities into rural areas. REA-financed cooperatives had the greatest impact in areas of the country where the costs of distributing electricity were high—areas where there were few customers per mile and where the consumption per customer was low. Thus, REA electricity is relatively unimportant in California and other areas of the West where the demand for pumping irrigation water is high. These are profitable areas for private companies to supply. Likewise, REA electricity is relatively unimportant in New England, where population density is high and privately owned companies have a major share of the rural market. On the other hand, in the South, the Midwest, the Great Plains, and the Rocky Mountain states, REA-financed cooperatives made their heaviest impacts on the total market for electricity. These are areas where the costs of distributing electricity are high, both because there are few customers per mile of line and because of relatively low consumption per customer.

REA-financed cooperatives were able to serve these high-cost areas primarily because they: (a) had long-term loans at low rates of interest from the federal government; (b) were exempt from federal incomes taxes; and (c) were preference customers in obtaining low-cost electricity produced by federal power projects. As a result, electrical service was extended to many farms that would not have been profitable customers for private power companies, and it is probable that rates charged by private companies to farm customers were lowered in some areas as a result of competition from REA cooperatives.

The distribution facilities financed by REA represented additions to the stock of capital available to farmers. However, a relatively high proportion of the electricity used on farms during the 1930's was for household purposes, and was much more important in raising the level of living of farm families than in increasing farm output. Nevertheless, the availability of a dependable, low-cost supply of electricity made feasible new laborsaving technologies, particularly on poultry and dairy farms, which made important contributions to expanding farm production in later years, and had some effects on raising farm output in the last half of the 1930's.

SOIL CONSERVATION

Since the mid-1930's, USDA has had two nationwide programs concerned with soil conservation. One of these is administered by the Soil Conservation Service (SCS) which provides information and technical assistance to farmers and landowners with respect to a wide range of conservation problems. The other was originated by the Agricultural Adjustment Administration (AAA), and is now administered by the Agricultural Stabilization and Conservation Service (ASCS). It provides direct payments to farmers for adopting approved conservation practices. Although the programs are quite different in aims and methods of administration, they both supply farmers with important inputs that tend to increase agricultural production.

Soil Conservation Service

This agency originated as the Soil Erosion Service in the Department of the Interior in 1933. Its main purpose, at that time, was to provide employment by utilizing Civilian Conservation Corps (CCC) personnel on projects to prevent soil erosion. Most of the work was done on publicly owned land. In early 1935, the Soil Erosion Service was transferred to the Department of Agriculture. Its functions were expanded; its name was changed to the Soil Conservation Service; and by an Act of Congress it became an important new agency within the Department of Agriculture. In the late 1930's, the SCS shifted the emphasis of its program from the construction of erosion prevention facilities with CCC personnel to furnishing technical advice and assistance to members of Soil Conservation Districts.

"By 1940 a permanent staff of more than 8,000 workers had been assembled in the Soil Conservation Service, and this agency received a regular appropriation of twenty-three million dollars . . . . Supplementary funds for submarginal land purchase and development, flood control work, civilian conservation corps, and related activities increased the total funds administered by SCS in 1939–40 to almost forty-nine million dollars." (13.)

During the late 1930's, the SCS personnel were engaged mainly in such activities as developing conservation plans for individual farms, providing farmers with technical guidance in adopting soil conservation practices, and in administering the work of persons in CCC camps who were engaged in conservation and forest improvement activities. By the beginning of World War II, the SCS had a field staff approximately as large as that of the Extension Service.

Agricultural Conservation Practice Payments

Under the authority of the Soil Conservation and Domestic Allotment Act of 1936, a program was initiated of paying farmers "for shifting acreage out of 'soil-depleting' crops and for adopting approved conservation practices. Heavy subsidies were involved, and it is clear that major considerations were the reduction of acreages in cash crops and the provision of a means for distributing public funds to agriculture." (5.) This program has continued throughout subsequent years.

In 1936, the year the program began, slightly over 3 million farms participated, and over $374 million was paid out to participants. By 1941, the number of participating farms had risen to

4.4 million, and payments totaled over $456 million. During the 6-year period, 1936 through 1941, approximately $2.524 billion was paid to farmers. Of this total, about $1.921 billion represented payments made to farmers for diverting land from such soil-depleting crops as wheat, cotton, corn, peanuts, and rice (1, p. 71). Their primary purpose was for holding down production and increasing farm income. They were direct income transfers to farmers and probably reduced the amount of funds which farmers would have borrowed for production purposes. The remainder, approximately $603 million, represented payments for soil-building and soil-conserving practices such as growing cover crops and applying lime and fertilizer to land used for pasture. Thus, they lowered the farmers' cost of inputs used in production.

COMBINED EFFECTS OF NONCOMMMODITY PROGRAMS, 1931 TO 1941

Clearly, the publicly sponsored programs which expanded the quantity, improved the quality, and maintained low prices for inputs used in agricultural production represented large and important segments of agricultural policy during the 1930's. The two most important inputs affected by these programs were technical knowledge and capital. Both tended to increase total farm output especially during the latter half of the 1930's. They, therefore, exerted downward pressures on farm prices and farm incomes. Thus, their main thrust was plainly at cross purposes with the programs aimed at raising farm product prices by restricting agricultural production. In other words, at the same time one set of programs was attempting to reduce agricultural production by restricting crop acreage, the education, credit, and conservation programs were aiding and encouraging farmers to expand the output of their farms.

There is no precise way of measuring the impact which the noncommodity programs had on total farm production during the 1930's. It is worth noting, however, that the acreage restriction programs, coupled with serious and widespread droughts in the mid-1930's, were successful in reducing the production of wheat, cotton, and tobacco between 1930 and 1940, and probably in holding down feed grain output below the level that would otherwise have been reached, but total farm output was not reduced. The total volume of farm production in 1940 and 1941 was about 22 percent higher than a decade earlier. This increase in output was brought forth on about 2 percent fewer crop acres, and with a 10 percent decrease in the man-hours of labor used for farm work. The result, of course, was a significant increase in output per acre and per man-hour of labor. Total output per unit of total input rose about 15 percent between 1930–34 and 1941 (6).

While these increases in farm efficiency were occurring, neither total gross nor net farm income, excluding government payments, reached as high a level in any year between 1930 and 1942 as they had in 1929. The decade of the 1930's was clearly a period in which the major gains in the productive efficiency of agriculture were being passed along to consumers in the form of lower prices for farm products or were adding to taxpayers' costs in the form of stocks held by the Commodity Credit Corporation as a result of its price-supporting activities.

The impacts of the noncommodity programs on the structure of agriculture are extremely difficult to evaluate during the 1930's because of the high rates of unemployment and general depression in the nonfarm sector of the economy and because of the countervailing influences of other farm and nonfarm programs. Nevertheless, they appear to have had at least three effects on the structure of the agricultural industry.

First, they were important in aiding thousands of farmers to maintain the ownership of the equities which they had accumulated in land and buildings and other forms of property.

Second, they encouraged farmers to substitute capital for land and labor. Moreover, they changed the capital-mix, mainly by speeding up the substitution of tractors, trucks, and automobiles for horsepower. In this way, they decreased the farmer's degree of self-sufficiency and made him more dependent on purchased inputs from the nonfarm sector of the economy.

Third, farmers with large acreage received relatively greater benefits than those with small acreage, tenants, sharecroppers, and farm laborers. Though the programs of the Resettlement Administration and the Farm Security Administration were aimed specifically at aiding the latter groups, they were small and ineffective relative to the other sources of funds and technical assistance. Thus, in total impact, the educational, credit, and conservation programs worked hand-in-glove with the acreage allotment and price support programs to widen the gap in incomes, assets, and production potentials between land-owning farmers and propertyless farmers. One indication of this tendency was the change in the tenure pattern. Between 1930 and 1940, the number of farmers who were full owners and part owners increased about 135,000, while the number of tenants decreased by approximately 304,000. Of the latter, about 235,000 were sharecroppers, that is, tenants who owned neither workstock nor equipment.

THE WAR AND IMMEDIATE POSTWAR YEARS, 1942 TO 1953

Agriculture was in a strong position to expand output at the outbreak of World War II. Farmers' debts had been adjusted downward, and many had been refinanced by the public lending agencies on terms and conditions that were adjusted to the low price level that characterized the depression. During the latter half of the 1930's, many farmers had purchased new tractors and power-driven machines. "Many new strains of seeds, hybrid seed corn, improved methods of livestock production including heavier feeding of better balanced rations to dairy cows and chickens, together with less use of feed for horse power, increased market supplies per acre of cropland harvested around 20 percent above ten years earlier. . . . In terms of productive capacity, agriculture was at an all-time high." (13, p. 19.)

Relatively soon after the outbreak of the war, it became clear that increased food output would be needed. The slogan "Food Will Win the War and Write the Peace," epitomized the nation's desire to expand farm output. The agencies administering the noncommodity programs were in the best position of any of the USDA agencies to swing into action quickly to aid farmers in increasing food production. They were the agencies that were supplying some of the most needed inputs to raise farm output. Early in the war effort, there was a shortage of new farm machinery because of the allocation of steel to the production of war materials, and it soon became evident that fertilizer, feed, and insecticides were in short supply relative to demand. It was especially important, therefore, that increased food production be brought forth by improved technologies and know-how, which required minimum amounts of these scarce inputs. This put a high premium on the work of the research and educational agencies—the producers and disseminators of new technical knowledge.

As has been pointed out earlier, the increased demand for food from war-torn countries around the world continued after the end of the fighting in 1945. At the same time, supplies of farm machinery, fertilizer, feed, and other purchased inputs became more plentiful. Consequently, surpluses of some farm products became a problem in 1948 and 1949, and the federal government again had to resort to price-supporting activities. But the Korean conflict again stimulated the demand for farm products, and most of the period from 1942 through 1953 offered unusually good opportunities for those public agencies that were primarily engaged in supplying farmers with technical knowledge and credit to make significant contributions to national welfare. They responded vigorously to these opportunities.

RESEARCH AND EDUCATION

Virtually all of the professional personnel of the agricultural experiment stations and the Cooperative Extension Service were trained in methods of increasing farm production, and were, therefore, an important national resource in the war effort. Although there were modest declines in the number of research workers in state experiment stations during the war years, their numbers increased from 4,927 in 1942 to 7,477 in 1953. Extension service employees rose from just over 9,000 to approximately 12,600 during the same period. Total expenditures—federal, state, and local—for agricultural research and extension activities increased from about $80 million in 1942 to $207 million in 1953, and expenditures for teaching vocational agriculture in high schools rose from $18 million to $48 million. In dollars of constant purchasing power, the total expenditures for agricultural research, extension work, and teaching of vocational agriculture were over 50 percent greater in 1953 than in 1942.[1]

The increases in numbers of persons engaged in research and educational activities by public agencies, or expenditures of funds for such purposes, though clearly showing substantial expansion in these types of public programs, are poor indices of the contribution which research and education made to increasing farm production. As producers and disseminators of technical knowledge, the work of research and extension personnel manifests itself in such ways as: the development and adoption of improved varieties and strains of crops, poultry, and livestock; better organization and management of farms; improvements in the breeding, feeding, and care of livestock; more efficient utilization of fertilizers, insecticides, and pesticides; and the improvement and development of new models of farm machines and equipment.

---

[1] Data in this paragraph are from annual reports of the experiment stations and extension services and from reports of the Office of Budget and Finance, USDA. The deflator used on the total of expenditures was the Consumer Cost of Living Index, 1957–59=100.

On all of these fronts, the research and educational programs made important contributions to increasing farm production. They, of course, were not the only input enhancement programs that made their impact felt in the same direction. Many significant contributions were made by private business firms engaged in manufacturing and selling farm production inputs.

CREDIT PROGRAMS

Many of the new technologies and farming practices recommended to farmers by the educational agencies required additions to farm capital. The shift toward a highly commercialized agriculture proceeded at a rapid pace between 1942 and 1953. Farmers increased their use of machinery, chemical fertilizers, insecticides, pesticides, oil, gas, electricity, purchased feeds and seeds, and similar forms of capital that had to be bought in the marketplace. The publicly sponsored farm credit agencies, therefore, were called upon to shift their emphasis from refinancing outstanding loans to supplying farmers with credit to be used for purchasing capital items that could be put to immediate productive use.

This shift in emphasis, plus the re-entry of insurance companies and other private lending agencies into the farm real estate financing field, is shown by the contrasting experiences of the Federal Land Banks and the Production Credit Associations. The outstanding loans of the Federal Land Banks totaled $2.723 billion at the beginning of 1940, and represented 41.3 percent of the total farm real estate debt. By 1950, their outstanding loans had dropped to $965 million, and were only 17.3 percent of the farm real estate debt. In contrast, the outstanding loans of the Production Credit Associations totaled $154 million in 1940, and were approximately 5 percent of the farmers' non-real estate debt. By 1950, they had risen to $392 million and represented 7.6 percent of the non-real estate debt of farmers. During the 12-year period 1942 through 1953 the Production Credit Associations loaned a total of approximately $9.87 billion. Much of this credit probably would have been supplied by private lending agencies had the PCA's not been operating. Nevertheless, a high proportion of it was used for the purchase of capital items used in farm production and contributed to an expansion of farm output.[2]

---

[2] Data in this paragraph are from Annual Reports of the Farm Credit Administration and Agricultural Statistics, 1962, USDA, pp. 596–607; The Balance Sheet of Agriculture, USDA, 1952 Issue, p. 3; 1966 Issue, pp. 26–27.

Although the Farm Security Administration, as a part of its war effort, was eager to put additional capital resources into the hands of small farmers whose labor supply was only partially employed, and was able to significantly expand its lending operations during 1941, '42, and '43, its activities resulted in a series of difficulties with Congress. As a result, several of its earlier programs were curtailed, eliminated, or significantly altered. For example, grants to farm families were eliminated, most of the resettlement projects were liquidated by selling the land and buildings to individual families, the migratory farm labor camps were transferred out of the Farm Security Administration and were later sold to private individuals or associations of farm employers, and the eligibility requirements for farmers to receive rural rehabilitation loans (later called farm operating loans) were raised. It was not until after the passage of the Farmers Home Administration Act of 1946, which brought an end to the Farm Security Administration, that the loan programs were again expanded. The objectives of the agency were then increasingly aimed at supplying credit to farmers who were generally in a higher income class and had greater productive potentialities than those who had been reached by the earlier programs.

The 1946 Act authorized the Farmers Home Administration to institute a program of insured farm ownership loans, by which private lenders—mainly banks and insurance companies—provide funds to selected borrowers while the loan supervision and collection functions are provided by the federal agency. By the Housing Act of 1949, the lending authority of the Farmers Home Administration was expanded into a new area by authorizing it to make loans to farm owners for the construction and repair of houses and farm buildings. And, in 1954, the water facilities program—which had been started in 1937 to make loans to individual farmers and associations of farmers in the 17 western states to enable them to improve and construct irrigation facilities—was expanded to include the entire United States, and the purposes for which loans could be made were broadened to include funds for soil and water conservation purposes.

During the entire period from 1942 through 1953, the Farm Security Administration and its successor, the Farmers Home Administration, loaned, or insured private loans, totaling $2.139 billion. Of this amount, $1.284 billion was in the form of rehabilitation or operating loans, a high proportion of which would not have been made available by other lending institutions to the kinds of low-income farmers served by these agencies, and were, therefore, net additions to the supply of agricultural credit available to farmers. Moreover, much of this credit represented a net addition to farm capital.

The lending activities of the REA were seriously curtailed because of the wartime shortages of copper and other materials during the period from 1941 through 1944. Following the end of the war, however, there was a rapid upsurge in REA lending, in the construction of rural electric lines, and in the amount of electricity used per farm. From fiscal year 1942 to 1953, REA loaned a total of $1.966 billion in its electrification program, of which $1.875 billion, or 95.4 percent, was loaned after 1944. Most of ths was used by REA-financed cooperatives for the construction of distribution systems. By 1953, approximately 93 percent of the farms in the nation were receiving central station electricity, and electric power was being utilized in numerous ways on thousands of farms to reduce labor requirements per unit of output.

SOIL CONSERVATION

The principal soil conservation activities of the USDA, during the war and immediate postwar years, continued to be carried forward by the Soil Conservation Service and the Agricultural Conservation Program. In terms of funds expended, the latter was much larger than the former. The Soil Conservation Service worked primarily through local Soil Conservation Districts, and furnished technical assistance to farmers in preparing and carrying out soil conservation plans on their individual farms. The Agricultural Conservation Program, as in earlier years, made direct payments to farmers for carrying out approved conservation practices.

During the war years, the expenditures of the Soil Conservation Service were at an annual rate of $20 to $27 million. Immediately after the war, however, SCS expenditures rose significantly. In 1953, they were $59.6 million (10).

Funds expended under the Agricultural Conservation Program, including acreage allotment payments, ranged from a high of $438.8 million in 1943 to a low of $124.5 million in 1948 (1). During most of the years, however, between 1942 and 1953, expenditures under this program ranged around $250 million annually. Payments were made to farmers for a wide variety of practices which were ". . . intended to: (a) protect farm and ranchland from wind and water erosion, (b) improve the productivity of the nation's agricultural resources, and (c) protect and improve the source, flow and use of water for agricultural purposes." (2). Among the measures for which large expenditures were made were: the application of lime and other inorganic fertilizers; the planting of green manure crops; the construction of mechanical erosion control facilities; and a large number of pasture and range improvement practices.

The funds expended under the Agricultural Conservation Program, including acreage allotment payments, from 1942 through 1953, totaled $3.149 billion, of which approximately 85.3 percent were for practice payments (1, p. 71). Virtually all of the practices for which payments were made had output-increasing effects.

COMBINED EFFECTS OF NONCOMMODITY PROGRAMS, 1942 TO 1953

The inputs emanating from the educational, credit, and conservation programs clearly made significant contributions to increased agricultural production during the period covered by World War II, the immediate postwar years and the Korean War. Moreover, during most of this time, the demand for farm products was expanding, the income elasticity of the demand for food was still relatively high (though it probably declined during the later years of the period), and unemployment in the nonfarm sectors of the economy virtually disappeared in 1943 and remained unusually low, except in 1949 and 1950. In short, this was a period when increased farm output not only served to strengthen the nation's war effort, but also improved the income position of both farmers and consumers.

The physical volume of total farm production had a rising upward trend throughout the period from an index of 80 in 1943 (1957–59 = 100) to 93 in 1953—an increase of over 16 percent (6). The increased output was brought about with quite minor increases in the acreage of cropland used for crops, and with large decreases in the number of man-hours of labor used for farm work. The latter declined approximately 32 percent between 1942 and 1953 (6). The major gains in output came from: (a) large increases in the amount of chemical fertilizers used by farmers, an increase of almost 203 percent; (b) improvements in strains and varieties of crops, which with the increased use of fertilizers raised crop yields per acre; (c) increased output per unit of feed consumed by animals and poultry; (d) more timely production practices on the part of farmers, much of which was made possible by the greater use of tractors and electricity on farms; and (e) more efficient organization and management of farms.

As a result of these and related changes, farm output per man-hour of labor rose about 69 percent between 1942 and 1953, and output per unit of total farm inputs increased approximately 10 percent. Real net income of operators per farm rose between 1942 and 1948, then began a generally downward trend, and was slightly lower in 1953 than in 1942 (11, Table 9H). Consumers' expenditures for food rose between 1942 and 1953, but at a slower rate than total personal consumption expenditures (3). Thus, the total increased efficiency of the agricultural industry was reflected not only in higher real incomes of farm operators and relatively low food prices to consumers, but most importantly in the release of manpower from agriculture to serve in the armed forces and produce nonfarm products, for which there was a greater demand than for farm commodities.

The substitution of technical knowledge and physical capital for manpower used in farming had important impacts on the structure of agriculture in the 1942–53 period. During these 12 years, the number of farms declined by almost 20 percent and the number of persons employed in agriculture decreased 29 percent. Although data are not available for the 12-year period with respect to the changes in farm numbers by size, tenure, and geographic location, it is evident from a comparison of 1940 and 1954 census data that: (a) the number of small farms declined more rapidly than large farms; (b) most of the decline in farm numbers occurred among tenant-operated units; (c) the greatest percentage decline in number of farms was in the South; and (d) the average size of farm, measured either in acres, value of output, or investment in land and buildings, increased in all regions of the country. By the end of the period, farming not only had become highly commercialized, but successful farmers were operators of large businesses with heavy investments in land and capital. By the early 1950's, the profit-making innovators among them were relying heavily on the research and extension agencies for new knowledge and on the government-sponsored credit agencies for loans with which to expand and modernize their farming operations.

THE PERIOD FROM 1954 THROUGH 1965

Demand and employment conditions during most of the period from the end of the Korean conflict through 1965 were of such a nature that increases in farm output were virtually certain either to depress farm product prices and total farm income, or to involve the government in costly price-supporting activities.

However, the educational, credit, and conservation programs, all of which tend to increase farm production, were expanded.

The research personnel in state agricultural experiment stations steadily increased in number from about 7,900 in 1954 to over 10,000 in 1965. Likewise, the number of federal and state agricultural extension workers rose from approximately 12,700 to almost 15,000 during the same period. Federal, state, and local expenditures for research, extension, and the teaching of vocational agriculture rose from approximately $270 million to $596 million during the decade from 1954 to 1964. The expenditures of the Soil Conservation Service, the other major USDA agency providing technical assistance to farmers, increased from $57 million to $108 million during the same decade, and the acres of farm land covered by SCS districts represented about 96 percent of the total land in farms in the United States in 1964, as compared to 84 percent in 1953.

Private business firms also expanded their agricultural research and development and extension-type activities rapidly during this period. In 1965, the estimated expenditures by private industry for agricultural research and development were larger than those from state and federal sources (9). In addition, there were a large number of fieldmen and salesmen employed by private businesses to promote the sale and use of farm machinery, chemicals, feed, seed, and similar inputs used by farmers.

To meet farmers' demands for credit, both public and private agricultural lending agencies expanded their operations. Outstanding loans of the Federal Land Banks at the beginning of 1954 totaled $1.18 billion. By the end of 1965, they had risen to $4.281 billion. Production Credit Association loans rose at an even faster rate. The amount of their outstanding loans at the beginning of 1954 was $550 million. Twelve years later, it was $2.598 billion. The lending activities of the Farmers Home Administration followed the same general upward pattern as that of the Farm Credit Administration. The outstanding real estate loans, both direct and insured, of this agency totaled approximately $346 million at the beginning of 1954, and had risen to $1.873 billion at the end of 1965. The amount of non-real estate loans outstanding of the Farmers Home Administration at the same respective dates were $387 million and $912 million.[3]

At the same time that the Federal Land Banks, Production Credit Associations, and Farmers Home Administration were increasing their loans to individual farmers, the Banks for Coop-

---

[3] Data in this paragraph are from Agricultural Statistics, 1966.

eratives were expanding their loans and the Rural Electrification Administration was increasing its loans to REA cooperatives. The total of loans made by the 13 Banks for Cooperatives from July 1, 1954, to June 30, 1965, was $8.882 billion. In the same period, REA made loans in the amount of $2.489 billion for the expansion and improvement of rural electrical lines and generating facilities. In 1965 about 98.2 percent of the farms in the country were receiving central station electricity, of which approximately 50 percent were served by REA-financed cooperatives.

In addition to the credit extended by the publicly sponsored lending agencies, farmers were also borrowing heavily from private sources. The amount of outstanding farm mortgage loans held by life insurance companies, commercial and savings banks, and other private lenders rose from $6.3 billion on January 1, 1954, to almost $16.3 billion on January 1, 1966. During the same time, short-term and intermediate loans to farmers held by all operating banks rose from $2.8 billion to almost $7.7 billion.

Not only were large amounts of credit borrowed by farmers in the years following the Korean conflict, but payments made to farmers under the Agricultural Conservation Program were also increased significantly. These payments rose from approximately $147 million in 1954 to $222 million in 1964, and totaled $2.322 billion for the 11-year period.

Clearly, this was a period in which both public and private agencies supplying new knowledge and capital to farmers were very active. It is not surprising therefore, that the physical volume of agricultural production rose by almost 24 percent—a simple average rate of about 2 percent per year. Total farm inputs remained relatively constant throughout the period. There were, however, important changes in the input-mix:

1. The number of man-hours of labor used for farm work decreased from 13.310 billion in 1954 7.976 billion in 1965—a decline of 40 percent.
2. The acres of cropland harvested decreased from 339 million to 295 million—a decline of 13 percent.
3. The quantity of nitrogen, phosphorus, and potassium fertilizer used by farmers increased from 4.3 million tons in 1954 to 8.5 million tons in 1965—a rise of 98 percent.
4. Liming materials rose from almost 19 million tons to 27 million tons—an increase of 42 percent.
5. The number of tractors and trucks on farms increased from 6,853 in 1954 to 7,550 in 1965, and the numbers of other farm machines also increased significantly (7).

These changes in the input-mix indicate quite clearly that land and labor became much less important as factors of production, while capital inputs increased greatly in significance. Largely as a result of the substitution of physical capital for land and labor, together with increased technical knowledge, total farm output per unit of all inputs rose about 23 percent during the 1954–65 period. This is a rough indicator of the increase in production efficiency of the national farm plant.

The large increases in farm output which occurred during the period involved the government in heavy expenditures to prevent farm product prices from falling to extremely low levels. Nevertheless, farm operators' real net income from farming, including direct government payments, was lower in all years between 1954 and 1965 than it was in 1953 (11). Thus, as a group, farmers were lowering their total net income by increasing farm output during the 1954–65 period and consumers were benefiting from low food and fiber prices. Also, nonfarm firms engaged in storing, processing, and transporting farm products had an increased volume of business, as did also the sellers of farm product supplies and equipment, which probably increased their total net income.

The squeeze on total net farm income, and the high investments necessary to establish and maintain farms of such sizes and types as to yield returns to labor and management comparable to those in nonfarm industries, resulted in a decreased number of farms. This was the main source of the decline in man-hours of labor used for farm work. The number of farms as reported by the Censuses of Agriculture, fell from 4,783,000 in 1954 to 3,158,000 in 1964, or 34 percent. All of the decrease occurred in farms with value of sales below $10,000 per farm. In fact, farms which had higher sales per farm increased slightly in number. Tenant-operated farms decreased at a more rapid rate—from 1,149,239 in 1954 to 539,921 in 1964, or 53 percent—than farms operated by full owners, and there was an increase in the proportion of farms operated by part owners.

Since the South was the region of the country with the highest proportion of small farms and of tenant-operated farms, it was the region in which the total number of farms declined at the fastest rate. The decrease in the number of southern farms was from 2,317,000 in 1954 to 1,372,733 in 1964—a decline of 41 percent. Farms operated by nonwhites (mainly Negroes) in the South, decreased from approximately 463,476 in 1954 to 184,653 in 1964, or 60 percent. This, of course, resulted in many Negro families moving to urban centers both within the South and in other areas of the country. The increase in the Negro population of most large urban centers in the North and West—an increase which has been proceeding at an unusually rapid rate during the past decade—is directly traceable to the declining number of Negro-operated farms in the South.

SUMMARY AND PERSPECTIVE

This chapter has centered attention on those segments of agricultural policy pertaining to the supply and pricing of scientific knowledge and capital used in farm production. Although there are numerous research programs financed by public funds which produce knowledge utilized in the production and marketing of farm products, the principal publicly supported activities of this nature are research and extension programs of the USDA, the land-grant colleges, and the Soil Conservation Service, plus the teaching of vocational agriculture in high schools. The major publicly sponsored sources of credit with which farmers purchase capital items are loans made by the Farm Credit Administration agencies, the Farmers Home Administration, and the Rural Electrification Administration. The direct payments made to farmers for carrying out Agricultural Conservation Practices are also important sources of funds for capital expenditures. In addition, large numbers of private business firms are regularly engaged in various types of activities which supply farmers with technical knowledge and capital.

During the period from 1932 to 1965, the expenditures of the USDA and state and local governments for agricultural research and extension, plus expenditures for the teaching of vocational agriculture in high schools and those of the Soil Conservation Service, totaled approximately $9.5 billion. Agricultural conservation assistance payments were approximately $8 billion. During the same period, the total loans made by the Farm Credit Administration agencies, the Farmers Home Administration and its predecessor agencies, and the Rural Electrification Administration amounted to about $86.9 billion. A substantial proportion of the funds that were made available to farmers by these publicly sponsored programs, particularly the loans made by the Farm Credit Administration agencies and the Farmers Home Administration following World War II, would have come from private sources if they had not been available as a result of public actions.

Nevertheless, the main thrust of all such public and private activities has been to enlarge the supply and to improve the quality of scientific knowledge and capital used in farming. Their immediate impacts, therefore, have been to lower prices for these two inputs relative to the prices of land and labor. The growing utilization of scientific knowledge and new capital by farmers has been a potent force in increasing the volume of farm production. Expanded farm output has, in turn, affected farm product prices, farmers' incomes, and the structural organization of agriculture.

The extent of such effects has been dependent on the nature of the demand for farm products and on the level of employment in nonfarm sectors of the economy. During the period from 1930 to 1965, there were only 10 to 12 years between 1942 and 1953 when the demand for farm products and employment conditions in nonfarm industries were clearly of such a nature that the increased farm output which stemmed from the application of scientific knowledge and new capital to farming made important contributions to the real incomes of both farmers and consumers. During the depressed 1930's, and again in the years following the Korean conflict, increases in total farm output exerted strong downward pressures on farm product prices and on total real income of farmers.

Most of these programs have been aimed at benefiting farmers by increasing their efficiency and raising their incomes, but it is almost certain that farmers as a group have not been the principal beneficiaries. It is impossible, in the present state of knowledge, to arrive at an accurate accounting of the net balance between benefits and costs of educational, credit, and conservation programs among various groups in society. Nevertheless, it is safe to conclude that, during most of the past 34 years, they have been of primary benefit to consumers, to those agri business firms whose earnings were raised as a result of increases in their volume of business, and temporarily to those farmers who were the early adopters of cost-reducing practices arising from the programs.

The benefits to consumers have been of two types: first, lower prices for farm products than would have occurred if these programs had not been in existence to increase farm production; and second, the release of manpower from farming for productive work in nonfarm industries. Because of this release of manpower from farming, the national production of nonfarm goods and services has expanded in quantity and improved in quality at a more rapid rate than would have occurred if the government had not implemented and subsidized the creation and dissemination of knowledge and credit for use by farmers.

There have, however, been significant costs associated with the publicly sponsored educational, credit, and conservation programs. They have been mainly of four kinds: first, the direct public expenditures—federal, state, and local—in organizing and administering the programs; second, a part of the public expenditures associated with government programs to maintain farm product prices above free market levels; third, the psychological and financial costs to large numbers of rural people who moved out of agricultural occupations, and often out of rural areas, because of their low earnings resulting from low farm product prices; and, fourth, a part of the public and private costs—such as welfare payments, expenses of specialized training programs, and increased expenses of city administration—which has been a result of the migration of low-income, poorly educated, rural people into metropolitan areas.

Though accurate measures are not available of the total benefits and costs arising from the impacts of the educational, credit, and conservation programs on farming, there is evidence which strongly suggests that the long-term benefits of these programs to society as a whole are quite high (8). Although farmers have not been the principal beneficiaries, it is reasonable to believe that the total social benefits of these programs far outweigh their total social costs.

It is clear that the technical knowledge and capital which stemmed from public programs have not been distributed equally among all farmers. There has been a strong tendency for those farmers who were in the higher income brackets, who controlled relatively large amounts of productive property, who were the best managers, and who were the most willing to take new and added risks to benefit most from the publicly sponsored input enhancement programs. Consequently, small farms, tenant-operated farms, and farms operated by Negroes have decreased at a faster than average rate, and maturing young men have been discouraged from starting to farm in competition with more mature and experienced farmers in command of a considerable bundle of productive assets. Thus, the average size of farms in all areas of the country has increased, and the average age of farmers has risen.

As a result of these kinds of changes, it is probable that farms are polarizing into two groups. At one extreme is a group

114   *James G. Maddox*

of large, highly capitalized, efficient farms, whose operators are actively seeking to expand the scale and efficiency of their operations. At the other extreme is a group of small, inefficient farms, many of whose operators are too old, too poorly educated, and too far out of touch with the available educational and credit agencies to reorganize their farms into efficient operating units. Although it can hardly be argued that the publicly sponsored educational, credit, and conservation programs have been the main causes of this polarization process, their combined impact has contributed to its rate of development.

LITERATURE CITED

1. Agricultural Conservation Program, Summary by States—1964, Table 19. USDA, ERS. 1964.
2. Agricultural Conservation Program, Summary Fiscal Year 1966, Agr. Stab. and Conserv. Serv., USDA. Jan., 1967.
3. Annual Report of the Council of Economic Advisers, U.S. GPO. 1967.
4. Annual Report 32 of the Farm Credit Administration. Pp. 67, 84, and 106. Washington, D.C., Feb., 1966.
5. Benedict, M. R. Farm Policies of the United States, 1790–1950. P. 396. New York: The Twentieth Century Fund. 1953.
6. Changes in Farm Production and Efficiency: A Summary Report, 1964. USDA Stat. Bul. 233. 1964.
7. Changes in Farm Production Efficiency, A Summary Report, 1966. USDA Stat. Bul. 233. 1966.
8. Griliches, Z. Research expenditures, education, and the aggregate agricultural production function (including refs.). Amer. Econ. Rev., Dec., 1964.
9. A National Program of Research for Agriculture. A report of a study sponsored jointly by: Assoc. of State Univ. and Land-grant Colleges and the USDA. P. 7. Oct., 1966.
10. Report B and FR—2321, Office of Budget and Finance. USDA. Oct. 12, 1964.
11. Farm Income Situation, USDA. July, 1966.
12. Report of the Administrator of the Farm Security Administration, 1941. USDA. Oct. 1, 1941.
13. Wilcox, W. W. The Farmer in the Second World War. Ames: Iowa State Univ. Press, 1947.

CHAPTER FIVE

Some Implications of Continuing Present Farm Price and Income Support Programs

DALE E. HATHAWAY

THE DIFFICULTIES of evaluating the impact of past agricultural policies are great and those of evaluating future policies even greater. This is especially true when the very parameters that one uses in such projections are—by definition—going to change in the years ahead. To attempt such a projection requires that one specify rather precisely the policies under consideration.

The policies to be dealt with in this discussion are those generally termed price and income support policies. They include price support programs, stock accumulation programs, compensatory payment programs, acreage restrictions, and multiple-pricing programs both at home and abroad.

The U.S. price support programs have operated for more than three decades. In general the price support levels have been set above the market-clearing price and the disequilibrium between prices and quantities that might be offered has been handled by stock accumulation, land withdrawal programs, and export subsidies of various types.

In the early 1960's there was a shift in the program emphasis. The market price supports on major commodities were dropped to or near market-clearing prices. Producers' incomes meanwhile were protected by direct payments on fixed quantities of products. These payments were made only to eligible producers—defined as those who comply with land retirement or other output restraints. This shift enabled us to reduce or eliminate export subsidies on major price supported crops without inducing continued stock increases or applying compulsory production controls. Of course, the continuation of large-scale concessional sales of grains to underdeveloped countries has served to buoy the domestic market price and make the program more palatable to producers.

Both the compensatory payments and the acreage control aspects of the current programs are tied to historical land bases. These bases are relatively recent for feed grains, but are tied to much earlier history for wheat and cotton.

There is a general consensus that the programs of the past twenty years have maintained gross farm income in most years at levels above that which would have been experienced in the absence of price support program (see Chap. 3). The effects of the program upon factor returns, especially labor, in agriculture are less clear. It has been asserted that the use of land restrictions as a method of production control, together with compensatory payments tied to a historical land use, have resulted in the artificial enhancement of land prices and little improvement in labor returns.

In the short run, with the bulk of our farms owner-operated, this kind of distortion of factor returns probably has had relatively minor adverse welfare effects within agriculture. The nature of the programs, however, has been to help most those in agriculture who are the best off, i.e., the landowners; and, it has done little to aid the lowest income groups in farming—the farm tenants and hired farm workers.

Past programs have contributed to the continued rise in land prices and the resulting capital gains for land owners. Whether this is good or bad depends upon one's point of view, but it certainly has implications for the future.

SOME REASONS THAT PRESENT POLICIES ARE LIKELY TO CONTINUE

Before turning to the probable effects of continuing the present policies, it is worthwhile to review some of the reasons that these basic policies are likely to continue, with modifications, of course, to meet changing conditions. These are primarily political in nature, but it will take strong adverse economic effects to generate enough political dissatisfaction to overcome them.

An effective agricultural policy must be understood and acceptable to those whose participation is required. The present program meets these criteria despite some farm organizations' claims to the contrary. This is a major reason the program is likely to receive continued support. The present program represents an evolution starting in the 1930's and it rejects both the extremes of withdrawing government support and extensive government control over farm operations. Farmers understand the present program and, if participation is a valid criteria, find it acceptable. Moreover, it is administratively workable under U.S. conditions, a feature that some proposals clearly have lacked.

Equally important, the present program is acceptable to both the bureaucracy and to agriculturally allied input-producing and marketing industries. Both groups are important in implementing or opposing program changes. Both prefer certainty to uncertainty insofar as government policies are concerned. Thus, the major agricultural groups with power understand the present program, are reasonably well adjusted to it, and would be highly unlikely to agree on major changes.

Another major reason for farmer opposition to marked changes from the present program relates to the effects of such changes upon asset values and income distribution in agriculture. As mentioned, much of the past program effects have been built into asset values in agriculture via the land market. Commercial farmers have a huge financial stake in maintaining a program which will at least protect these asset values. Thus, there would be strong opposition on the part of all organized farm groups and from agricultural financial institutions to any program which threatened to reduce the returns to land and historical production bases.

The current programs have distributed income primarily on the basis of contribution to farm output. While the programs have redistributed income from nonfarm to farm people they have not been designed to redistribute income significantly within agriculture. Whenever suggestions have been made that the programs ought to be operated to change income distribution in agriculture, the farm organizations have voiced strong opposition. This opposition seems more likely to grow than diminish as the relative power of commercial farmers grows within the general farm organizations and as the power of specialized commodity groups increases.

A final point supporting continuation of the present program is its general acceptance by the nonfarm public. Even though it is not clearly understood, urban representatives have generally come to accept and support the present program. Given the present and future urban domination of the Congress, this acceptance is likely to be important. Urban representatives are likely to view major program changes with skepticism, although the present program may generate increasing dissatisfaction on some counts.

In general, it will probably require major and obvious undesired results in order for the present programs to get into major political difficulty. Let us turn to some of the probable program consequences to see if they appear to be of this magnitude.

INCOME DISTRIBUTION AND FOOD PRICES

The consolidation of farms is likely to continue in the years immediately ahead, perhaps at an even faster pace as the percentage of farmers reaching retirement age increases. This is likely to result in an even greater concentration of agricultural production on farms in the two top economic classes, those selling over $20,000 of farm products annually.

This increased concentration of production on the larger commercial farms is likely to result in some serious questions about the equity of redistributing income from the nonfarm population to the owners of these larger commercial farms. For instance, the USDA estimated that in 1965 the average family income of farm operator families on farms selling over $20,000 of products annually was $15,793.[1] Since this is more than twice the nonfarm average, it is likely to become increasingly difficult to convince urban legislators that such transfers are justifiable. The move to direct payments for at least part of the income transfer will tend to magnify this concern, for it will become increasingly obvious that our commodity price support and income supplement programs primarily benefit those with the highest income in agriculture.

Opposition to the programs will be intensified when and if the USDA releases its calculations on parity income. These will

[1] Data taken from Table 5D, Farm Income Situation 203, July, 1966.

show that these larger commercial farms on the average were earning at least enough to cover their opportunity costs on all of their resources in recent years.

Maintenance of the present programs in the years ahead at present price levels will certinly result in favorable incomes for the larger commercial farms and in resource returns on many of these farms that will substantially exceed opportunity costs for the resources involved. Both are likely to be increasingly difficult to justify and maintain.

Food prices have become a politically sensitive issue, especially as consumers increasingly believe that food prices are related directly to government policy. This sensitivity is likely to preclude any attempts to shift more of the income transfers to the market where their income distribution effect is less visible. Indeed, this sensitivity regarding prices is likely to put sharp limits on the kinds of self-help and bargaining programs that Congress will authorize for farmers as well as upon direct government price support levels.

Thus, continuation of the present program is likely to bring increasing concern from urban consumers about its income distribution effects and its effects upon food prices. It does not follow that these pressures will result in major changes, but the interaction between the program and the changes in agriculture will generate increasing pressure from nonagricultural groups for change.

INPUT PRICES, RESOURCE USES, AND RESOURCE RETURNS

A continuation of the present program will have continued impact on input prices, resources uses, and resource returns. As long as the income supports are based upon historical bases tied to land, and use land retirement as the major method of production control, the relative price of land will be increased. When these pressures are added to the pressures on land prices arising from the economies of farm enlargement, it appears that farm land prices will continue to rise. The capitalization of the program benefits into land prices means that the returns to labor are likely to continue to remain relatively low for the operators of many farms. Moreover, the primary beneficiaries of the program will be the original owners of the land on which the capitalization of the benefits occurs. As long as the program continues, society will either have to cover these increased costs to each successive owner or some of these future owners will incur large capital losses.

The capitalization of program benefits into land raises the question as to whether it might not be possible to divorce the real asset prices from the capitalized values of the income stream generated by the program. In principle this would not be difficult. Government bonds could be issued to the holders of present feed grain, wheat, cotton, and other crop bases, the bonds equal in value to the capitalized value of the base. This would protect the income and asset value of the present base owners and relieve the future purchasers of the land from the obligation of having to acquire the capital to finance the purchase of the bases. It would leave unchanged the net returns to future purchasers.

There is one drawback to such a scheme, however. The granting or withholding of the compensatory payments is the most powerful incentive for participation in acreage reduction programs. For the government to buy out the bases would require that voluntary acreage control be dropped as a method of production control. If one is going to divorce the income flows from the program effects on land prices, the use of acreage restrictions as a production control device would have to be dropped or altered markedly. With few exceptions commercial farmers have steadfastly resisted the use of quantity control restrictions. Dropping of the acreage allotments tied to the payments would remove the only workable supply management program thus far devised for the major crops.

From the point of view of the economy as a whole the relative inflation of land prices makes little sense. The results of the program indicate that the opportunity costs for agricultural land are high. This leads to the conclusion that the land input should not be reduced relative to labor and capital. In reality, however, most farm land has low economic value outside of farming. Both capital and labor, however, have relatively high nonfarm value in a full employment economy. Thus, the program will tend to make dear in agriculture that resource which has little value elsewhere and tends to encourage the farm use of those resources which have the most value elsewhere.

Continuation of the program will not only perpetuate or worsen the resource mix within U.S. agriculture, but it may also accentuate the tendency for the entry of excessive resources. The consequent problem is excess output. As mentioned earlier, many of the larger commercial farms appear to be earning more than the total opportunity costs for their present resources. Thus, these farms have a great incentive to add more productive resources and add to the excess capacity problem in agriculture. The present program is better in this regard than some of its predecessors, inasmuch as the earlier programs provided very high price supports for all production. It is possible, however, that in the foreseeable future, price supports for corn at just over a dollar per bushel may prove to be just as attractive to new resources as was $1.40 corn a decade ago.

THE OWNERSHIP OF AGRICULTURAL ASSETS

Historically, with the exception of the plantations of the old South, U.S. agriculture has been a system of predominately owner-operated farms. It has been possible over the lifetime of an individual for farmers to acquire ownership or a major equity in the total resources required to put together a viable commercial farm.

Economic conditions in modern agriculture are rapidly moving in a direction that raises questions as to whether this system can and should be continued. The very high capital requirements of modern agriculture together with the low labor returns in the industry make it very difficult for an individual to enter farming successfully unless he has major capital available beyond that which can be saved from his individual labor returns. This would be true even if the farm program benefits were not capitalized into farm land prices, but this capitalization will make the problem even greater.

This development could lead to either of two trends in the future. Either commercial farming will be restricted primarily to those individuals who inherit or marry enough capital to finance a viable commercial farm; or the ownership and operation of farm land will be separated, just as the ownership and management of nonfarm businesses generally are.

The development of a class of commercial farmers who achieve this status primarily by inheritance would not be a new development in the world, in fact it is a common one in many other countries. Such a system continues the owner-operated tradition, but it essentially excludes those not born into the system from entering it. This would represent a sharp departure from the present image of our agricultural society, although it probably would not represent a marked departure from past reality.

The shift to outside ownership of much of the capital required for agriculture would represent a rather marked shift from our past experience. Again, this system is not unique and is fairly common in certain countries. However, as long as the returns on commercial farms fail to cover the opportunity costs of all of the capital and labor involved, a system of outside ownership can evolve only if either the capital or labor is forthcoming at less than its possible opportunity costs in nonfarm markets. In some countries this has been possible because nonfarm owners are willing to hold farm land for zero or negative real returns and rent the land to operating farmers. It is doubtful in the years ahead if farm labor or tenants will be willing to work in a full employment economy at much less than they might earn elsewhere, especially if they have lost the potential capital gains that have accrued to farm owners.

If the earnings on commercial farms in the years ahead are generally large enough to cover the opportunity costs for all resources, there will be a powerful incentive for the entry of nonfarm capital into the ownership of farm production assets. We already have seen such movement into poultry and egg production, beef feeding, and dry-lot dairying in some areas. It has not become common in that part of agriculture where land is the major capital item, but this does not mean it may not.

Thus, it is somewhat ironic that the present program—designed to protect the owner-operated family farm—may be a significant element hastening the demise of the system. If the program successfully maintains "parity income" in farming it will make the entry of capital from outside the industry more probable. To the extent the program contributes to further increases in land prices, it will limit entry into commercial farming by persons lacking access to substantial capital.

It is doubtful that alterations in the price and income support programs would have a marked impact upon either the speed or direction of the change in our agricultural system. Much of the change is due to economic forces apart from the price and income supports, and these programs only serve to accentuate the changes. Our price and income policies have never contained an explicit policy decision about the structure of agriculture; and only an explicit policy, operated with specific structural objectives, can alter the trends in resource ownership in agriculture.

INTERNATIONAL TRADE
AND INTERNATIONAL RELATIONS

In some ways our policy makers have recognized a fact that academic workers have been reluctant to admit regarding international trade in farm products. International trade in farm products has never been organized and is unlikely to be, primarily on the basis of comparative advantage that operates for industrial goods. There are many reasons for this, including the crucial role that food and fiber play in the sheer existence of an economy or political system.

The present price and income support programs in the United States are more nearly consistent with international trade in farm products along the lines of comparative advantage than have been our policies for almost forty years. If our domestic prices are allowed to remain close to the "world" price level, we will not have to resort to large export subsidies to engage in commercial trade. This certainly improves our moral position insofar as international trade negotiations are concerned, even if it doesn't help our political bargaining.

A continuation of the present programs leaves the question open as to the program impact upon our international relations. The disappearance of our excess stocks in 1965 and 1966 has made it possible for the United States to put its food aid program on primarily an aid basis. Yet there are tremendous domestic political incentives from farmers and allied interests to provide such aid at a level in excess of the long-run interests of the recipient countries.

The food aid program provides the United States with a tremendous force in international diplomacy which can work for good or not, depending upon its use. Because it is such a force, it must be used carefully and this means by those responsible for our total foreign policy. Excessive congressional restrictions on the use of food aid—such as limiting its extension on the basis of political ideology—place major limits on its effectiveness. Excessive pressures to increase volume or to include certain commodities have the same effect.

Basically, if the program is to have its maximum international effect it must be made more flexible than in recent years. This means that its effects upon domestic agricultural prices and incomes cannot be the sole criteria upon which either congressional or administrative decisions are made.

ADMINISTRATION AND BUDGET CONTROL

The mid-1960's was a period in which the threat of ever-growing federal expenditures for farm price and income support programs was reduced if not removed. The cessation of the open-ended price supports at high price levels brought a leveling off of expenditures for price and income supports. It does not, however, promise an end to such expenditures or even a significant reduction in them.

Even if commercial agriculture could be brought into approximate adjustment in terms of resource use and earnings, there will be great opposition by some to the ending of compensatory income payments. This will be even more difficult as these bases are tied into the capitalized value of farms and become fixed assets to the succeeding generations of resource owners. To end the stream of program benefits would cause a substantial deflation of farm assets and be regarded as breaking faith with the owners. Thus, the prospects of future downward adjustments in budget costs are not great.

On the other side, the present program does contain the possibility of preventing sharp increases in federal budget costs under the program. The fixed quantity of products covered by direct income supplements prevents large unplanned budget costs due to changes in crop size. Lower price supports and the powerful incentives to participate in supply management programs should prevent large and expensive unwanted stock accumulations. The placing of foreign food aid on a need basis makes its costs more predictable except in cases of widespread emergency.

Despite these factors, budget costs for the present programs may spiral slowly upward and continue unchanged in the years ahead. The present program (1967–68) requires large direct payments to producers of wheat and cotton regardless of the market price of those products or of acreage restrictions. As resource productivity and yield per acre increase in the years ahead, either the payment per acre will have to rise or the product price be lowered in order to induce farmers to participate in the acreage diversion program. Barring a continued surge in commercial export demand, the problems of excess supplies, stock accumulation, and rising budget costs could appear at present market price levels.

The present programs have proven administratively feasible, although there is much that could be done to simplify administration at the individual farm level. There was, in the early 1960's, some push for restrictive nonvoluntary production controls on individual farms. One of the great problems of that approach is the administrative difficulties it would entail at all levels. Agriculture has used an unusual elective-appointive system of local people to administer price and income support programs at the local level, and it is doubtful whether this system could and would successfully operate an effective system of restrictive direct controls.

SUMMARY AND CONCLUSIONS

The present price and income support program for commercial agriculture in the United States appears workable in the years ahead. It is understood, accepted by farmers, administratively feasible, and subject to a fair degree of budget control. Thus, it does not carry inherently the seeds of its own political destruction. It is perhaps best adjusted to the international scene of any program we have had in recent years. This does not imply that it is perfect, however. It will create some increased tensions and could lead to serious economic and political difficulties. The program does not and will not reduce income disparities within agriculture, in fact it may increase them. The program benefits will largely go to the owners of land, so that it tends to distort relative factor prices within agriculture and contribute little to increased rewards for labor in farming.

This program has and will contribute toward increased barriers to entry in farming and add to the pressures for an agricultural system with land ownership separated from farm operation. All of these goods and bads are matters of degree, for it is rare to find a program which can make everyone in the economy better off and achieve all the values sought from such programs. Only with the ability to predict the future in all respects could one tell if the present program will endure for some period of time. The best guess is, however, that those hoping for its quick demise are destined to disappointment.

CHAPTER SIX

Transforming Rural Policies To Mesh With Future Goals and Values

EMERY N. CASTLE and WALTER R. BUTCHER

"Faiths are the Genes of Society"—KENNETH BOULDING, *The Image,*
p. 172.

THE TITLE of this chapter is capable of many interpretations, depending upon one's views about the policy-making process. One possible view is that future goals and values can be predicted by the people or groups who will transform rural policies and that the relationship of policies to goals and values can be known. If one further holds that the people affected will readily accept the "ideal" policy designed by "intellectuals" or "planners" then it follows that policy transformation is largely an intellectual accomplishment.

Another view is that knowledge about "what is," "what will be," and "what should be" is more difficult to obtain than the above position would seem to imply. As a result, policy formation and transformation is a complex process involving much more than intellectual analysis.

We believe that the "complex" view is the more realistic

description of the policy-making situation. Thus in this discussion of policy transformation emphasis is made on the indirectness and complexity of the transformation process. However, it is not held, as some may, that the complexity is so great as to preclude any useful discussion of the areas in which policy transformations are needed. Thus, some problem areas are suggested where a transformation of policy is clearly indicated by analysis of present and prospective outcomes under existing policies.

THE OBJECTIVES OF POLICY—GOALS AND VALUES

It has long been a respected viewpoint in the scientific community that science is not mainly concerned with value formation. This viewpoint holds that science is somehow neutral with respect to "what should be" and that positive rather than normative investigations are the respectable outlet for scientific efforts. Admittedly, there have been difficulties in maintaining this code. In the social sciences—economics, political science, sociology— there has long been concern over difficulties of performing usefully as scientists without slipping into the role of telling people what should be. And there have been examples of deliberate use of sciences—especially psychology—as a tool to manipulate people's tastes, goals, and values. But the sciences have not involved themselves in the business of shaping men's minds and reordering society's goals to any large degree.

Despite this desire of scientists to accept society's goals and values as given and to work from there, science, through the development and application of knowledge, has been a most powerful force for change in goal patterns. How can this be? How can a neutral instrument do more to change goals and aspirations than all of the theologians in the country? Kenneth Boulding in *The Image,* says: "We shall delude ourselves if we think that the self-perpetuation of images through the apostolic succession of authority is unknown to science" (5).

First, science changes our perception of reality. Scientific discoveries and developments change the "facts," "limitations," and "possibilities" which make up the conditions of production and other elements of the boundaries which determine the extent to which various goals can be attained. As a result, some goals— such as high school education for all—that were previously unattainable can now be reached. Other goals—such as the simple, unencumbered, and free life—become relatively more costly when measured in terms of what must be foregone to attain them. The altered relations among different goals and values cause some of them to become inconsistent with one another.

We may be forced to choose between two goals or values of almost equal desirability because they are in direct conflict in the altered "environment" given to scientific and technological changes. In general, the knowledge and technological change provided by "neutral" science are a force requiring reappraisal and change in the "mix" of goals and values held by individuals and society. The classic treatment of conflict among values caused by changes in conditions over time was made by J. M. Brewster (6, 7, and 8). Science-caused changes in the *means* by which values are realized thus lead, without question, to changes in the values which are realized. Barzun (2) says: "Yet science is an all-pervasive energy, for it is at once a mode of thought, a source of strong emotion, and a faith as fanatical as any in history."

Science may also become involved in goals and values through serving as a means of ascertaining what values exist at a point in time. Although economists are aware of the difficulties of establishing a social welfare function, it may be possible to make useful statements about the relative values people hold. This point is not developed in depth here. For more complete treatment, the following are recommended: (4, 14). If this is so, we then have science engaged in the formulation of statements about what values people hold. Not only is science affecting the means by which values are achieved but also, it is contributing to the discovery of values. The final, ultimate value question remains unanswered by science—what values should we hold? If science can induce change either by affecting ends or means, what changes should be unleashed? While there may not be answers to these questions in science as such, the scientific community has a particular responsibility to consider them and to point out the consequences of alternative choices. Kenneth Boulding has said the method of science consists of substituting unimportant questions which can be answered, for important questions which cannot be (5). However, it would also be in the Boulding tradition to say that it is appropriate for some to struggle with the important questions from time to time, even though we may not have a high degree of confidence that an answer will be obtained.

POLICY CHANGE AS A PROCESS

Changing goal patterns or changes in the means of attaining goals and values create a situation in which policy changes may be desirable. In this country, the process by which these changes of policy are brought about is one of continuous, interlocking adaptations and revisions.

This process goes forward without receiving a great deal of attention or creating concern. Change is an accepted characteristic of our culture. Many minor changes from the customary ways of doing things are accepted without even being considered "policy change." However, there inevitably and periodically arises call for changes so noticeable as to be viewed as *basic* policy changes. Fundamental changes in means and goals or ends may lead us to such a discrete "turning point."

A small change in a "sensitive" policy can have the same effect. So can the cumulative effect of several adaptations within an existing policy that become so weighty as to constitute substantial changes of the policy itself. These more basic policy changes are questioned much more thoroughly than are discrete minor modifications. Often, when some goal can only be achieved by a fundamental policy change, there is a long delay in its achievement or, in fact, it may never come about.

What is it about these fundamental policy changes that makes their lag time so long? Complexity and a need to untangle and account for potential or imagined side effects contribute to some delay. However, the main deterrent seems to be the complicated merging that takes place over time with goals or ends and the means which are used to achieve them. Means and ends become intertwined, either for the individual or for the group. For example, the rural school is a means invented by man to provide opportunity for individual development of rural youth. It served well to that end for many years and came to be venerated—it achieved the status of an end rather than a means. In time, conditions changed so that the same end of individual development could now be better achieved in many instances by means other than the rural school. But the rural school had come to represent an end itself quite apart from its contribution to the goal for which it was created. There were, and still are, valiant efforts to preserve the rural schools regardless of whether the ultimate end of individual development could now be best achieved in other ways. The ultimate end came to be sacrificed to the means-become-end.

Many instances of this sort could be cited. The term "institution" has been used to describe these human arrangements that are designed to serve as means for some purpose but which are also regarded as ends. Clarence Ayers' use of the term "sacred" to define an "institution" is descriptive of what we are trying to convey.

It seems to be generally true that the institutions that have grown up with or around a policy have greater durability than do the conditions that created the need for the policy. Once the policy becomes institutionalized, it may prove exceedingly difficult to alter it as quickly as desired to take advantage of opportunities and needs to be served by the potential new policy (4). Where there are strong institutions there are generally lags due to the continuation of policies after change has occurred in the conditions calling for the policy.

It becomes clear upon close examination that much policy conflict stems from disagreement as to what constitutes mean and what constitutes ends. The intellectual or planner often errs at this point because he is inclined to isolate the ultimate goals and consider all else as means to ends. His analysis and conclusions as to what should be the policy are unencumbered by the sentiment, emotion, and desire for individual or local power that is associated with the preservation of institutions such as the rural school, church, or county government.

If social scientists aspire to the role of "transformers of policies," they must do a better job of recognizing the strength of institutions and the *apparently* irrational aspirations (ends) of different interest groups. It sometimes seems that only the Bureau of the Budget and a few academic economists adopt the "national point of view." To transform policies one must reconcile the "national viewpoint" with that of individuals and smaller groups who affect decision making.

The transformation process then very much involves political issues. It is the process by which group and individual interests are harmonized so that change can occur. One must distinguish this process from the procedure of the intellectual or planner who assumes or states a goal of society, logically and objectively considers the alternative means of attaining that goal, and presents the result as a new "policy." This is not to detract from the value of such plans. They can be exceedingly useful to the policy-making process.

The point is that the work may not be relevant to the aspirations of all who participate in the policy transformation process. The reasons are many, but without doubt institutions and all that which is associated with them often become identified with the existing power structure. The two become mutually reinforcing and each represents to the other a way of life rather than being partners in adventurous change.

The origin, design, functioning, and decline of institutions appear to be of crucial importance to policy changes. If institutions could be viewed as a means to accomplishing the ends of policies, highly specialized institutions would be the most efficient for achieving their intended purpose of providing a mechanism to permit man to achieve rather fundamental values. When the particular purpose of one of these specialized institutions had been served, it would be quickly replaced by a more efficient means when policies were changed. But the tendency for institutions resulting from yesterday's policies to become "ends," or have associated with them the values of the day, means that quick replacement of outdated institutions simply does not happen. Further, we believe these "lags" are an inevitable part of the way of life in a democratic society. Thus, for long-run efficiency, it is imperative that emphasis be placed on the design and adoption of those institutions that are not only efficient for achieving the end in view but also have great flexibility and adaptability. The point has been made elsewhere that analytical economics stemming from the logic of the marketplace may have considerable value in the analysis of institutions. For examples of this type of approach, see: (3 and 9).

The price and market system is an example of an institution which is both effective and flexible. Advanced technology results in a division of labor and exchange. To the extent that material goods and services are important to man, he needs an effective system for coordinating the many resulting activities. To this end, the market has proved to be remarkably effective and useful. It appears in a variety of conditions and cultures. There is no proven alternative arrangement for coordinating a complex economy. Capitalist and socialist countries alike have need for the services of this remarkable development by man. The common need for this type of coordinating device is now a great force bringing about an economic organization in the countries of Eastern Europe that is similar to that of Western democracies. We conclude then that the price system is based on the desire for people to have material goods and services or, to put the same thing another way, efficiency is a rather fundamental value of modern man. This statement may be inaccurate in a strict logical sense. Rather than efficiency being a value of man, it may more accurately be a description of man himself. If man is rational (that is, his means are consistent with his ends), he will behave in an "efficient" manner. In this sense, observed efficiency may simply be a manifestation of an innate rationality.

The price system also has a remarkable capacity to accommodate and generate change in tastes and preferences, the distribution of income, and in the conditions of production. This adaptability has given the system great durability. Sufficient capacity to absorb exogenous and endogenous changes make it unnecessary to construct a new system and fit each new set of conditions. Nevertheless, the Western democracies have never relied exclusively on the market as constituted in its "purest" form. They have recognized that the market operates within a broader framework and have not hesitated to change or modify the conditions of market operations. They recognized "externalities" and other market imperfections. It seems that it was known intuitively, long before economists brought proof, that under laissez-faire market conditions, the ratio of marginal costs and returns to the individual decision maker may not always be proportional to the marginal social costs and returns.

The political process by which the market was adjusted and modified in the Western democracies is another example of an institution having both effectiveness and adaptability. The fundamental value in a democratic political process is the belief that if an individual is affected by an action, he should have a voice in deciding what the action is to be. Another way of saying this is that political decisions should not be imposed on persons not represented in the decision process.

This dualism of the price system and the political process tends to explain the unique fabric of life in the Western democracies. This is not to say that one cannot exist without the other (6). It is to say that they have existed side by side in the United States and have operated with considerable success. One who wishes to change policies must recognize the fundamental allegiance we have to these two basic institutions. The institutions are interwoven and tend to counterbalance one another on crucial issues.

The political process may be relied upon to counteract against undesirable market effects either by general or specific actions. By the same token, the market has provided a means whereby those who did not have political power might have an achievement outlet. Obviously the two did not always have a counteracting influence. There have been instances when political power was used to influence the market so that the two have complemented one another to achieve highly questionable objectives.

The American Negro has suffered not only from a less than open economic system, but also from a political system that did not provide recourse. But the bulk of the evidence is on the other side. Political power has been used more to right inequities of the market than to accentuate them.

It is submitted that since these two institutions are both effective in permitting man to realize fundamental values and also adaptable to conditions of change it is highly likely that they will persist and remain strong. Policy and institutional changes will, to some extent, be designed explicitly to protect and strengthen the basic institutions. Policy changes for other purposes will be watched for their effects upon these basic institutions and some otherwise desirable changes may be forestalled for fear of seriously damaging the market or the democratic process.

Thus looking to the future, it is anticipated that the market will continue to be the principal allocator of resources and distributor of economic rewards in rural America. But the specific rules under which the market operates will be subject to change. Some of the changes will result from direct intervention. In other instances, developments such as vertical integration and other forms of coordination will shift the focal point of the market in the production-consumption chain and lead to changes in the relative strength of various forces in the market transactions.

On the political side, there will continue to be a strong defense of those institutions and policies that give the individual a voice in decisions that affect his own welfare. In particular there will be support for policies that extend special assistance to persons who for one reason or another have been left out of the mainstream of economic and political activities.

NEEDED POLICY TRANSFORMATIONS

To some extent, the need for policy transformation arises because changes in goals or values render the old policies inappropriate. More often we simply find by experience that an enacted policy is not leading as effectively as anticipated toward society's goals. But the most common reason that policies become obsolete is that the structure of the economy has changed. New stresses arise that the old policies cannot handle. "Facts" that the old policies are based upon change and leave the policy acting as a hindrance to attainment of desired goals.

The major dissatisfactions in the economic sphere center in three areas: (a) mobility of resources, (b) income distribution, and (c) investment in social overhead capital. For reasons mentioned above, it is not possible for an economist to say with any degree of finality that policies should be. However, it is possible to point out some areas in which present policies seem to be performing inefficiently or with important undesirable side effects.

Some of the major problem situations that face rural America with opportunities for substantially greater goal achievement through careful transformation of policies will be discussed.

POLICIES TO DEAL WITH THE DOWNWARD ADJUSTMENT OF AGRICULTURAL LABOR

The rising productivity of labor used in U.S. agriculture has probably been the single most important development in the employment picture of the whole U.S. economy. From 1900 to 1963, output per man-hour in agriculture rose to more than five times its earlier level. Associated with this rise in productivity has been a dramatic fall in the share of the total labor force employed in agriculture. Lebergott (11) has estimated that from 1900 to 1958, 22 million workers were "released" from agriculture by rising productivity and that these released workers made up three-fourths of the work force added by expanding industries such as trades and services. Thus, to an important extent, declining farm employment has provided the labor force for the growth industries.

People in and connected with agriculture have not been altogether pleased with this exodus of labor from agriculture and the consequent decline in the share of total employment that has been made up by farm employment. That is understandable. No one likes to see his profession or chosen employment declining relative to other fields.

As a result, the shift of labor out of agriculture has occurred without help from official policies designed to ease the cost and difficulty of the transfers or increase the probability that the individuals involved will find the employment for which they are best suited. In fact, the weight of policy has worked to impede rather than ease the shift. Farmers, farm workers, and farm youth have been encouraged to stay on the farm despite bleak income prospects, and the "educational deck" has been stacked in favor of their staying by making available training and employment services to prepare them for agricultural employment but not for nonfarm employment.

By now, sufficient experience has been gained to make it obvious that a policy of "keeping them down on the farm" is unworkable and undesirable. A large number of the young people, trained more or less exclusively for a life in agricultural employment, have moved to nonfarm employment despite handicaps and hindrances. Once there, their lack of preparation has proven to be a personal liability causing a disappointingly large concentration of these farm-to-nonfarm migrants in the lower income, semiskilled and nonskilled positions. These individuals go through life performing at less than their capabilities and receiving less than the maximum reward for their services.

In addition, a policy of "keeping them on the farm" works against those who would stay under any circumstances. Observation of the employment policies in other occupations and industries indicates that employees prosper most in professions which follow a policy of keeping people out of their ranks rather than of keeping them in. Witness the high level of wage earnings in those occupations which have strong unions with difficult entry conditions.

Looking back on the policies toward education and career choice in rural areas, it appears that substantial weight was given to the goals of pride in one's profession and economizing in time and money costs of education. Those are laudable goals, still deserving of consideration. Under the right conditions, a policy based almost solely on those goals would have had few undesirable repercussions. But conditions have turned against a narrowly prideful and economizing educational policy. It is doubted that there has been much change in the relative importance that rural people attach to these goals. Rather, the change has come in economic conditions which now require substantial occupational and geographical mobility for farm and rural town people to achieve economic returns comparable to those of other groups. The market has exerted very powerful pressure for outmovement of labor from agriculture and rural areas. As a result, the goals of economic progress for individuals and the economy are being sacrificed to a substantial degree for the attainment of other goals.

Mobility is partially competitive with pride of profession and economy of investment in occupational preparation; or, at least, it is competitive with some methods of achieving those goals. Thus one would expect that a policy transformation would be desirable. In fact some changes are beginning to be made.

The agricultural education curriculum in rural high schools is undergoing some change to adjust to the needs of farm youth. Greater emphasis is being given to the skills desired by nonfarm agricultural businesses where many farm youth eventually find employment. General educational standards of rural schools are being improved and the school attendance record of students from rural farm areas is improving so that more are completing high school. There also is growing recognition of the need for informing rural youth of nonfarm as well as farm work opportunities. Still, there remains much to be done before farm youth are adequately prepared to enter nonfarm occupations.

A continuing problem that is more difficult and will take longer to solve is that of individuals 35 years old and older who are now excluded by a lack of training, preparation, and experience from entering occupations which could give them profitable employment at this stage in their life. Retraining of these individuals is very costly, both in terms of time and out-of-pocket expense and also in terms of the severity of the personal adjustment involved. But against this must be weighed the fact that, without retraining, their personal achievement and contribution to the economy are going to be negligible.

REDUCING THE FOCUS OF POLICY UPON LAND

Past farm income support policies have keyed upon the land input as a lever to control supply and support prices. Even the names of major programs indicate that this is so—for example, *Soil* Bank Program, *Acreage* Allotment Program, and *Cropland* Conversion Program.

Controlling land use has seemed like a logical avenue to controlling commodity supplies and thereby allowing farmers to receive higher prices and higher incomes. After all, land is the common input in all farm production; and if there is no land there is no production. It seemed logical to reduce land use and thereby cut production.

But the rise of technology has brought into importance several other inputs that can substitute for land to an extent not even imagined when the direction of control programs was being established. Increased use of fertilizers, high-yielding varieties, and chemicals to fight weeds, insects, and disease has increased crop production per acre by 35 percent in the past 10 years.

The influence of these other inputs has caused farm policy geared to land to become less and less effective in attaining major goals of farmers and the nation. The presence of important highly mobile inputs that can "substitute" for land makes it very difficult and expensive to control output for long periods of time simply by controlling acreage. And thus crop acreage control has become less useful as a tool to be used in price income support programs.

A further deficiency of acreage-based controls is that much

of the benefit from the control program accrues to the land owner. Studies have shown that an acre of tobacco allotment had a market value in 1957 of $1,000 in one area and $2,500 in another. A landlord or farmer who is operating his own land is in position to benefit from the program. But tenant operators or the next generation of farmers who must pay for the capitalized value of the allotment get little benefit.

Policies should be adjusted to achieve output control by means other than land withdrawal. Direct control through marketing quotas is one oft-suggested method that should be reconsidered. At the other extreme, policies designed to bring about a more desirable level of total resource commitment to agriculture rather than control output have much to offer in the long run. These long-run policies should give particular attention to the human resource.

POLICIES TO DEAL WITH DEPOPULATION OF RURAL AREAS

As a direct outcome of the decline in labor used on farms there has been, during the past 25 to 30 years, a substantial decline in population of many rural areas. Depopulation is particularly severe in areas that are isolated from industrial centers and specialized in agricultural production. Population loss due to decreased labor on farms has been magnified by the resulting loss of associated business and population in small rural towns. Local booster policies and federal programs such as the Rural Area Development program have attempted to counteract the outmovement from rural areas by introducing nonfarm industries to provide an alternative employment base. Experience indicates that there is some opportunity for successfully supporting and maintaining the population of rural areas in this way. However, experience would also indicate very clearly that this is not a universally satisfactory approach. In many rural areas, the present lack of industry is due to a lack of the basic factors that make for successful industrial enterprise. It is unfortunate, but true, that the very fact that an area is "rural" indicates that it does not have the materials, markets, and skilled labor pools that attract large agglomerations of industry and create an urban rather than rural area. In exceptional cases a rural area may be able to offer an advantage to an industry through the availability of cheap (by industrial-urban standards) land and water or a large pool of inexpensive, unskilled labor. However, in the main, rural areas must face the fact that they are not going to reverse the present trends to depopulation.

The major threat posed by the depopulation of rural areas

is to the continuation and successful performance of rural institutions and public services. The cost per capita of providing roads, schools, welfare, and local government services tends to rise when the population density of an area falls. This is especially true if the population is highly dispersed throughout the area and if the institutions and services were originally formed to serve a larger population. Thus, in a sense, one could say that depopulation of rural areas creates for them a comparative disadvantage in the provision of basic community services and institutions. Modern developments in data processing and the growth of opportunities for specialization of labor in public services, schools, churches, utilities, and governmental functions are serving to further accentuate the comparative advantage of areas of concentrated population in providing these services. The local depopulated community, struggling to provide community services, is forced to accept either a higher rate of local taxation to provide services or a less extensive and lower quality service unless outside assistance is received.

We have had, historically, policies at both national and state levels to support the provision of basic community services and facilities in rural areas. Farm-to-market roads, the REA, federal farm credit programs, rural free delivery of mail, and vocational education for agriculture are all examples that come to mind of outside support to basic rural institutions.

Recently the political base for support of endangered or disadvantaged rural institutions has been weakened. For one thing, the general shift of the population from a rural to an urban residence and orientation has reduced the political power of rural areas. Recent reapportionment decisions have strengthened and accelerated this shift of power. Furthermore, there is a growing feeling that disadvantaged individuals and areas within cities and even the cities themselves need outside support. Thus, there will be increasing competition with rural areas for federal and state funds, and it becomes increasingly important that policies designed to aid and support rural institutions be well thought out and carefully supported.

The primary danger to rural areas is that in the onrush of urbanization and the exodus of people from rural areas, some people are stranded without the economic and political base to support adequate institutions and with no substitute institutions to which they can turn. Allowing communities to die a natural but slow death can be very costly. Thus it is important that a solution be developed to provide a way out for the people of these areas. In some cases the hard decision to cut back quickly will have to be made. When this country was being settled, there was no presumption of a fixed pattern of roads, schools, and local jurisdictional areas but rather a utilitarian policy of providing services where needed and when feasible. School consolidation has already come in many areas. There are undoubtedly opportunities for net gains from a policy of consolidating roads where a too dense network of service roads is causing an unnecessarily large maintenance expense (2). There have been several reports of the relative inefficiencies of governmental functions in small, sparsely populated counties. However, the accepted policy throughout rural America has been to resist any efforts toward county consolidation on the grounds of protecting the local voice in local policies. When a policy of unyielding resistance leads to low performance and an abdication of responsibility and power to state and federal government levels, the local area often ends up losing the very autonomy that it was seeking to defend.

Another local institution that is being greatly affected by depopulation is the local businesses who service farmers and residents. Many small villages have actually suffered a decrease in population and business activity that is more than proportional to the decline in rural farm population. They have been caught not only by the decline in population in their market area but also by changes in the marketing structure which favor larger firms and concentrations of businesses in the larger county seat or area trade center. The decline of many of these small villages appears to be so inevitable that efforts to resist it are futile. Some within driving distance of urban centers will experience some growth as outlying bedroom communities, but many have already decayed to the point where they are not even attractive to this potential source of economic life.

POLICIES TO DEAL WITH RURAL POVERTY

Despite some encouraging trends, there is still a disappointingly large number of rural people living on unsatisfactorily low incomes. In 1959, one-third of all rural families had incomes of less than $3,000 (1). This is twice as high as the rate of poverty incidence in urban areas. High rates of unemployment or underemployment, labor immobility, and lack of resources for adjusting to changing economic conditions are all to prevalent causes of low income in rural areas.

Fortunately, the forces of economic change are working in

the direction of lessening the incidence of poverty among U.S. farmers and farm workers. The very small subsistence farm is rapidly disappearing from the scene as their operators have increasingly taken on other jobs. Some are continuing to operate the farm and depend upon it for a place to live, some home-grown food, and a supplement to their nonfarm income. Many others made a complete switch from farm to city living and their farm is typically consolidated into the larger operation of a more prosperous neighbor. The poorly paid seasonal farm workers are also dwindling in numbers as machines take over more and more of the hand labor tasks and the farm labor needs shift in the direction of a smaller number of more skilled and higher paid workers.

Policies are needed that will capitalize upon and bolster the favorable trends. But these favorable developments should not be taken to indicate that no policy adjustments are needed to deal directly with rural poverty. There is still a great deal of self-perpetuating poverty and underachievement in rural areas that will take literally generations to correct through the unaided adjustment process.

Any judgment of inadequacy in past urban poverty policies must apply much more to rural areas where there has been even less of an effort to help the poor to rise above their situation.

LITERATURE CITED

1. Bird, A. R. Poverty in rural areas of the United States. USDA, Agr. Econ. Rpt. 63, Washington, D.C. P. 15. 1964.
2. Barzun, J. Science: The Glorious Entertainment. New York: Harper and Row. 1964.
3. Bator, F. The anatomy of market failure. Q. J. Econ. 72:351–79, Aug., 1958.
4. Bergeson, A. Essays in Normative Economics. Cambridge, Mass.: The Belknap Press of Harvard Univ. Press. 1966.
5. Boulding, K. The Image. Ann Arbor: Univ. of Mich. Press. 1956.
6. Brewster, J. M. The impact of technical advance and migration on agricultural society and policy. J. Farm Econ. 41:1169–84. 1959.
7. ———. Society values and goals in respect to agriculture. In: Goals and Values in Agricultural Policy. Ames: Iowa State Univ. Press. 1961.
8. ———. Value judgments as principles of social organization with special reference to the rural scene. A paper presented at a meeting of the Southwestern Soc. Sci. Assoc. in Galveston, Texas. March, 1958.
9. Castle, E. N. The market mechanism, externalities and land economics. J. Farm Econ. 47:542–56. Aug., 1965.

10. Clawson, M. Factors and forces affecting the optimum rural settlement pattern in the United States. Econ. Geog. Oct., 1966.
11. Lebergott, S. *Manpower in Economic Growth; The American Record Since 1800.* New York. McGraw-Hill. 1964.
12. Lindblom, C. E. Handling of norms in policy analysis. In: Allocation of Economic Resources (essays in honor of Bernard Francis Haley). Stanford, Calif.: Stanford Univ. Press. 1959.
13. Maier, F., J. L. Hedrid, and W. L. Gibson, Jr. The Sale Value of Flue-cured Tobacco Allotments. Vir. Agr. Exp. Sta., Tech. Bul. 148. 1960.
14. Misham, E. J. A survey of welfare economics. Econ. J. June, 1960.
15. Schumpeter, J. Capitalism, Socialism, and Democracy. New York: Harper and Row. 1942.

CHAPTER SEVEN

Political Forces in American Agriculture: The Present and a Look to the Future

ROSS B. TALBOT and CHARLES W. WIGGINS

IN THIS CHAPTER the major political forces affecting American agriculture in the next ten years are analyzed and further, an attempt is made to sketch out the types of policies which are most likely to dominate American agriculture within that time period.

Political science, in terms of its ability to predict future policy trends with any high degree of accuracy, is hardly an exact science. Indeed, if political predictions are made they need to be of a short-run variety if a useful degree of reliability is to be attained. Like the Weather Bureau, it is best to say the political climate has: some sunshine, various cloud patterns, possibly light rain or even heavy showers, with winds shifting in direction and varying in intensity.

So many variables, or factors, are involved in future political situations that only predictions based on certain assumptions

---

The authors have benefited from the comments and criticisms of our colleague, Don F. Hadwiger.

can be made. These may or may not prove to be accurate. They are what the philosopher would call "if-then" propositions.

Relative to future farm policies, for example, one cannot be at all certain about the future in terms of: wars—limited, conventional, or thermonuclear; drought—why cannot 1934 and 1936 occur again; and diplomatic politics—after all, there were real differences in international strategies and tactics between Theodore Roosevelt and Woodrow Wilson. There are further uncertainties about scientific and technological developments. It could be that General Mills will prove that "synthetic" foods can be "manufactured" so that they will be satisfying to the consumer in terms of price, taste, and aesthetics. Consumer demands may change—we may question the reality of subliminal perception, but it does seem evident that our eating and drinking patterns change because of things read about and heard of. Interest group goals and plans of operation also cause uncertainty—for example, it is not certain whether a holding action will be called by the National Farmers Organization, or whether, if it is called, it will succeed or fail.

The above examples are only a few among many which point to the complexities of predictions. One thing seems certain, however, in the world in which we live (East as well as West): major and minor social, economic, and political changes are occurring and will continue to do so. The challenge of trying to discover the direction, extent, and implications of these changes is exciting.

Political scientists have for a long time made certain assumptions about the nature of man, from which they have constructed ideal, yet avowedly realistic, political systems. James Madison, for example, was an intensive student of history and philosophy, as well as an astute and practicing politician. His studies led him to conclude that man is a political animal who is constantly engaged in conflict and who forms factions in order to try to get what he wants. Moreover, said Madison, "the most common and durable source of faction is the unequal distribution of property." He believed that this new nation (then just becoming the United States of America) should be a strong and dynamic nation, but, being fearful of large concentrations of power, he advocated a political system characterized by checks and balances so that men would have the freedom to form factions. However, these factions would be so limited in power that policy (legislation) would almost invariably have to be in the form of compromise.

Some political scientists are convinced that Madisonian

democracy is inadequate for the United States' role of world leadership today, as well as for the dynamic role government must play in the maintenance and sustenance of a welfare, full-employment economy. These accomplishments must be brought about, they contend, in a political environment in which majoritarian rule can become operational (1).

Their criticisms may, or may not, be valid. Our concern is simply to contend that all of us do have within us an outlook on life which is based on a more or less clearly perceived conception of the nature of man which in turn leads us to a conception of the nature of what is right and wrong and which evolves then into certain positions about policy matters.

MAJOR POLITICAL FORCES AFFECTING AMERICAN AGRICULTURE, 1967 TO 1977

Within this perspective, then, the political forces which seem most significant today in the development of agricultural policies are outlined in this chapter.

First, there is need to point out a possible pitfall—many of the political forces which influence agricultural policies are not directly involved in farming. There is what might be called an *infrastructure* of food politics, and such has been the case throughout our history. Land owners and land speculators, the railroads, banking interests, and storage and marketing interests have all been a part of our so-called agricultural history. The situation today makes for a more complex and fragmented power structure than was true in the past. The fertilizer industry, the farm implement industry, electric power (public and private), the chemical industry (insecticides, pesticides, and herbicides), food exporting and importing firms, research institutions (public and private), some concerned with the natural sciences, others concentrating on the social sciences, all are involved in the development and execution of farm policies. And this list is only indicative, rather than comprehensive, of the intricate political environment which surrounds the modern farming industry.

Moreover, these interests have organized themselves into national and sometimes international organizations which play a direct and active role in public policy. This emphasis will be primarily on farm politics as such, but it needs to be kept constantly in mind that food politics is far more than who gets what, when, and how in terms of the actual production of food and fiber. Although it is a rather biased and somewhat out-dated study, Wesley McCune's *Who's Behind Our Farm Policy?* is worth reading if only in terms of its recounting of all those who have been involved in the passage or defeat of what we too glibly refer to as farm legislation (7).

What strikes one rather forcefully when he studies the political forces in American agriculture are the differences, antagonisms, and conflicts which become apparent. The agricultural industry in America is far from being monolithic, either in terms of interest or ideology. On all sides one observes differences, name-calling, charge and countercharge. Over the years, increased specialization in the commodity production and marketing fields has usually resulted in greater economic interdependence. In turn, this interdependence has resulted in increased—often conflicting—demands being made for policies that will protect agricultural interests from present or anticipated economic and sociological insecurities. Attention will be primarily directed toward these conflict situations.

IDEOLOGICAL DIVISIONS

Someone has said long ago that men divide themselves into two main categories in terms of their philosophical outlooks on life— some are Platonists (only a few can understand truth, and only they should govern); others are Aristotelians (all individuals and especially groups and classes of individuals have a justifiable claim to power; therefore, government should be constructed so that their claims can have a fair hearing). Recently, Theodosius Dobzhansky has used the categories of "dreamers" and "practical men," and concludes: "unfortunately, we do not know to what extent the differences between the 'dreamers' and the 'practical men' are caused by variations in their genes and in their environments. Probably both are involved to some extent (4).

With a sense of uncertainty it is suggested that a somewhat different categorization is useful to classify farmers (and the rest of us) into two groups: the egalitarians and the qualitarians. The first looks upon man in terms of his intrinsic and innate qualities and views differences largely in terms of environment. This phrase was often found in the early literature of the Farmers Union: as the twig is bent, so the tree inclines.

The qualitarians stress the basic and innate differences found in man. They are not by any means as rigorous as Plato, in terms of his stress on heredity, and then the "right" environment. Rather, it is the strains and stresses of a "free society" which prove whether or not one has the stuff which makes for the successful farmer. Still, "one cannot make a silk purse out of a sow's ear," and many of the mistakes in modern public policy (farm policy as well as other varieties) come about because misguided politicians try to do what cannot be done.

The leadership of farm organizations seems to embody this ideological division, although it must be admitted that the judgment here is based primarily on observation, casual and limited interviews, and a study of farm organizational literature.

These categories could be used to develop a picture of the ideological split in farm politics today. However, it would be more fruitful if the reader tests out this analysis for himself. Essentially, however, the leadership of the Farm Bureau is qualitarian, while that of the Farmers Union, the Grange, and with less certainty, the National Farmers Organization, is egalitarian. To those who are born to be, or become, philosophers or ideologists, beliefs and valuations are matters of momentous importance. This leadership group, it should be stressed, appears to be a relatively small, yet powerful, minority (3).

ANTAGONISTIC INTEREST AND ORIENTATIONS

This position holds that most of us are not ideologists, or at least not in any systematic and dogmatic sense. It is assumed that most of us are concerned with such material matters as security, wealth, and status primarily for ourselves and our families. This is not really a revolutionary theory on our part. Thucydides said the same thing; Plato was fearful that Thucydides was right; and the data of the University of Michigan's Survey Research Center seem to provide a fairly solid empirical base for the belief.

Consequently, farm organizations are wise to develop cooperatives and other business concerns which enhance the economic and social condition of those who participate. So a farmer ships to the Grain Terminals Association, or buys his automobile insurance from a State Farm Bureau agent, or doesn't ship his milk until the National Farmers Organization leadership is ready; most of us calculate or rationalize in terms of our own self-interest.

Sectional controversies, commodity differences, disputes between REA's and private utilities, along with many other types of conflicts found within the broad confines of farm politics can be explained in terms of the ideology—interest dichotomy. No attempt is made regarding judgments relative to the "goodness" or "badness" of these conflict situations.

POLITICAL PARTISANSHIP

American political parties are hardly noted for their ideological purity, but the Republican Party is usually the haven of the qualitarian ideologists while most of the egalitarians find refuge within the Democratic Party. The South is an impressive exception to that generalization, but this can be explained largely in terms of the Civil War and the Negro. With a steady increase in the size of the Negro electorate in the South, that section will again join the Union in terms of having a two-party system within which ideologies and interests are fought out through periodic, and reasonably free, elections (6).

Relative to farm politics, the Farm Bureau leadership consistently supports the conservative Republican-Southern Democratic coalition, while the Farmers Union, in particular, and the Grange and National Farmers Organization, less certainly, support the liberal Democratic-liberal Republican coalition.

The voting behavior of the farmer members is another matter. Not being as ideologically motivated in terms of their political behavior, they tend to vote (if they vote at all) according to their material interests, at least as they understand those interests, and their conception of the underlying dynamics of political parties in terms such as war and peace, full employment and recessions. Consequently, and especially since the New Deal farm programs, the farmer has shown a considerable degree of variability in voting behavior. His vote has fluctuated in terms of changing calculation relative to his economic and social interests, although at times ideology (e.g., religion, in 1960) will persuade him—and especially his wife—to uphold the "truth" of his Protestant heritage.

ALLIANCES AND COALITIONS WITH OTHER INTEREST GROUPS

The ideology-interest framework holds together quite well here. "If you can't beat 'em, join 'em," is commonplace in American politics with one strong amendment—who is it that you want to beat, and with whom can you join hands. If the Farm Bureau leadership has ever uttered a favorable word about the United Auto Workers, or the Farmers Union about the National Association of Manufacturers, we have neither heard nor read it. Likewise, one can quite accurately predict how farm organizations will evaluate individual legislators. With almost as much accuracy, one can judge the way in which an individual legislator will evaluate a farm organization.

Note, too, that these coalitions have both a materialistic and an ideological basis. Again, the leadership is attracted by the ideological affinities, while the membership is not much concerned about, or has meager knowledge of, the coalition in any respect.

SUPPORT BY GOVERNMENTAL INSTITUTIONS: FEDERAL OR STATE

The ambivalent attitude of farm organization leaders toward federal and state political institutions is quite a broad topic in itself. The essential ingredient, however, seems to be again both ideological and interest-oriented. The Farm Bureau looks forward to the election of a Republican President and a Republican Congress, and anticipates the rebirth of a conservative Supreme Court. For just the obverse reasons the egalitarian farm leaders desire that the same institutions be under different party and ideological control. At the state level the relationship is less exact but still quite evident, although southern Farm Bureaus—like the Democratic parties in the southern states—require a rather special analysis on this point.

Again it makes a significant difference as to who occupies the top policy positions in the administrative departments, like the United States Department of Agriculture, or the independent regulatory commission, such as the Interstate Commerce Commission and the Federal Power Commission, or the state Departments of Agriculture.

Also, the farmer-voter has more political power than we may realize. Who is elected to public office does make a difference in terms of policies enacted, as well as the way those policies are administered. Often a national election is, usually in a modest way, a revolutionary act.

ATTITUDES OF URBAN CONSUMERS

Pictures of urban housewives picketing grocery stores were abundant in the late summer and fall of 1966. Urban families like "cheap" food, and the votes are in the cities, or so runs the political cliché.

The urbanite seems to be caught on the horns of an ideological interest dilemma. On one hand, there appears to be a considerable residue of nostalgic agrarian fundamentalism in metropolitan America. A Gallup poll, published in March, 1966, indicated that only 22 percent of us desired to live in cities, 49 percent preferred to live in small towns or the farm, and 28 percent favored life in the suburbs. A recent Louis Harris poll showed that 73 percent of the respondents felt that rising food costs had little to do with prices paid to farmers. A survey made for the American Dairy Association indicated that 77 percent thought food was a "good buy," 81 percent agreed that today's farmer is an efficient and progressive businessman, and 82 percent were of the opinion that farmers were not overrepresented in our state legislatures.

On the other hand, recent farm programs—feed grains, wheat certificates, CCC sales, as examples—have had the effect in the last year or two of maintaining farm market prices at a relatively moderate level. All the while, of course, the urbanite has been becoming more affluent. This has meant that, since 1947, the percentage of disposable personal income spent on food has declined from nearly 26 to the present 18. The economic interest of the urban family is favored, at least in the short run, by low food prices.

One could enter into a volume of speculation as to what this will mean in terms of the urban housewife as a political force, relative to future farm policies which probably should be referred to as food policies. Neither political parties nor involved interest groups can afford to neglect this new political force. If a price rise on food proves to be gradual, the urban repercussions may be quite modest; if they are as precipitous as was true for ham and bacon in late 1966, then the unrest may be somewhat rebellious.

THE INTERNATIONAL SITUATION

Farm prosperity, resulting from the dramatic increases in production per acre or animal unit and the low demand elasticity for food, depends heavily on a growing foreign demand for our food products. Throughout our history, U.S. foreign policy has been an important factor in determining the state of the rural economy. This condition has simply been accentuated in recent years. There are so many "ifs" here that we can only summarize them into two groups. First, relative to the sale of farm exports for dollars, the American farmer is certainly affected by U.S. foreign policies relative to such vital matters as the Kennedy Round negotiations in Geneva, the future policies of the European Economic Community and the European Free Trade Association, and the farmer's limited access to the food markets of Communist nations. Second, what happens in terms of population and food production growth rates in the so-called developing nations will be a dramatic force in the determination of American food policies.

In summary, and in over-all terms, the future looks more optimistic for the qualitarians than the egalitarians, in either ideological and interest terms because they will be likely to survive the constant and continuing reduction in the number of farmers due to their ability to absorb and apply the new technologies. Thirty-two million people lived on U.S. farms in 1920; the estimate is 9.7 million by 1972. Percentagewise this means a decrease from 30 to 4 percent. Farming is not yet a part of our corporate economy, nor will it be by 1977. The trend is, nevertheless, perceptibly in that direction. The farmer who will both survive and prosper needs to be a competent scientist, a skillful user of modern technology, a qualified economist and businessman, and a person who has ready access to adequate capital.

The egalitarians may be able to adopt their agrarian fundamentalism to that realistic prototype. To do so, leaders wise in political calculations and prudent in matters of economics will need to develop within their memberships an attitude of organizational self-discipline, and infuse that same attitude into a very sizeable number of commercial farmers who are not members but pork-choppers (those who will act only, or largely, in terms of their own self-interest). The present vigor and dynamism of the National Farmers Organization, in particular, leads one to the position that this *could* happen. A study of the historical development of the United States farm economy leads one to doubt that it *will* happen.

POLICY TRENDS
—A LOOK AT THE NEXT TEN YEARS

For reasons already stated, one must make several assumptions before entering into the hazardous task of peering into the future. Forecasting and prophecy have a genuine fascination, however, so it is with little reluctance, and with a paucity of humility, that the course of some American food policies in the next decade is charted. Before trying to sketch out this policy course six generalizations are made which are intended to furnish a frame of reference for the policy guide.

One needs to look at forces first, then policies. Long ago Thomas Hobbes deduced that "power is the present means to achieve some future apparent good." It is true that we may not agree on what the future apparent good is; nor, for that matter, would we necessarily agree as to what means would be effective (or ethical) in order to attain even a commonly acceptable "good." Within rather indefinable limits this is heartening. James Madison stated well the authors' value position on this issue: "Liberty is to faction what air is to fire, an ailment without which it instantly expires."

This leads to the second generalization: there are two "faces" in the world of farm politics; for the want of a better nomenclature we have called one face egalitarian, the other qualitarian. *Every* farm policy that changes the structure of rural power, or if farm leaders only *perceive* it to do so, is the seedbed, and then probably the hotbed, of political conflict.

Third, there is a kind of "Congressional timetable" when it comes to policy decisions, and especially their removal. All these timetables have a particular history, but an estimate of the future made in 1965 may not prove to be accurate in 1969—an example might be the Food and Agriculture Act of 1965 which expires in 1969. The pro-P.L. 480 (Food for Peace—or Freedom) forces wanted a four-year extension in 1966, but they had to settle for two years and another fight in 1968. With the Democrats losing 47 House seats in the 1966 elections—and 8 of those losses were Midwest Democrats on the House Agriculture Committee—this means what was fairly difficult to accomplish in 1966 may be extremely difficult to achieve in 1968.

The next three generalizations pertain to issues that are more directly on the policy side. First, this nation is probably moving into an economy of balance as far as food is concerned. The state of the national larder may well be a top-priority issue in the years ahead. At the moment our land reserves (feed grains and wheat programs, conservation reserve, cropland adjustment, etc.) seem to give us a reasonable margin of safety. Except for cotton and tobacco, which are hardly edible items, the national larder is decidedly on the scanty side.

Next, as a nation we are just beginning to face up to the issue of Rural Poverty. Many agricultural fundamentalists have grudgingly, if not meanly, acknowledged that rural people are, per capita, poorer in health, education, public welfare, transportation, housing, and cultural advantages than their urban neighbor. The social Darwinists are just not much concerned. Fresh air, fresh water, and possible aesthetic advantages are listed on the plus side of the rural ledger. Nevertheless, rural poverty is found in rather extensive geographical areas, and is a growing source of national concern. (Or, are we saying that it should be?)

The principal trend all over the world is for the rural poor to congregate in vast urban slums, a movement only partially completed here and just getting underway in the developing regions.

Finally, this is a very "hungry world" that we live in. Such a condition creates an emotional and ethical issue of international import in this world of nation-states. When David Hume remarked that "reason is, and ought to be, the slave of the passion," he was stating both a normative and an empirical proposition. To believe that a rampantly hungry world will not bring about serious challenges to the prevailing world power structure is just as foolish as believing that the United States must involve itself in a self-proclaimed, full-scale effort to feed this hungry world. Hunger needs to be attacked on many fronts, simultaneously. The "science" of nation building is wonderfully intricate; in fact, no firm answers are yet available. One can be hopeful, without being optimistic. If political scientists have not yet been able to comprehend the grinding difficulties involved in cultural change, and notably so in agrarian-type political systems, then there is some serious weakness within the educational structure of our discipline.

UNITED STATES FOOD POLICIES

With those generalizations as background, the major policy trends relative to United States food policies are now examined briefly.

CHEAP FOOD

There are many political anomalies intertwined in this issue. The qualitarians clamor against the use of CCC stocks to keep market prices at a "reasonable" level. At the same time they advocate an end to government production control programs (although some indefinite kind of a land retirement program is advocated) which would really bring about cheap food prices—although not as cheap as a substantially lower farm income might seem to dictate. The egalitarians, who need to maintain their political allies, believe that a fair market price can only be brought about through government-administered and public-financed production control programs, and advocate that all this be done through direct payments.

However, the paradox here is that this program only works when the "big farmers" receive the huge portion of the payoff, because they produce most of the surplus. It is possible, theoretically, to turn off the flow of public dollars at a certain point ($50,000, e.g.), but this is difficult to do politically, would depress market prices, and might slow down technological advances in agriculture, although the last consideration would not discourage the egalitarians. Besides, direct payments require a handsome public subsidy, and we are finding it tedious, irksome, and expensive to finance both a war in Viet Nam and Great Society programs at home.

What will happen depends to a considerable extent on the international situation. Who controls the Presidency and Congress in 1968 and 1972 is an important political consideration. Fenton contends that we are moving toward national issue-oriented political parties (5). Stephen K. Bailey observes the same trend (2). Both analyses were made prior to the 1966 Congressional elections. Some of the actions of the First Session of the 90th Congress indicate a return to Republican-Southern Democrat coalition politics.

BALANCED FOOD DEMAND AND SUPPLY SITUATION

The USDA is engaged in a tremendously difficult piece of gamesmanship—how to stand in the middle of the teeter-totter and keep both ends a fair distance off the ground at the same time. In a reasonable and modest sort of way, the USDA seems to be saying that, under their gentle guidance and direction, we can have a planned food economy which will give us the best of all possible worlds, at home and abroad, in terms of a higher farm income, moderate food prices, and sufficient stocks of exportable food surpluses. The Farmers Union seems fairly willing to go along with this concept, although they question whether there is political muscle sufficient for the task without "unjustly" favoring the consumer at the expense of the farmer. The National Farmers Organization doesn't believe the USDA really intends to balance the teeter-totter on the side of the farmer, so it plans to develop its own set of political muscles in order to "right" the balance. The Farm Bureau contends that it represents a large majority of bona fide (commercial) farmers, and that the proper role of the USDA is to do production research and agricultural extension, engage in modest production control activities for brief periods, and enforce marketing regulations—all the while intending to develop its own marketing control institutions, gradually but effectively. At home, the qualitarians are mercantilists, at least in terms of imports of items like beef and dairy products; abroad they are free traders, with the law of comparative advantage as the sword of truth. Again, the international situation and the next two Presidential elections seem to be the political keys to future policy trends.

FOOD FOR PEACE PROGRAMS

For the first time in its political career this program is facing the great test of truth: Why did we begin the program, and do we now really want to continue it? In the enlightened self-interest of the United States, should this program be extended, leveled off, or decreased in emphasis? Born out of surpluses and nourished by a national ethic that the hungry should be fed, we have now arrived at a situation in which the national larder is only adequate under certain assumptions. The possibility of feeding a hungry world of gigantically increasing proportions is not credible, even over the rather short run and with known technology. Besides that, to make an all-out effort to improve the production and marketing of food in the developing nations, along with considerable assistance in establishing effective birth control measures, in order to alleviate the vast pockets of hunger, fear, and discontent would be a tremendously expensive enterprise. More than that, it might not work, although we citizens should rightly ask why we do not make a national effort which is at least roughly comparable to the vast commitments we have undertaken in Viet Nam.

At the moment, a great deal of political hanky-panky is going on around this issue. Congress extended the Food for Peace Program for two years, although the President proposed a four-year extension and wanted to change "Peace" to "Freedom," presumably because we obviously do not have peace. It might be argued that one cannot have both peace and freedom, at least at the same time over a very long period. According to Thomas Jefferson, "The tree of liberty needs to be fed each generation with the blood of tyrants; that is its natural manure."

However, the USDA hardly seems about to implement any wholesale increase in Title I expenditures. Mrs. Dorothy Jacobson, Assistant Secretary for International Affairs in the USDA, remarked at the Agricultural Outlook Conference in late 1966 that "this avowed policy of the United States to stimulate, encourage, and assist the developing nations of the free world to improve their own food production . . . is a new policy. . . ." This statement, at best, has a relative amount of accuracy. What the USDA really seems to be saying is: the nine criteria in the new legislation for the determination of whether we will ship food to the developing nations will be useful tools in that we will now be able to tell these nations why we cannot ship them this food. This blackjack device might work, but there is nothing new here except a legislative threat which—in a real "crunch"— we would probably refuse to enforce.

The qualitarians may have bred the P.L. 480 program but they have been suspicious of their progeny for a long time. It is just another device, in their opinion, to impose a controlled economy on the unsuspecting farmer. One should not, their reasoning goes, deny those who are hungry. Rather the United States government, now that the national larder is on the relatively short side, should buy needed foodstuffs *in the market,* at market prices; the cost should then be budgeted for national security rather than against the farmer. This is a neat proposal, one must admit: we can eat steak, they can eat wheat and perhaps a little more rice; and all the while our conscience is clear because our actions are in the national interest in terms of both domestic and foreign policy.

The egalitarians have their own troubles here. They have an ardent moral commitment, but it is difficult for them to believe that what their ethic calls for should be accomplished at the expense of the farmer's pocketbook. That is, if the farmer is to produce more, and he should, then the United States should uphold this noble action through substantially higher price supports in order to bring about more intensive farming and higher production. This might be viewed as a new form of hedging. In any respect, treasury costs would be increased considerably, which would jeopardize even further the funding of Great Society programs.

Clearly the authors slip into a moral judgment at this point. This nation has only been involved in the puniest sort of efforts to bring about meaningful social, economic, and political development in the new nations. It was perhaps unfortunate, in terms of hindsight at least, that a Marshall Plan was ever undertaken. Its remarkable success created a set of pictures in the minds of political leaders and intellectuals, which was of meager value when we began to concern ourselves with the realities of poverty such as illiteracy, cultural and religious taboos, poor soil, scarcity of water, and archaic tenure systems. We could, in the next ten years, *begin* to assist these new nations to do what they cannot do by themselves. Ironically, to be sure, whether we made the effort may well depend more on what happens in the Soviet Union and Communist China than in the United States Congress.

EXPORTS FOR DOLLARS

In some respects this is a remarkable success story. The value of farm exports in fiscal 1967 is approximately $7 billion; the future seems bright, with a few shadows of doubt. Not only is the total value of farm exports increasing, but the relative percentage of these commodities sold for dollars, rather than giveaways has increased. In calendar 1965, $4.8 billion was exported commercially, while $1.4 billion was shipped under government-financed programs.

In terms of our balance-of-payments situation, there is much to be said for increasing our dollar exports of food and fiber. Although causation for improved export conditions must surely be complex here, the principal reason appears to be the general advancement of prosperity in certain geographic areas, almost all of them Western, with the exception of Japan and possibly Taiwan.

The Common Agricultural Policy (CAP) of the European Economic Community (EEC) really has not hurt the American farmer, except in terms of reduced wheat and poultry shipments. There are good reasons, to be sure, to fear this CAP and its subsequent implementing regulations, but thus far a rather constantly rising per capita income has meant that the EEC member-states have kept increasing their purchases of United States food products. Under different circumstances, the same has been true for Japan. What this seems to mean is that those who are concerned with the protection of U.S. farm interests in such matters as the Kennedy Round negotiations might give more heed to regional economic trends and less to technical matters like target and intervention prices and variable levies.

RURAL POVERTY AND COMMUNITY DEVELOPMENT PROGRAMS

Congress and the USDA have been directly involved in establishing and administering programs of this type since the early New Deal years. Still, it is difficult to conclude that Congress, in particular, has ever been very serious about this matter. In fact, there have been instances where influential members of Congress were wrathful and vindictive in their reactions toward the quite limited number of research and extension projects in rural poverty undertaken by the USDA.

The poor have always been handicapped in American politics—poorly organized, inarticulate in their demands, unlikely even to vote, migrants in a culture where power comes primarily to those who have roots and status in that culture. Even an acceptable definition of what poverty is has been impossible to achieve, but using the $3,000 per family annual income figure, there are as many rural as urban poor.

The qualitarians have really never recognized rural poverty as a social and, therefore, political issue; the egalitarians have had an abundance of "good intentions," but their built-in bias has been that the thing to do was to find a way to make a poor farmer into a middle-class farmer.

Great Society programs have proliferated all over the Washington bureaucracy until at the moment it is difficult for even the Secretary of Health, Education and Welfare to know just who is to do what, how, and when. One count of 1966 programs put the over-all figure at 152. Many of these are only of peripheral or tangential interest to the rural poor, but a substantial number are of direct concern.

The future seems fairly optimistic for community development programs such as the type admistered by the Farmers Home Administration—rural (including small towns) water and sewage systems, housing, even golf courses. This outlook should be tempered by the fact that even in the 89th Congress the USDA was unable to get its Community Development Service bill out of committee. Direct and magnanimous programs for the hard-core indigent will probably have to await the next gush of liberalism—an event which hardly seems predictable at the moment.

URBAN FOOD-WELFARE PROGRAMS

School lunch, school milk, food stamp, and food-welfare distribution programs have tied together farmer interests with those of urban middle- and low-income groups. Even those who could afford to pay for these services seem to prefer them to be socialized; witness President Johnson's reputed remark to the effect that he was opposed to providing subsidized milk to the "rich kids," and Congress' reaction in terms of refusing to pass any means test for the distribution of milk in public or parochial schools.

Whether these programs are extended or stabilized will probably depend a great deal on which political party controls the Presidency and Congress, and the margin of the majority. If the national larder becomes really bare, the programs might

 be scaled down. The egalitarians are attracted to these pro-
ams in terms of ideology and interests. The qualitarians suspect they are simply another way for the USDA to intervene in,
if not control, the decision-making process, but they recognize
that advantages from the programs do accrue to the major producers.

SOIL AND WATER CONSERVATION PROGRAMS

Another anomaly in farm politics may be the attitude that soil
is more precious than people to this nation. As indicated earlier,
the significance of the "love of the land" myth among urban
people, as well as rural, is both impressive and curious.

The old (1936) Agricultural Conservation Program (ACP)
still costs around $250 million a year and, so some contend, is of
meager value to the cause of soil conservation, and may have
aggravated the farm surplus problem of recent years, although
the USDA denies the validity of that contention. ACP payments
have become rather built-in subsidies now to middle-class farmers; as a student remarked in a jesting but pointed manner,
"Don't fool around with that program; it buys my mother a
washing machine every two or three years."

ACP payments will probably continue on, but the future
lies with the small watershed program (the Watershed Protection
and Flood Prevention Act of 1954, P.L. 566). This multiple-pur-
pose program has both an urban and a rural orientation, and is
therefore both politically and bureaucratically attractive. The
qualitarian interest groups have viewed it either apathetically or
skeptically, but the "whirlpools of power" which have built up
around the program seem to guarantee its continuance, and indicate the likelihood of its advancement.

The policy trends in the American food economy have not
been exhausted. This has been an attempt to induce the reader
to perform his own diagnosis and then extend his analyses
into new policy areas. The programs of the Rural Electrification
Administration are now a part of the rural-urban/public-private
power complex. Farmer cooperatives are involved in the struggle of farmers to acquire countervailing power—political and
economic. Vertical integration, contract farming, and packers
and processors as producers are all phenomena that were not
conceived of at the time the Farm Bloc passed the Capper-
Volstead Act in 1922. Recent Supreme Court decisions have
aroused the farmer interest groups to see if they have the political strength to revise that act in their own interest. It is

interesting to note that the egalitarians and the qualitarians were by no means in agreement as to whose interests and ideologies were being served by S. 109 (89th Congress), which would have revised and strengthened the Capper-Volstead Act. Because of this basic disagreement the bill never left the Senate Committee on Agriculture and Forestry.

Also, there is the important question of the future of the USDA as an institution. Secretary Freeman contends that "two-thirds of the Department's annual expenditures and about 90 percent of its man-hours are devoted to services of benefit to the general public." Farm organizations tend strongly to view the USDA as "the farmer's agency." More expansive in vision, the USDA seems to desire the roles of protector of the rural poor, preserver of the nation's topsoil, and worldwide purveyor of farm products, to say nothing of the several roles of the Forest Service, the research bureaus, and the lending and regulatory agencies. It is by no means clear as to who could play these roles most effectively.

STATE GOVERNMENTS AND PROGRAMS AFFECTING RURAL INTERESTS

After the Supreme Court declared that the denial of legislative reapportionment was a denial of equal protection of the laws (Baker v. Carr, 1962), a few political scientists began to conjecture on the impact of this decision on the policies and programs of state legislatures, as well as those of the U.S. Congress. Then in Reynolds v. Sims (1964), the Court announced its famous "one-person, one-vote" rule, in both houses of the state legislature, and applied that ruling to the United States House in Wesberry v. Sanders during the same year. By that time there was considerable speculation, not to say prediction, that the interests and ideologies of rural America would now be subordinated to those of the cities.

However, current political research indicates that these prophecies were exaggerated, and possibly just downright wrong. In a somewhat casual manner, letters were written to knowledgeable officials in nine states that had some limited experience with reapportioned state legislatures. The responses were almost entirely in terms of a negative correlation. That is, the reapportionment had, if anything, enhanced the involvement of rural America in public programs, disregarding the value question as to whether this involvement was "good" or "bad." For example, rural education and public welfare programs may well have received more financial and technical assistance because of the legislation and appropriations passed by a reapportioned, urban-dominated state legislature.

Colorado indicated no observable shifts from rural to urban types of legislation, other than the passage of a daylight-saving-time bill. Delaware "did not notice any significant curtailment of state programs affecting rural interests in the last General Assembly." Kentucky reported increases in appropriations after reapportionment for such things as rural roads (over $25 million in 1962–63 to nearly $34 million in 1966–67) and for the agricultural extension service (over $3.7 million in 1962–63, to almost $5.5 million in 1966–67). Massachusetts claimed that the complaints of rural and urban communities tended to be much the same—need for more state revenues to alleviate the local tax burden, and revisions of school aid formulas, as examples. The verdict from Michigan seemed to be that rural programs had neither been restricted nor improved because of reapportionment. Oklahoma saw no significant changes; the statewide closing of open range might be viewed as due to reapportionment, but this legislation was well on its way to being passed even under the old power structure. Quite to the point is a statement from Oklahoma to the effect that "there is no 'urban consciousness,' as such, in this state and thus the full impact of apportionment in relation to urban affairs, will probably not be felt for several years."

Oregon expressed the position that the impact of reapportionment had been "negligible" thus far, and concluded that "agriculture plays an important role in the economy of Oregon, a fact apparently as well recognized by urban legislators as by rural legislators." West Virginia reported "no significant changes." State legislative districts in Wisconsin have been on a one-man, one-vote basis since the beginning of statehood in 1848, although this has not precluded some reapportionment controversy in the late 1960's. In Iowa one important rural-urban fight shaped up in the 1966 legislative session—the distribution formula for the road-use tax. The Iowa League of Municipalities wanted a 20 rather than a 13 percent cut; the Iowa Farm Bureau led a vigorous and well-organized opposition to the proposed change.

Thomas Dye's conclusion is one to which we, at least, can subscribe: "The moral case for equality of representation is as compelling as it ever was. The impact on reapportionment of public policy, however, may be somewhat less sweeping than many expect" (5). Moreover, and importantly, the reapportioned legislatures may now regain a new aura of legitimacy, an attitude of rightness and respectability because the operative ideal of majority rule is again being observed.

This conclusion is reached with some of the same doubts and uncertainties expressed initially. In external affairs, the United States is now a superpower struggling to make the thermonuclear era one in which no major war will be fought, primarily because of the continuing presence of a balance of terror. Within that overwhelmingly crucial policy framework, food and fiber play important secondary roles because this is, and will be, also a world of hunger. It is too simple to say that hungry people start major, or minor, military conflicts and political turmoils. It is too nearsighted to claim that hunger is not an impressive factor in an age of revolutions and revolts.

Inside the United States, farmers as a political force are dwindling. A recent study of the U.S. Senates' Republican Policy Committee (*Where the Votes Are*) calculates that in less than ten years more teachers will be eligible to vote than farmers and—we might add—much more likely to vote. However, the power lost at the ballot box may be regained, and perhaps even increased, at the bargaining table. A decision here is in the process of emerging. This automation era at home will continue to push the farmer into the city. The fewer farmers the better, probably, just in the sheer terms of game theory and bargaining power, although at the moment the situation is confusing and debilitating, in political terms, because several organized interests are trying to play the rural "hand."

This chapter closes with a word of caution and a plea. The caution concerns ideology. Farm interests would be foolish to forsake the myths of the family farm, love of the land, the rural community, and the beauty of open spaces. Food and fiber in an economy of wealth are looked on as auxiliary items; their abundance is assumed (glibly, to be sure) on a rather a priori basis. The myth of the rich farmer driving a Cadillac and cashing huge government checks may titillate those who know better, but in political terms it breeds the likelihood of regulatory, if not repressive legislation. The old myths are still the best, politically speaking.

The plea concerns poverty agriculture, and those who will surely be leaving the farm for the city. The first have never been accorded an equal opportunity in American agriculture or out of it. As for the second group—and the two groups may well merge into one in many instances—it is a violation of both the egalitarian and the qualitarian ethic to send the uneducated and untrained into a metropolitan environment which demands both knowledge and expertise. If the one ideological tradition must doubt that a man is his brother's keeper, it does not deny that a man should be in a position to keep himself.

LITERATURE CITED

1. Burns, J. The Deadlock of Democracy. Englewood Cliffs, N.J.: Prentice-Hall, Inc. 1963.
2. Bailey, S. K. The New Congress. New York: St. Martin's Press. 1966.
3. Campbell, A., *et al.* The American Voter. New York: John Wiley and Sons, Inc. 1960.
4. Dobzhansky, T. Human nature as a product of evolution. In: Abraham H. Maslow, New Knowledge in Human Values. New York: Harper and Row. 1959.
5. Dye, T. R. Malapportionment and public policy in the states. J. of Pol., p. 601. Aug., 1965. An excellent background on this issue can be found in: Alexander Heard (ed.), State Legislatures in American Politics. Englewood Cliffs, N.J.: Prentice-Hall, Inc., for the American Assembly. 1966.
6. Fenton, J. H. People and Parties in Politics. Glenview, Ill. Scott, Foresman, and Co. 1966.
7. McCune, W. J. Who's Behind Our Farm Policy? New York: F. A. Praegar, Inc. 1956.

CHAPTER EIGHT

Emerging Goals and Values for Rural People in an Urban-Industrial Society

LUTHER G. TWEETEN

In two centuries this nation has been transformed from a society with nearly 19 of 20 people on farms to one with 19 of 20 people living in villages, towns, and cities. The term "urban-industrial" society has been widely used by social scientists to depict the dominant U.S. culture. The term is a misnomer if "industrial" refers to "manufacturing." The term "industrial" is used in a broader sense in this paper. Other terms that might be used to describe emerging U.S. society are megalopolitan (extended city), technocratic (technical-scientific), affluent, and rurban. The latter recognizes the fact that the U.S. population growth is taking place primarily neither in the central city nor rural farm areas but in between. In general, the definitions of

The author has profited from the useful suggestions of William Jones, Roger Gray, Bruce Johnston, and Paul Mandell of the Food Research Institute, and of the authors of other chapters. However, this does not mean that the above persons necessarily agree with the judgments found in this chapter.

rural used in this paper conform to the 1960 U.S. Census definitions. The *rural farm* population is comprised of persons living on farms, where a farm is defined as a place of less than 10 acres yielding agricultural products sold for $250 or more the previous year, or on places of 10 acres or more yielding agricultural products which sold for $50 or more in the previous year. The *rural nonfarm* population is comprised of all remaining rural residents not urban. The *urban* population is comprised of residents of incorporated municipalities of 2,500 inhabitants or more, urban fringe areas, and other "dense" population areas designated by census definition.

"Farm" is used herein in a generic sense in many instances. For example, "farm" boys in several surveys were classified in that group because the students stated on questionnaires that they lived on a "farm." It is useful to distinguish the "low income" from the "commercial" farm population. This is done in some instances, but data limitations preclude extensive use of this breakdown.

This process of economic growth has brought radical changes to the environment in which people live, notably from primary economic activity strongly dependent on man, soil, and nature to secondary and tertiary economic activity dependent more nearly on machines and science. The rise of the city has led to increasing mobility, crowding of people, division of labor, large-scale industry, separation of occupation from family life, and increasing interdependence of man upon man. These environmental factors produce differences between farm and city people in their goals, values, beliefs, and attitudes (68).

These in turn have important future economic ramifications for farmers in a nation increasingly dominated by urban society.

This chapter examines the differences and their meaning for farm people. The first section is a comparison of fundamental rural and urban philosophic positions, and is followed by documentation of differences in demographic, economic, and personality characteristics. The conclusion is an interpretation of the major issues posed for farm people living in an urban-industrial society.

THE RURAL-URBAN TRADITION

More persons have lived in cities (over 2,500 population) than on farms for approximately a half century in the United States, yet a strong agrarian tradition has permeated society. Agrarian goals and values have persisted because (a) basic values of a once agrarian culture have powerful inertia and yield slowly to pressure for change, (b) agrarian values often have coincided with the values of the growing and influential business interests, (c) a large portion of urban dwellers have been of rural origin and have not forgotten these roots (over one-fifth of the current nonfarm residents have lived on the farm, and nearly twice as many farm-reared adults are living off the farm as on the farm [cf., 24]), and (d) political representation and power have responded slowly to changing rural-urban proportions.

The goals and values of this nation including farmers are increasingly dominated by the urban-industrial sector for several reasons. First, through modern transportation facilities and by the sheer magnitude of people and economic activity, the urban sector has a powerful influence. Second, mass communication media such as television, movies, magazines, and textbooks are almost universal. These media are of urban origin and reflect urban values, but fall equally on the senses of farm and nonfarm elements. A Wisconsin survey showed that, on the average, farmers spent one hour and 19 minutes per day listening to the radio and one hour and 42 minutes watching TV. Fuguitt concluded that there was little difference between rural and urban families in this respect (25). Third, the dynamic forces of research, education, and industry growth that underlie many of the changes in the structure of society (and which indirectly influence goals and values) also have their origin in the nonfarm sector. Fourth, farmers interact continually with the nonfarm organizations and people that provide farm inputs and market farm products. Two of every five farmers hold nonfarm jobs. Half of the farm inputs are supplied by the nonfarm sector. Mass communication and transportation insure that farm people are exposed to nonfarm values and modes of behavior. Finally, a number of nonfarm residents, especially girls, move to the farm after marriage.

Confrontations between rural and urban political interests have been traditional. The compromises that result depend not only on the size and power of the respective groups, but also on the goals, values, and interests of each. Supreme court reapportionment decisions such as Baker vs. Carr and Wesbury vs. Sanders speeded political adjustments that were perhaps inevitable, and shifted the balance of power. It is apparent that to understand and predict what will happen to agriculture in the next decade, it is essential to examine the structure and attitudes of the urban-industrial sector. It may well be argued that farming is increasingly an extension of that sector.

INTERDEPENDENCE OF FARM AND CITY

City and country are interdependent in the process of social and economic growth. The relationship is clearly mutually beneficial. This fact has not kept one group or the other from taking an occasional fundamentalist position, maintaining that one sector was inherently superior to the other—that one sector was host and the other parasite. In the words of Green, "The antagonism of the country bumpkin toward the city slicker mounted from the late 1750's onward, a hostility that would endure for two hundred years until automobiles, telephones, radio, and television largely obliterated basic differences between rural and urban life in America." (27, p. 46.)

Farm Fundamentalism

Farm people have condemned the city for its slums, race riots, crime, congestion, air pollution, business exploitations, secularism, disintegration of the family, corrupt government, and impersonal atmosphere. In turn the farm people have prized the open country which fosters individuality, independence, puritanical virtues, solitude, forthrightness, closeness to nature, a somewhat classless society, and democratic ideals.

Urban Fundamentalism

City people have in turn criticized farm life for being phlegmatic, isolated, uncultured, and unprogressive. They have accused farmers of being undemocratic in withholding equal political representation and tax treatment, and of being unsympathetic to problems of the city.

The position of urban fundamentalism is apparent in the words of Douglass:

From the earliest dawn of social life it has been felt that the clash of wits, especially in the marketplace, sharpens them. The mind stagnates in isolation, is speeded up in association. The man whose business is trade has always felt keenly his sophistication and acumen in contrast with the slower movement of the rustic mind. The typical townsman still implicitly claims this advantage over the farmer. The townsman feels his superiority as the keeper of the ideals of the community and of their peculiar symbols. He has—to paraphrase Prof. Galpin—not only its pantry and shop but also its safe, its medicine chest, its playhouse, and its altar. All keepers of ideals tend to hierarchical pride and a sense of class prerogative (22, p. 10).

A quote from W. Arthur Lewis further elaborates on the foundation for urban superiority:

The atmosphere of towns is also alleged to be more favorable to the attitudes and beliefs which favour growth. The fact that large numbers of people are thrown together in towns, in a competitive struggle for existence, weakens kinship ties and excessive respect for status; encourages impersonal economic relations and a willingness to trade wherever opportunities are favourable; and sharpens the wits.

In addition, the fact that towns develop a great range of arts and entertainments means that the opportunities for spending money are virtually unlimited, that wealth tends to acquire as much prestige as birth, and that ambition is stimulated. Townsmen are also alleged to be more open minded and less superstitious than countrymen, and therefore to be better placed to pursue those scientific enquiries which result in improved techniques. The countryman is impressed by the power of nature, since nature so often frustrates all his work, with its droughts, its floods, its storms, its epidemic diseases of crops, and other signs of its strength. The town, on the other hand, is created by man, who has learnt enough of the secrets of nature to be able to erect great buildings, to trap water in great reservoirs and transport it where he wants it, to summon electricity out of the skies to be his servant, and so forth. So the townsman is more easily tempted to believe that man can do anything he wants to do, if he tries hard enough (39, p. 151).

Slocum states:

It [urbanization] has released great creative forces; for example, most modern technological developments are urban in origin. It has forced the individual from the tyranny of inbred values and close social surveillance; it has brought increased leisure (60, p. 233).

There is a feeling that the urban society is the source and vanguard of the dynamic forces of science and culture that shape our social and economic environment. According to Landis, " . . . these two philosophies of existence dominate the minds of men: One holds that what has been will always be; the other holds that what man has accomplished is only the beginning, that on the basis of what he has accomplished he will build a bigger and more efficient way of life . . . . the one [first philosophy] is agrarian; the other, urban industrial." (36, p. 114.)

Urban fundamentalism can provide a growing impetus for

federal programs for cities as the superiority theme is coupled with feelings of frustration over urban problems.

These fundamentalist viewpoints contain certain elements of truth which are supported by more objective investigations of rural-urban differences which we shall examine later. A basis exists for both rural and urban pride. But this should not lead to oversimplification of issues, nor to valuing one sector as inherently superior to another. Rather, a statement of basic positions can be the springboard to greater appreciation of the problems and promise for all society posed by two essential, highly interdependent sectors.

FORMAL CONTRASTS OF RURAL AND URBAN CHARACTERISTICS

Several formal attempts have been made in the past to isolate those social characteristics that distinguish rural from urban living. One approach is the *Gemeinschaft-Gesellschaft* framework suggested by Tönnies (66) and extended by Parsons (50), Loomis (41), and Levy (38). Tönnies calls all kinds of associations in which the natural will predominates *Gemeinschaft;* all those which are formed and fundamentally conditioned by the rational will, *Gesellschaft* (66, p. 17). By means of political and other intellectual organizations promoted by town and city life, the Gesellschaft characteristics gradually permeate the mass of society (66, p. 29).

Polar types are used to distinguish Gemeinschaft from Gesellschaft in Table 8.1, but it is important to stress that the

TABLE 8.1. Polar types distinguishing societies*

Gemeinschaft	*Gesellschaft*
Traditional	Rational
Sacred	Secular
Spiritual	Materialistic
Particularistic	Universalistic
Ascriptive norms	Achievement norms
Affective selectivity	Affective neutrality
Functionally diffuse	Functionally specific
Occupation-generalistic	Occupation-specialistic
Responsible	Individualistic
Intimate	Impersonal
Nonhierarchical	Hierarchical
Atomistic	Bureaucratic

* Source: Adapted from: (38), (41), (50), and (66). For a critical evaluation of polar typologies, see the chapter by Oscar Lewis in (35).

gradient is not dichotomous. It is continuous. Societies can be characterized by the profile outlining where they lie between the polar types—no society is completely Gemeinschaft or Gesellschaft! Rural farm characteristics tend to lie more nearly toward the Gemeinschaft pole, urban society more nearly toward the Gesellschaft pole. Commerical farm areas are farther to the Gesellschaft pole in Table 8.1 than are low income (poverty) farm areas. In certain attributes, city slums may lie closer than commercial farm areas to the Gemeinschaft pole. The process of economic growth can be expected to be accompanied by movement to the right in Table 8.1. In the following discussion of polar characteristics, it is well to keep in mind that the farm community will, in the future, move toward the right—hence the table is a type of predictive device.

The "man-made" production and consumption process in the city has been characterized by terms of "rational" and "secular." This is in contrast to the more traditional and sacred orientation of particularly the low income rural areas. Rational orientation characterizes emphasis on education, research, and application of scientific processes to extend man's dominance over nature and to promote economic growth.

The urban-industrial society is characterized by universalist-achievement norms. An efficient, smoothly functioning "mass" society requires widely accepted universalist standards of suitability for jobs, evaluation of status, and norms of behavior. The impersonal, mobile, urban environment leads to less stress on affective evaluation of individuals on the basis of ascribed status (e.g., family) and emotionally involved criteria, and to more stress on evaluation on the basis of economic achievement and material display.

Intense division of labor in the urban-industrial environment is characterized by functionally specific roles. The occupational specialities often require a high degree of formal training. The result is considerable vulnerability to changing technology and business fluctuations. Division of labor and mass production economies are best achieved in an environment of considerable concentration of consumers and workers. Economies of scale lead to industry concentration, bureaucracy, and bargaining power. Increased bargaining power in industry is countervailed by bargaining power in the hands of labor and government. Concentration of people in a small area plus high mobility lead to more impersonal and individualistic relationships among people, partially to preserve privacy. The breakdown of the extended family unit, interdependence of elements in the economy to satisfy economic wants, and the impersonal human interrelationships in urban society, contribute to the demand for government welfare services to cushion the impact of unemployment, injury, illness, or death.

The central city, the origin of many of the mass cultural media, exerts a large impact on American values, beliefs, and attitudes, is inhabited by more than average proportions of the highly educated and talented who function in the commercial and cultural centers there located. A second major group located in the central city is the comparatively uneducated and unskilled people from lower socioeconomic status groups who carry on the "housekeeping" chores in the broadest sense, many of whom are Negroes. These two groups are not identified closely with the middle-class American culture and take a less than sacrosanct attitude toward traditional agrarian goals and values. Pressures of a different environment and a malleable outlook of these urbanites toward cultural change set the stage for adjustments in goals, values, and attitudes that ultimately touch farmers.

SOCIOLOGICAL RESEARCH ON RURAL AND URBAN CHARACTERISTICS

Results of opinion sampling and sociological studies tend to support many of the notions of rural and urban differences reported above. Decades ago, sociologists talked of the rural-urban dichotomy as if they were two separate and distinct cultures (cf., 66). The dichotomy later was rejected in favor of a rural-urban *continuum* (cf., 21, 62). Differences in rural and urban society were regarded as differences not so much in kind as in degree. The degree of difference could be explained as continuous variables relating goals, values, and attitudes to density of population and economic activity centered on primary versus secondary and tertiary industry. The next step was to admit the continuum between city and farm, but to say that the differences were relatively unimportant. Some social scientists are now asking whether there is any difference at all. The following discussion suggests that there are.

Tables 8.2 to 8.6 depict rural-urban differences in racial representation, age distribution, birthrates, size of family, education, communication, transportation, income, and mobility. The Negro population, once heavily rural farm, is now largely urban (Table 8.2). In 1920, over half of all U.S. whites but only

TABLE 8.2.   **Selected characteristics of the U.S. population, by residence, 1960***

Characteristic	Urban	Rural Nonfarm	Rural Farm
Total population (mil.)	125.3 (69.9)	40.5 (22.6)	13.5 (7.5)
White population (mil.)	110.4 (69.5)	36.5 (23.0)	11.9 (7.5)
Nonwhite population (mil.)	14.8 (72.2)	4.1 (20.0)	1.6 (7.8)
Average size of family	3.56	3.81	3.96
Children ever born/1,000 ever married women 35–39	2,514	3,034	3,469
Aged 65 and over	(9.1)	(8.9)	(9.3)
Median age (years)	30.3	26.7	29.6
Household characteristics (occupied units):			
With home freezer	(13.0)	(26.0)	(52.7)
With telephone	(83.1)	(67.1)	(64.2)
With automobile	(76.1)	(83.7)	(87.3)
With television†	(89.0)	(88.0)	(76.0)

* Unless otherwise indicated, data from (78). Percentage figures appear in parentheses.
† Data from: (25).

one-third of all U.S. Negroes lived in urban areas. Currently a higher percentage of all Negroes than of all whites live in urban areas. The migration rate to cities has been considerably higher among Negroes. Birthrates are higher in the rural farm than in other sectors, but sizeable outmigration of farm youth and of retired farmers washes out differences in the age patterns in Table 8.2. The high proportion of rural farm households with autos, telephones, and television sets demonstrates the considerable communication and transportation potentials of farmers.

This mobility potential also is apparent in Table 8.3. However, rural farm people move around less than other groups: 71 percent of them reported living in the same house in 1960 as in 1955, whereas approximately 50 percent of the urban and rural-nonfarm residents so reported. In 1958, 17 percent of the U.S. civilian nonfarm population 18 years of age and over were farm born (Table 8.3). However, 32 million or 30 percent of the survey population had either been born on the farm or spent at least one year on a farm. More than one-fifth of the sample farm population in Table 8.3 reported nonfarm origins. A sizeable portion of these were nonfarm girls who married farm boys.

Approximately one-sixth of all farm-born farm residents have lived in the nonfarm sector at some time. Combining two categories of farm residents (a) farm born with some nonfarm

TABLE 8.3. **Distribution of the civilian population 18 years of age and over, by residence, farm and nonfarm birthplace, and color, U.S., 1958***

	Percentage Distribution		
	Total	White	Nonwhite
Total	100.0	100.0	100.0
Farm-born	23.7	22.6	33.8
Nonfarm-born	75.0	76.3	63.5
Not reported†	1.3	1.1	2.7
Farm residents	100.0	100.0	100.0
Farm-born	78.5	76.4	94.9
Entire life on same farm	42.9	40.2	63.2
Some moves between farms	20.5	20.4	21.9
Some nonfarm moves	15.1	15.8	9.8
Nonfarm-born	21.5	23.6	5.1
Nonfarm residents	100.0	100.0	100.0
Farm-born	17.2	16.3	25.2
Nonfarm-born	82.8	83.7	74.8
Entire life nonfarm	79.4	80.1	72.4
Some farm moves	3.4	3.6	2.4

* Data from: (2, p. 2).
† Place of birth and/or residence not reported.

moves and (b) nonfarm born, it is apparent from Table 8.3 that 39.4 percent of white farm adults and 14.9 percent of non-white farm adults have been exposed to nonfarm living. The interaction between the two sectors is indeed great.

ECONOMIC CHARACTERISTICS

The net exodus of farm people to the city has been pushed by diminishing economic opportunities on the farm and pulled by attractive jobs elsewhere. Some reasons for the shift in employment reported above are apparent from the economic data in Table 8.4. The unemployment data are not meaningful because they fail to reflect underemployment, which is great in farming. Differences in economic measures between rural and urban sectors are accentuated by a higher proportion of rural people in the South than in other geographic areas. The percentage of female employment is larger in urban areas. These factors only partially explain differences in incomes, however. Including in a "poverty" category all individuals in families with less than $3,000 annual cash income and individuals (not classified with families) with less than $1,500 annual cash income, 35 million Americans were in poverty in 1962 (5). Of these, 16 million were rural residents and about 6 million were rural farm residents. Nearly half of all farm families were within the poverty

TABLE 8.4. Selected economic characteristics of U.S. population by residence

	Urban	Rural Nonfarm	Rural Farm
Percent unemployed, 1960*	5.1	6.1	3.0
Percent of females in labor force, 1960*	37.2	28.7	22.9
Median income of husband-wife families*	$7,188	$5,809	$3,929
Distibution of U.S. family income in 1959 by percent*			
Under $2,999	29.0	39.1	50.7
$3,000 to $5,999	29.8	32.5	29.4
$6,000 to $9,999	27.3	20.8	13.7
$10,000 to $24,999	12.7	6.9	5.7
$25,000 and over	1.2	0.6	0.5
Total	100.0	100.0‡	100.0

* Data from: (78).
† Data from: (79, p. 10).
‡ Does not total exactly 100.0 due to rounding.

category. The within-sector incidence of poverty was nearly twice as frequent in the rural farm as in the urban sector.

EDUCATION

Migration from the farm has been rapid and in 1958 substantially more farm-born adults were nonfarm residents (16.3 million) than were farm residents (9.5 million). Still, outmigration has not closed the income gaps and brought equilibrium factor use and returns among sectors (cf., 69, 77). This is at least partially due to another characteristic that differentiates farm and nonfarm groups—educational attainment. Whether measured by median education completed or dropout rates, rural farm areas rank low (Table 8.5). Not so apparent are basic rural-urban differences in quality of education. Also not apparent are substantial differences in the quality of schools within agriculture. A study (57) of eastern Kentucky migrants out of rural areas to cities found that high school graduates were doing no better than school dropouts. One explanation is that the quality of education was so low that both dropouts and graduates found themselves severely disadvantaged in seeking productive nonfarm employment. Another explanation is that the sample was taken in 1960 of persons who were in the eighth grade in 1949–50. Thus high school graduates may not have been out of school long enough for their salaries to exceed those of dropouts who were longer established in an occupation.

TABLE 8.5. Measures of education by residence groups, U.S.

	Urban	Rural Nonfarm	Rural Farm
5-year-olds enrolled in kindergarten, 1960 (percent)*	46.0	23.4	15.8
7- to 13-year-olds enrolled in school, 1960 (percent)*	97.8	97.1	97.2
Age 25–29 with 4 years high school or more, 1960 (percent)*	63.8	53.0	51.4
Median school completed by persons 25 years and over, 1960 (years)*	11.1	9.5	8.8
Estimated school dropouts among 16–24-year-olds, 1960 (percent):†			
1950 Total	35.0	50.4	55.5
Male white	33.8	50.7	54.3
Male nonwhite	63.6	79.7	88.6
1960 Total	27.6	37.6	34.5
Male white	25.8	35.9	32.0
Male nonwhite	47.4	61.3	69.9

* Data from: (78).
† Data from: (18, Table 3).

Data in Table 8.6 show a significant association between education and earnings. Farmers stand at the bottom of both the income and education ladders. Persons of farm origin rank low in educational attainment for several reasons. First, many farm youth become farmers, and few of these see the need for higher education. The day is approaching, if it is not already here, when a college education will be a profitable investment in management skills to operate large commerical farms. Second, more farm youth plan to farm than are able to secure an adequate economic opportunity in farming, and belatedly become aware that their educational attainment is too low for successful competition in the nonfarm labor market into which they have been thrust. Third, farm youth who do not plan to farm often have inadequate formal and informal advice, and too late realize that their educational background is not adequate for the occupation which they had planned to enter. Again the problem of inadequate counseling and narrow academic program limits opportunities, especially in areas characterized by rural poverty (70).

Of more than passing concern is the poor showing of farm-reared elements in adjustment to city life. Schnore (55, p. 136) concludes, after reviewing previous studies "that the farm-reared migrants to the city enter the urban class structure at or near the

TABLE 8.6.   Earnings and education by occupational group, U.S. males

Major Occupational Group: Males, 25–64 Years Old	Median Earnings, 1959*	Proportion With 12 or More School Years Completed, 1959*	Median Schooling, 1962†
	(dollars)	*(percent)*	*(years)*
Professional, technical, and kindred workers	6,978	91	16.2
Managers, officials, and proprietors, except farm	6,855	66	12.5
Sales workers	5,747	67	12.5
Craftsmen, foremen, and kindred workers	5,444	36	12.5
Clerical and kindred workers	5,216	63	12.5
Operatives and kindred workers	4,645	25	10.1
Service workers	3,799	31	10.8
Laborers, except farm and mine	3,504	16	8.9
Farmers and farm managers	2,447	30	8.8
Farm laborers and foremen	1,577	12	8.5

* Data from: (16, p. 13).
† Data from: (46, p. 34).

bottom, whether the measure is education, occupation, or income." This appraisal is especially critical because of the heavy outmigration of farm youth to cities. One study reports:

For farm males 15–24 years old, it was concluded that: in the North Central and Northeast less than one-half of the surviving farm males 15–24 years old in 1960 might be expected to remain in the farm population over the next 10 years. By the same logic, for the West, 1 of 3 may remain. The ratio for southern whites is 1 in 5. The extreme is found for southern nonwhites, only 1 in 16 of whom are expected to remain in the farm population (6, pp. 15, 16).

Inadequate education of farm people is of concern to all segments of society. Through migration the problems of rural America become the problems, sometimes intensified, of urban America. There are indications that assimilation and acculturation are rapid for migrants from commercial farming areas (cf., 70). But problems of migrants from rural poverty areas, especially of Negroes, are severe and are an important element in the crime and slum conditions of central cities.

Sewell and Haller attribute the problem of inadequate preparation of rural migrants to cities to ". . . relative geographic isolation and its attendant features such as relatively poor schools [and] few occupations visible to the youth. . . ." (59, p. 166.) The major concern in rural education is not only the quality of schooling but also the associated problem of finance. A major burden of financial support for local schools in most states is on property taxes in the local community. These taxes are inadequate because the community is poor, and the community may be poor because the schools are inadequate. This cycle of perpetuated rural poverty will continue unless federal and state aid to education becomes a more prominent supplement to local tax support.

PERSONALITY CHARACTERISTICS

A considerable number of comparisons have been made between personality characteristics of farm, village, and urban youth. These studies have been made in Michigan (30, 31), Minnesota (33, 43), Wisconsin (59, 63), Iowa (13), Florida (44), and Ohio (42).

These studies generally support the conclusion that farm boys rank lower than nonfarm boys in occupational and educational aspirations and they are more withdrawn and reserved. They place a lower value on geographic mobility and tend to believe that man has limited control over events. On over-all social adjustment, including lack of nervous tension, farm boys ranked high.

Urban boys had the higher score on occupational and educational aspirations, dominance, aggressiveness, self-confidence, and radicalism. They take a positive attitude toward geographic mobility and tend to believe that man has control over events. They generally ranked lower in measures of over-all social adjustment than farm boys, however.

A study by Clark and Wenninger reported by Polk gives some insight into the nature and extent of juvenile delinquency among farm and nonfarm youth. The conclusion from the study of adolescents was that:

. . . this questionnaire would indicate that rural boys differ very little from urban boys in the extent to which they "confess" to minor theft, the telling of lies, loitering, beating up other youngsters without specific reason, the use of narcotics (in all samples rare), and arson (also rare in all groups). In contrast, rural-farm youth engage less, according to this study, in such activities as major theft, the consumption of alcohol, taking money on the pretense that it would be repaid, and skipping school. On the other hand, rural youth were inclined to engage somewhat more in trespassing and tampering with another person's car, tractor, or bicycle without permission. These differences are especially pronounced when a comparison is made between the urban working class group and rural youth (52).

MISCELLANEOUS CHARACTERISTICS

Sweeter's analyses (64, p. 169) show that in the transition from rural to urban, the extended family gives way to independent nuclear family units. Urbanization leads to "matrimonial asymmetry," according to Sweeter, with closer ties to the wife's than to the husband's family. Greater economic independence of women in urban areas contributes to the higher divorce rates. Separation of residence from work leads to diminishing presence and influence of the father, and, along with growing education and independence of the mother, moves toward a more democratic and somewhat matriarchal urban family structure. Divorce rates are considerably higher among urban than among rural families (14). However other measures of marital success rate urban marriages more successful than rural marriages (10, pp. 217–18).

Sociological studies also indicate that farm people attend church more frequently, are more conservative in their religious beliefs, and are more active in church than nonfarm people (12).

A final characteristic of interest is how farm people view their occupation. The results reported in Table 8.7 are suggestive but are from opinion polls which are neither very scientific nor current. Farmers showed satisfaction about equal to that of

TABLE 8.7. Selected results of opinion polls taken in 1946–50*

Statement	Least Approve		Farmers	Most Approve	
	(group)	(percent)	(percent)	(group)	(percent)
If beginning again, would enter same work	Manual workers	46	70	Farmers, profess. and businessmen	70
Satisfied with lot in life	Manual workers	71	84	Professionals and executives	88
Satisfied with present housing	Residents of large cities	50	84	Farmers	84
Farmer is better off than city dweller	Residents of large cities	66	83	Farmers	83
Farmer is happier than man in city	Residents of large cities	55	73	Farmers	73
Would want son to go to college	Farmers	53	53	White collar workers	77
Young men need college training	Wage earners	38	48	Professionals and executives	74

* Data from: (3).

persons in the professions and business with their choice of occupation and lot in life. Two-thirds of city residents agreed that the farmer is better off than the city man. This result is partly explained by the fact that the opinion polls were concentrated in the 1946–50 period when farmers experienced unusual prosperity.

VALUES OF RURAL PEOPLE IN MODERN PERSPECTIVE

According to Beers, opinion polls support the contention that farmers exhibit values of Puritanism, individualism, national loyalty, and traditionalism. In this section, the position of agrarian values in an urban-industrial age is analyzed in a quite different way (3). Statements of agrarian values in America are keenly articulated by Brewster (9). These values, as interpreted by Brewster, are paraphrased briefly below and contrasted with emerging urban-industrial values. The following four creeds are idealized value judgments that permeated both rural and urban society in 19th-century America. However, these guides to individual behavior consistent with the respect of self and society today more nearly characterize rural than urban society.

WORK ETHIC

The work ethic contains four component judgments. The *work imperative* is a judgment that the proper way to fulfill status striving is to be proficient in one's chosen field, and backward or easy ways are not to be placed above love of excellence. The *self-made-man ideal* is worthy of respect and emulation, and precludes any dependence of status deserts on family pedigree. The work ethic contains the value judgment that men and nations alike possess sufficient means to improve the lot of the common man to close the gap between present circumstances and aspirations. To be unwilling to strive to close that gap belittles the promise of American life. Finally, the work ethic includes the value judgment that society owes to each man the value of his contributions (commutative justice), and equal access to the means of developing creative potential (distributive justice) (9, pp. 117–18).

The work ethic has antecedents in the Protestant ethic and the "liberal" economic philosophy of Adam Smith. These antecedents have been characterized in the United States by some authors as the Puritan tradition. A recent *Time* essay states:

If there is anything left of the Puritan tradition it is hard to detect. Perhaps its strongest remaining element is what sociologists call the "work ethic." . . . At the same time thrift is no longer a virtue—it is, in fact, subversive—pleasure is an unashamed good, leisure is the general goal and the subsidized life, from government benefits to foundation grants, is largely welcomed (49).

Even the work ethic has not been as durable a part of the Puritan tradition as the above quote implies. The work ethic, strictly interpreted, placed an essentially religious value on labor *per se*. In the Puritan tradition, work was valued for its moral qualities as an end in itself, irrespective of the monetary gains. Americans still work hard, but the work ethic is becoming less the underlying reason. Work is increasingly motivated by the desire to purchase material goods as a means toward enjoying the good life and displaying status. According to Williams, the lower value that contemporary society places on asceticism "leads to enjoyment of leisure without the guilt and ambivalence it carried in a 'puritan' ethos." (82, p. 436.)

Other value components of the work ethic are found in urban-industrial society, but the emphasis differs from the agrarian tradition. Urban-industrial society is increasingly concerned about distributive justice (providing equal access, through education and termination of racial barriers, to means of getting ahead) and is less committed to commutative justice. That is, legislation is increasingly concerned with need, not with ability to pay or to be employed productively.

DEMOCRATIC CREED

The democratic creed contains two component value judgments: all men are of equal worth and dignity, and none, however wise or good, is good or wise enough to have dictatorial power over any other. Included is the idea that all deserve an equal voice in shaping the rules which are deemed necessary for the sake of general welfare (9, pp. 118–19).

There is little evidence that urban society is less committed than rural society to this creed. In fact, in broad world perspective, the predominantly urban-industrial countries of the world are today more democratic in forms of national government than are the predominantly agrarian countries. However, there is no denial that the transient nature of city life and the indifference toward local government that attends it is a breeding ground for "boss" or "machine" rule.

THE ENTERPRISE CREED

The enterprise creed entails four component value judgments: (a) the individual or his immediate family ought to be responsible for his economic security throughout life, (b) a prime function of the government is to prevent the imprudent from pressing either government, business, or other organizations into sharing the burden of an individual's economic security, (c) proprietors deserve exclusive right to prescribe the rules under which their production units operate, and (d) a prime function of the government is to prevent anyone, including the government itself, from infringing upon the managerial power of proprietors (9, pp. 119–20).

It is apparent that one of the major issues in American politics today, reflected in conflicting ideologies of farm organizations, is the enterprise creed. The characteristics of the urban-industrial society increase the vulnerability of the individual to economic circumstances with which he finds it difficult to cope. The individual calls on the government for welfare assistance or countervailing economic power. This request for increased government involvement is to no small extent a result of industrialization. And the call for commodity programs by commercial farmers also, in part measure, stems from industrialization of the farm.

CREED OF SELF-INTEGRITY

The creed relates to the status of dissenters. Its central judgment is that in the case of conflict, both the individual and his group are responsible for seeking new modes of thought and practice that will unify the hitherto conflicting views of each. In line with this judgment, the community prizes its dissenting members as its agents for achieving new knowledge and practices. The individual and his group share the common judgment that the highest responsibility of the individual is to follow the dictates of his own exceptional insights (9, p. 121).

The high status of dissenters in agrarian society was afforded primarily to men whose insights were of *practical* significance. The intellectual and nonpractical innovators often were scorned. Studies reveal that farm dwellers are less tolerant of nonconformity than town, city, and metropolitan residents (45, pp. 93–94). Urban society more highly values the intellectual, and is more tolerant of deviant behavior. It is partially due to tolerance inherited from urban-industrial society that rural America today increasingly accepts a pluralistic society.

LONG-TERM IMPLICATIONS
FOR THE FARM ECONOMY

Urban-industrial society, though poetically speaking born of rural parentage, is now affluent and robust. The personality of urban society is also depicted as rational, pragmatic, dynamic, and basically healthy though troubled with crime, slums, race problems, air pollution, and transportation difficulties. It will be increasingly difficult to impress upon urban people beleaguered by their own problems the urgency of farm legislation.

The foregoing discussion shows that while rural and urban differences are not large and appear to be diminishing, they are nevertheless important. Many of the differences cited above are basically sociological, nevertheless their thrust is also economic and has important long-term meaning for the farm economy. The emergence of the nonfarm sector as an overriding political, economic, and cultural force has major significance for U.S. agriculture in at least four areas: (a) commercial agriculture and commodity programs, (b) low-income agricultural and welfare programs, (c) the family farm, and (d) political alliances.

COMMODITY PROGRAMS

The major goals of Americans are freedom, justice, security, and progress (including economic growth). While these are major goals for all sectors of almost any society, the emphasis as well as the means for achieving them change in the process of industrialization. It is difficult to see how any of the four goals can be satisfactorily attained in a society that lacks adequate food supplies. The nature of demand suggests that food, clothing, and shelter are basic necessities. The price inelastic demand for farm commodities indicates that society places a very high value on having enough food, but once needs are met, places little value on having more. The strong implication is that a scientifically-oriented, affluent society such as the United States that looks promisingly toward a 30-hour work week is unlikely to tolerate inadequate food supplies. It will take whatever measures are necessary to insure having plenty of food. Food production is increasingly being released from dependence on land inputs. Production will move at a more rapid rate toward nonland-based, synthetic, factory-made foods if conditions warrant.

Under current circumstances, the least expensive means of increasing food output is through improved technology and unconventional inputs (from research and education) to farmers rather than through higher prices for food to bring more conventional inputs into farming. Experiment stations and nonfarm industry can be expected to release a regenerating supply of improved inputs to farmers. These inputs can be profitable to farmers though farm labor and land are earning low returns. It is very difficult to predict the appropriate investment in science and technology. For society an error on the abundance side is clearly superior to an error on the scarcity side (cf., 74). Also, stockpiles of farm commodities (possibly "stored" as land diverted from production) well in excess of free market levels are likely to be carried over as insurance against drouth, wars, or other disaster. The result of those efforts described above to maintain reserve capacity will not always be successful, and periods of high prices and favorable economic conditions can be expected for farmers. But this is not the anticipated dominant long-term outlook—the one that is expected over the next 20 years. Stockpiling of reserve capacity tends to depress farm prices, other things being equal. Pressures to maintain reserve capacity are expected to keep returns on conventional farm resources below returns in other sectors.

Farm commmodity programs are designed to stabilize markets and provide some security against a sharp shift in demand and supply. The economic structure of commercial farming is increasingly intolerant of highly unstable prices. In the past, farmers weathered economic crises by deferring returns to equity capital and family labor. As cash production expenses mount as a percentage of costs, as capital requirements become larger, and as farm people become psychologically less tolerant of economic crises, the demand for economic stability in farming grows. And this demand comes at a time when urban society sees little purpose in commodity programs. Farmers can react positively to this urban backlash in two ways. Either they can improve their public image and continue to receive government help, or they can make a determined effort to improve their own market power and do without government supports.

Apologists for farm programs have in the past stressed that public investment in farm research and technology has vastly benefitted the consumer and left the farmer relatively though not absolutely worse off. Thus consumers can compensate farmers through commodity programs and still remain better off. While this argument has much validity and appeal, a better approach is to stress those aspects of commodity and poverty programs that farm and nonfarm elements find mutually beneficial.

Urban-industrial society wants these things from farmers: ample quantity and quality of food at reasonable costs, and sufficient reserve production capacity to meet emergencies. Farm commodity programs in the future cannot be forced through by farm political muscle alone, or justified as welfare measures alone, but must be sold to the public (if indeed they are to be sold at all) on the basis of serving the two objectives above.

There is a growing body of evidence that past farm programs have not caused inefficiency in farming (cf., 67, 75). In a recent study, Tyner simulated the operation of the farm economy over a 30-year period (a) under free markets and (b) under commodity programs. Less farm labor was employed with commodity programs than with free markets. The economic stability, security, and capital provided by programs permitted purchase of large machines and other improved inputs which substituted for labor. The larger, more efficient farm operator found it profitable to purchase or rent the farm of his less efficient neighbor who perhaps found a nonfarm job or retired early (75).

Also, land prices inflated by capitalized benefits of programs constituted a major barrier to entry into farming. Thus programs have not slowed outmovement of labor from agriculture, nor have they increased costs per unit of farm output according to the analysis. Programs have helped farmers bear the cost of reserve capacity which society appears to value highly. Farm programs that are administered efficiently with supports designed to stabilize prices in line with production costs (thus avoiding capitalization of benefits into land prices), and to maintain reserve capacity for emergencies in agriculture without undue government treasury costs are in the interest of farmers and consumers alike, and can be "sold" to society.

We are at a crucial juncture for agricultural policies. In a period when crises of either abundance or scarcity could emerge, it is essential that *flexibility* be maintained in farm programs. The growing call for funds to aid the really poor in cities and farms at home and abroad will mean growing difficulty in justifying subsidies to large farmers in periods when demand presses supply. The justification for the lion's share of program benefits going to the large farms (because those who produce the most must be included to control production) will disappear in periods when demand presses supply. Unless payments to large farmers are deemed essential for efficiency, there is no justification for continuing direct payments to these farmers in times of farm prosperity.

More emphasis should be placed on those voluntary farm programs that remove the most production per government dollar. This means a shift away from direct payment programs which do not require acreage diversion. Attention must be given to slippage in programs. If reserve capacity is to be efficiently maintained, slippage in programs must be reduced so that limited funds for commodity programs will hold more reserve capacity. Appointment of a "Hoover Commission" to examine possible ways to streamline the administration down to the local ASCS office of farm programs is overdue. A farmer now virtually needs a lawyer to interpret the complex features of programs.

The farm community would do well to reappraise critically the whole structure of farm programs. Programs that unduly benefit narrow interests, cause undue inefficiencies, and promote regressive income redistribution will need to be revised. Agriculture will need to: place more emphasis on society's goals of reserve capacity, efficiency, and flexibility; streamline commodity program administration; and clear up inequities or face embarrassing questions from the nonfarm policy. In all likelihood, nonfarm interests will demand and get more reasonable farm policies than the piecemeal prescriptions of the rural written legislation.

The growing influence of the urban-industrial sector has important implications for the market structure of farming, particularly bargaining power. Taking their cue from urban-industrial society, few farmers today adhere to the code of a purely competitive economy for agriculture. The fundamental conflict in agriculture is not over whether farmers should have more bargaining power, but rather over who should provide it. The Farmers Union at least currently favors a strong government role to give farmers strength in the marketplace. The Farm Bureau and National Farmers Organization place emphasis on bargaining power through a cohesive organization of farmers themselves. I have predicted that the lack of farm empathy with government efforts to raise farm income, plus growing disenchantment of the nonfarm sector with farm commodity programs will lead to an effective organization of farmers themselves to regulate production and marketing in perhaps 20 years (67).

The declining relative voice of farmers in the voting mechanism and the increasing urgency of city problems can only lead in the long run to less dependence of commercial farmers on government transfer payments. These factors, plus the changing value structure of farmers, will lead to a struggle for indigenous economic power in agriculture. The government's role will be to provide enabling legislation. Antitrust action likely will not interfere with farmers' efforts as long as plentiful food and fiber supplies are provided at reasonable prices.

WELFARE PROGRAMS

Further departure of urban-industrial society from the early agrarian laissez-faire tradition means support will grow for welfare programs in the urban sector. A concern is with welfare programs for farm people. For a useful extension of the discussion of welfare programs, see T. W. Schultz (56). Farmers have only belatedly secured benefits of Social Security. It is of considerable significance, because it supplements an important past retirement fund—capital gain—which has been a highly inequitable source of income (cf., 73). Also increased separation of farm ownership from operation may in the future restrict capital gains to a very small group of farmers.

The most important element in welfare legislation is broader financial support for education in rural areas. The foregoing discussion shows clearly that farm boys and girls are receiving neither the quantity nor quality of education needed to equip them for living in an urban-industrial environment. Yet a majority of farm youth will eventually live and work in the nonfarm sector. To fail to give farm youth adequate education will mean continued exporting of farm problems to the city. As stated earlier, sociologists have found that a surprising proportion of the social problems in the city can be traced to people of farm origins, mainly immigrants from rural areas of low income rather than from commercial farming areas. The fact needs to be stressed that rural poverty problems become more intensified city problems when rural migrants are not preequipped for urban jobs and culture, and that the economic payoff is potentially large from public policies to improved rural education. One estimate places the value of alleviating rural poverty at $156 billion (70).

Sizeable federal aid to education may be the only feasible way to raise education to acceptable levels. Federal aid for general education has not been politically acceptable to low-income areas which have received welfare grants of other types—much of them federal in origin. Meanwhile, urbanites are vocal in calling for federal aid, and pressures now are great for the government to provide more assistance to urban communities. Depressed rural communities need to realize that for economic progress, they too have a stake in education and training in the skills that are a concomitant of the urban-industrial process.

The poor in urban and rural areas have many characteristics in common. Both are "isolated" and both suffer from the anomie of social alienation. The U.S. poor have often been called "invisible" because they have few advocates and have been politically inert. This may once have been true for all but it is not now true of the poor in city slums. A riot makes a group stand out like the proverbial sore thumb. The political indifference of the rural poor is permitting the war on poverty to be less than a skirmish in the countryside. Unless farm leaders speak out with a louder voice than in the past, aid funds will increasingly pass the rural poor and will go to the vocal, urban poor.

The American people have traditionally supported the underdog elements in society. The welfare orientation will provide a reservoir of concern of American society for the disadvantaged in agriculture. Needs must be articulated by farm leaders, however, to draw from this reservoir of concern. It is a kind of perverse agrarian fundamentalism that attempts to retain people in agriculture and preserve rural poverty by refusal to accept federal programs to aid local schools that would better equip rural youth for productive employment elsewhere. It is the rising new generation that pays the cost of this fundamentalism. It is also this younger generation which most surely will perpetuate the problems of rural poverty unless rural elements accept the inevitability of living in an urban-industrial society.

THE FAMILY FARM

A third issue of particular relevance to farm people in an urban-industrial society is the family farm. One definition of the family farm is the nostalgic concept of an economic unit where a family can be independent, free from the hustle and bustle of city life, and commune with nature. Here a man can have autonomy and freedom from the pressure of the urban world—he can be an individualist. With some effort and a minimum of formal training, a hard-working, frugal family can provide sufficient income to lead a complete and wholesome life. Here is the moral and political foundation and sustenance for the democratic, free-enterprise society.

Unfortunately, this nostalgic concept is a myth and may never have existed. Today on the one hand are the large, hardheaded business operations of the adequate commercial farm which are basically an extension of the industrial system to the country. On the other hand are the farms which are classified in the poverty category. The top four economic classes of farms, now comprising approximately half of all farms, fall in the first category. The other half of all farms fall in the second category of inadequate farms. A category of farms in between these two groups might conform to the nostalgic concept of the family farm, but this category is small. Society will not long support farm programs to preserve the romantic concept of the family farm.

A second definition is very much alive however, and has shown vitality and durability. The USDA defines a family farm as a farming unit in which the majority of the labor and management is provided by the operator and his family. This family farm will be preserved as long as it is economically efficient and not just because it provides "the good life."

The family farm (second definition) has proved durable because (a) economies of scale are not so great but that youth can obtain sufficient financial help for a start from parents, (b) the high value of apprenticeship versus formal training for farming, (c) the large requirement for operational versus organizational management and attendant complementarity of manual labor with management, and (d) low returns in farming and in some instances legal restrictions have discouraged nonfarm corporations from large investment operations. The capital requirements for an efficient, adequate family farm are large and expanding. Efforts of farmers to improve management and efficiency almost invariably contain elements of the industrialization, and move farmers even closer to the urban-industrial structure. A dilemma facing family farmers in the future is how to increase efficiency—a major barrier of the family farm against inroads of corporate farming and vertical integration—without at the same time losing the identity of the family farm.

POLITICAL ALLIANCE

A final relationship of importance is identification of farmers with major power groups in society. Farmers have been traditionally distrustful of "big business," and have attempted to form political alliances with nonfarm groups such as in the Populist Party movement. These efforts largely have failed, and for example the close prewar relations have for some time been broken between the American Federation of Labor on the one hand and the American Farm Bureau Federation and Grange on the other.

The cleavage between farmers and the labor movement has grown in recent years for several reasons. The term "farmers" refers to operators and their families, and this group could be classified in either the labor or management camp. However, for at least two reasons, farmers increasingly wish to identify with the business community rather than with labor. First, the labor-management struggle is being brought close to farming by minimum wage legislation and intensified efforts of unions to organize hired farm workers, and by the wage-price spiral reflected in rising farm input prices. Second, the management input of the farm operator is rising relative to his labor input. Thus he can be expected to lean increasingly to the management position.

The fact that farmers have historically been highly vocal in denouncing big business and have ostentatiously sided with labor on certain issues hides the fact that the basic economic philosophy of the majority of farmers is closer to that of the business community than to that of organized labor. Based on a substantial number of opinion polls in the postwar period, Beers concluded that ". . . farmer distributions of opinion on the economic role of government were more like the distributions of executives, proprietors, businessmen, and white collar samples than like the distributions of sample laborers." (3.) Farmers have adopted the liberal position on specific issues when the economic pinch is severe. They face a severe dilemma in trying to preserve rugged individualism in a society in which bargaining power and public welfare measures are an accepted reality. This leads farmers to a more than usual frustration of being conservative in general and liberal in specifics (cf., 71).

The fertilizer, machinery, and other industries supplying inputs to farmers proved an important lobby for extending Food for Peace. Business interests are likely to be a continued ally of the Farm Bureau and the commercial family class of "haves" or believers in "qualitative" politics described by Wiggins and Talbot. But the struggle for welfare assistance to the disadvantaged in agriculture is likely to receive much more support from organized industrial labor than from industry. Thus, opportunities for political alliances for agriculture do not lie wholly within either labor or management. Farm political alliances to gain more political power appear to have no clear-cut doctrinaire direction, but must be based on opportunism.

CONCLUSIONS

This paper is based on the proposition that the future economic structure of farming can only be understood in the perspective of our now dominant urban-industrial society. Data and analysis show that differences are small but important between rural and urban sectors in demographic characteristics, education, attitudes, and values.

City people have cast the farmer as the underdog and last vestige of the early American agrarian culture—as independent, thrifty, and Puritanical. One reason why city people have not vetoed sizeable public programs for agriculture is that they wish to preserve this farm way of life. It is increasingly recognized that farming is no longer a way of life however but a business—an extension of urban-industrial society. Farmers no longer conform to the agrarian image—they must seek a new one.

Urban-industrial society has been depicted as affluent and security conscious. It places a high value on an efficient agriculture that provides adequate food at reasonable prices and that has sufficient reserve capacity to meet unforeseen difficulties. Commodity programs for agriculture have been consistent with these objectives for agriculture. Programs have not impeded labor outmovement nor increased farm production costs. Programs have maintained reserved capacity—land withdrawn from farm production should not be viewed entirely as a wasted resource but as one having value in that "nonuse" by a society which places a premium on flexibility and security. Low supply elasticity of farm output, high reserve needs, uncertainty, and the imperfect structure of the market create a situation where the social benefit-cost ratio exceeds the private benefit-cost ratio of maintaining reserve capacity in agriculture in the form of buffer stocks and land withdrawals.

But all is not well with commodity programs. They cost too much—the benefits to farmers and society could be achieved at less cost if some of the more conspicuous weaknesses of farm programs were removed. The emphasis should be flexibility in government spending in response to changing supply-demand conditions. The emphasis should be on government payments to remove land from production rather than on direct payments not tied to production adjustments. Also, farm programs cost too much in the sense that more funds are needed to alleviate poverty.

The intent of the authors and supporters of commodity programs was to promote equity, though it was believed that these programs would cause inefficiency. The opposite result has occurred. And as so often is the case, we find ourselves doing the right thing for the wrong reasons—the public ordered equity but got efficiency. Programs must be faulted for diverting income from the taxpayer who earns (say) $10,000 annually to one among the top 100,000 farmers who on the average earn a net income of $20,000 a year. This top 3 percent of farmers receive about one-third of the farm program benefits. Urban-industrial society is interested in preserving farming efficiency but also is concerned about equity issues. Program costs might be justified if they are necessary for efficiency and holding reserve capacity in agriculture, but hardly can be justified as direct transfer payments that continue even if supply is in line with utilization at acceptable prices in agriculture.

The urban press is unsympathetic to farm commodity programs. Unless the more conspicuous weaknesses of commodity programs can be corrected, and unless the public is convinced that programs are consistent with national goals of flexibility, efficiency, and stockpiling for emergencies, then programs will be in jeopardy. City people will not dictate future farm programs. But public policies for agriculture will increasingly be those of which urban-industrial society at least does not disapprove!

Farmers too are not entirely happy with federal programs, and would like a change. The dilemma is that efforts to gain collective independence—through farmer-controlled, cohesive bargaining groups—means an increasing sacrifice of personal independence. To keep the family farm efficient, farmers must adopt urban-industrial characteristics of self-preservation through larger and more mechanized farms, increased bargaining power, and government welfare legislation. Thus ironically, in the process of attempting to maintain the farm identity, the last vestiges of the traditional agrarian society tend to be lost.

The consumer is becoming a more visible participant in the farm policy milieu. Evidence of this is reflected in the ubiquitous revolts of housewives over the nation in 1966 against high food prices. There is talk of renaming the USDA the U.S. Department of Food and Agriculture—apparently to give more recognition to consumers. Also in 1966, the Secretary of Agriculture was severely taken to task by farm groups for allegedly lowering farm prices by reducing government purchase of pork for servicemen. The new feature is not that he was berated for his action, but that the consumer should have rated that much attention.

The rise of consumer bargaining power, coupled with the squeeze imposed by rising costs for hired labor and other farm inputs, puts further pressure and limits on the farmers' economic prerogatives. To be tolerated, supply administration by any farm group will need to be more concerned with stabilizing economic conditions for agriculture than with appreciably or precipitously raising prices.

Farm fundamentalism has served a useful purpose—it has contributed to the dignity, self-respect, and well-being of farmers.

But like most fundamentalist positions, it has sometimes led to myopia. It has led to greater interest in preserving the farm than the family. It has shielded farm people from the reality that most farm youth will find their place in a nonfarm environment. Inadequate schooling and other preparation for that environment can only lead to a legacy of socioeconomic difficulties that sometimes takes generations to correct.

LITERATURE CITED AND BIBLIOGRAPHY

1. Baker, C. B. and L. G. Tweeten. Financial requirements of the farm firm. In: Structural Changes in Commercial Agriculture, Center for Agr. and Econ. Development, No. 24. Pp. 27–51. Ames, Iowa. 1965.
2. Beale, C., J. Hudson, and V. Banks. Characteristics of the U.S. Population by Farm and Nonfarm Origin. USDA Econ. Rpt. 66. Dec., 1964.
3. Beers, H. Rural-urban differences: some evidence from public opinion polls. Rur. Soc. 18:1–11. 1952.
4. Bertrand, A. Rural communities under confrontation by mass society. In: The World Population Explosion. Pp. 81–86. Dept. of Agr. Econ., Louisiana State Univ., Baton Rouge. 1966.
5. Bird, A. R. Poverty in Rural Areas of the United States. USDA Econ. Rpt. 63. Nov., 1964.
6. Bishop, C. E. and G. S. Tolley. Manpower in farming and related occupations. Prepared for the President's Panel of Consultants on Vocational Education, Washington, D.C. U.S. GPO. July, 1962.
7. Bonnen, J. National policy for agriculture. In: Increasing Understanding of Public Problems and Policies. Chicago: Farm Foundation. 1965.
8. Breimyer, H. F. Individual Freedom and the Economic Organization of Agriculture. Urbana: Univ. of Ill. Press. 1965.
9. Brewster, J. Society values and goals in respect to agriculture. In: Goals and Values in Agricultural Policy. Ames: Iowa State Univ. Press. 1961.
10. Burchinal, L. G. Dialogue. In: Farm Goals in Conflict. Pp. 217–18. Ames: Iowa State Univ. Press. 1963.
11. ———. Differences in educational and occupational aspirations of farm, small town, and city boys. Rur. Soc. 26:107–21. 1961.
12. ———. Farm-nonfarm differences in religious beliefs and practices. Rur. Soc. 26:414–18. 1961.
13. ——— and P. E. Jacobson. Migration and adjustments of farm and urban families and adolescents in Cedar Rapids, Iowa. Rural Soc. 28:364–78. 1963.
14. Cannon, K. and R. Gingles. Social factors related to divorce rates for urban counties in Nebraska. Rural Soc. 21:34–40. 1956.
15. Cowhig, J. D. Age-Grade School Progress of Farm and Nonfarm Youth, 1960. USDA Econ. Rpt. 40. 1960.

16. ———. Characteristics of School Dropouts and High School Graduates, Farm and Nonfarm, 1960. USDA Econ. Rpt. 65. Dec., 1964.

17. ———. Early occupational status as related to education and residence. Rural Soc. 27:18–27. 1962.

18. ———. School Dropout Rates Among Farm and Nonfarm Youth, 1950 and 1960. USDA Econ. Rpt. 42. Sept., 1963.

19. ——— and C. B. Nam. Educational Status, College Plans, and Occupational Status of Farm and Nonfarm Youth: October 1959. Farm Population, USDA, ERS P-27, No. 30. Aug., 1961.

20. Cox, H. The Secular City. New York: Macmillan Co. 1965.

21. Dewey, R. The rural-urban continuum: real but relatively unimportant. Amer. J. of Soc. 66:60–66. 1960–61.

22. Douglass, H. P. The Little Town. New York: Macmillan Co. 1919.

23. Fite, G. The historical development of agricultural fundamentalism in the nineteenth century. J. Farm Econ. 44:1203–11. Dec., 1962.

24. Freedman, R. and D. Freedman. Farm-reared elements in the nonfarm population. Rural Soc. 21:50–61. 1956.

25. Fuguitt, G. V. The city and countryside. Rural Soc. 28:247–57. 1963.

26. Goldsmith, H. F. and J. H. Copp. Metropolitan dominance and agriculture. Rural Soc. 29:385–95. 1964.

27. Green, C. McL. The Rise of Urban America. New York: Harper and Row. 1965.

28. Haer, J. Conservatism-radicalism and the rural-urban continuum. Rural Soc. 17:343–47. 1952.

29. Hallenbeck, W. C. American Urban Communities. New York: Harper and Row. 1951.

30. Haller, A. O. Occupational achievement process of farm-reared youth in urban-industrial society. Rural Soc. 25:321–33. 1960.

31. ——— and C. E. Wolff. Personality orientations of farm, village, and urban boys. Rural Soc. 27:275–93. 1962.

32. Hathaway, D. and A. Waldo. Multiple Jobholding by Farm Operators. Mich. Agr. Exp. Sta., Res. Bul. 5. East Lansing. 1964.

33. Hathaway, S. R., E. D. Monochesi, and L. A. Young. Rural-urban adolescent personality. Rur. Soc. 24:331–46. 1959.

34. Hauser, P. Urbanization: an overview. In: P. Hauser and L. Schnore, eds., The Study of Urbanization. New York: Wiley and Sons, Inc. 1965.

35. ——— and L. Schnore, eds. The Study of Urbanization. New York: Wiley and Sons, Inc. 1965.

36. Landis, P. H. Social Problems in Nation and World. Chicago: J. B. Lippincott Co. 1959.

37. Larson, O. and E. Rogers. Rural society in transition. In: J. H. Copp, ed., Our Changing Rural Society. Ames: Iowa State Univ. Press. 1964.

38. Levy, M. J., Jr. Modernization and the Structure of Societies. Princeton, N.J.: Princeton Univ. Press. 1966.

39. Lewis, A. W. The Theory of Economic Growth. Great Britain: Simson Shand, Ltd. 1955.

40. Lipset, S. M. Social mobility and urbanization. Rural Soc. 20:220–28. 1955.

41. Loomis, C. P. Social Systems. Princeton, N.J.: D. Van Nostrand Co., Inc. 1960.
42. Mangus, A. R. Personality adjustment of rural and urban children. In: P. Hatt and A. Reiss, Jr., eds. Cities and Societies, 2nd ed. Pp. 603–14. Glencoe, Ill.: Free Press. 1957.
43. Martinson, F. Personal adjustment and rural-urban migration. Rural Soc. 20:102–10. 1955.
44. Middleton, R. and C. M. Grigg. Rural-urban differences in aspirations. Rural Soc. 24:347–54. 1959.
45. Miller, P. A. Social, economic, and political values of farm people. In: Problems and Policies in American Agriculture. Ames: Iowa State Univ. Press. 1959.
46. Moore, E. J., E. L. Baum, and R. B. Glasgow. Economic Factors Influencing Educational Attainments and Aspirations of Farm Youth. USDA Econ. Rpt. 51. Apr., 1964.
47. Nam, C. B. and J. D. Cowhig. Factors Related to College Attendance of Farm and Nonfarm High School Graduates: 1960. Farm Population. USDA, ERS P-27, No. 32. June, 1962.
48. Nelson, L. Rural life in a mass-industrial society. Rural Soc. 22:20–30. 1957.
49. On Tradition, or What Is Left of It. Time, p. 42. Apr. 22, 1966.
50. Parsons, T. The Social System. Glencoe, Ill.: Free Press. 1951.
51. Payne, R. Development of occupational and migration expectations. Rural Soc. 21:117–25. 1956.
52. Polk, K. An exploration of rural juvenile delinquency. In: Rural Youth in Crisis. U.S. Dept. of Health, Ed. and Welfare, U.S. GPO. 1963.
53. Redfield, R. The Folk Society. Am. J. Soc. 52:293–320. 1946–47.
54. Ruttan, V. Agriculture in an affluent society. J. Farm Econ. 48:1100–20. 1966.
55. Schnore, L. F. The rural-urban variable: an urbanite's perspective. Rural Soc. 31:135–43. 1966.
56. Schultz, T. W. Urban developments and policy implications for agriculture. Investment in Human Capital Series Paper 65:08. Dept. of Econ. Univ. of Chicago. 1965.
57. Schwarzweller, H. Education, migration, and economic life chances of male entrants to the labor force from a low-income rural area. Rural Soc. 29:152–67. 1964.
58. ——— and J. Brown. Education as a cultural bridge between eastern Kentucky and the Great Society. Rural Soc. 27:357–73. 1962.
59. Sewell, W. and A. Haller. The educational and occupational prospectives of rural youth. In: Rural Youth in Crisis. U.S. Dept. of Health, Ed. and Welfare, U.S. GPO. 1963.
60. Slocum, W. L. Agricultural Sociology. New York: Harper and Row. 1962.
61. Spiegelman, R. Analysis of Urban Agglomeration and Its Meaning for Rural People. USDA Econ. Rpt. 96. June, 1966.
62. Stewart, C., Jr. The rural-urban dichotomy: concepts and uses. Amer. J. of Soc. 64:152–58. 1958–59.
63. Straus, M. A. Societal needs and personal characteristics in the choice of occupation by farmers' sons. Rural Soc. 29:408–25. 1964.

64. Sweeter, D. A. The effect of industrialization on intergenerational solidarity. Rural Soc. 31:145–70. 1966.
65. Taylor, L. and A. Jones, Jr. Rural Life and Urbanized Society. New York: Oxford Univ. Press. 1964.
66. Tönnies, F. Fundamental Concepts of Sociology. (Trans. by C. P. Loomis.) New York: American Book Co. 1949.
67. Tweenten, L. G. Comparing effects of U.S. and Canadian farm policies: discussion. J. Farm Econ. 47:1152–59. 1965.
68. ———. Socio-Economic Growth Theory. Dept. of Agr. Econ., Oklahoma State Univ., Stillwater. 1966. (Mimeo.)
69. ———. The income structure of U.S. farms by economic class. J. Farm Econ. 47:207–21. 1965.
70. ———. The Role of Education in Alleviating Rural Poverty. Background paper for Research on Rural Poverty. USDA, ERS. July, 1965. (Mimeo.)
71. ——— et al. Summary of Press Releases of 1964 Wheat Survey. Dept. of Agr. Econ., Oklahoma State Univ., Stillwater. 1965. (Mimeo.)
72. Tweeten, L. G. and F. K. Hines. Contributions of agricultural productivity to national economic growth. Agr. Sci. Review. 3:40–45. 1965.
73. ——— and T. R. Nelson. Sources and Repercussions of Changing U.S. Farm Real Estate Values. Oklahoma Agr. Exp. Sta. Tech. Bul. T-120. Stillwater. 1966.
74. ——— and J. S. Plaxico. Long-run outlook for agricultural adjustments based on national growth. J. Farm Econ. 46:39–53. 1964.
75. Tyner, F. A Simulation Analysis of the U.S. Farm Economy. Unpublished Ph.D. Thesis. Lib., Oklahoma State Univ., Stillwater. 1966.
76. ——— and L. G. Tweeten. Excess capacity in U.S. agriculture. USDA Agr. Econ. Res. 16:1. 1964.
77. ——— and ———. Optimum resource allocation in U.S. agriculture. J. Farm Econ. 48:613–31. 1966.
78. USDA. A Summary of Selected Characteristics of the Urban and Rural Populations, by States, 1960. ERS-174. Mar., 1964.
79. ———. The Farm Index. Vol. 3, No. 11. Nov., 1964.
80. ———. The Farm Index. Vol. 5, No. 8. Aug., 1966.
81. Weber, M. The Protestant Ethic. London: George Allen and Unwin, Ltd. 1930.
82. Williams, R. M., Jr. American Society. New York: Alfred A. Knopf. 1965.
83. ———. American society in transition. In: Our Changing Rural Society. Ames: Iowa State Univ. Press. 1964.
84. Zeisel, J. The job outlook for rural youth. In: Rural Youth in Crisis. U.S. Dept. of Health, Ed. and Welfare, U.S. GPO. 1963.

CHAPTER NINE

Developing Economically and Politically Consistent Policies: The Problem of Equity

EARL O. HEADY

THE BASIC PROBLEM underlying American farm policy, even if unrecognized by the public, has been that of inequitable distributions of the gains and sacrifices from technical progress and reorganization of agriculture under economic growth. This problem continues to exist. Policies that are both politically acceptable and economically most reasonable are unlikely to prevail until equitable distributions are attained. This will be necessary over all of the major groups whose incomes and welfare are affected through the structural changes and intersectoral relations of agriculture.

PROGRESS AND DISTRIBUTIONS

Broad attempts of American society to rectify inequitable distributions of gains and sacrifices stemming from changes and reorganizations of agriculture had their beginning in the major income transfer, production control, commodity storage, and price support programs initiated in the 1930's and continued to this time. By the late 1920's, society at large was just beginning to realize the very great payoff from its investment in technical change and progress of agriculture. The public investment for these purposes has continued and the societal payoff has been accentuated. From its investment in improved technology, society has realized a return estimated to range from 50 percent to 100 percent (4, pp. 595–603; see also, 2).

Recognizing this problem of contrasting gains and losses in welfare, American society has invested over $60 billion for this purpose in programs of direct payments, price support mechanisms, and surplus disposal, both domestic and international over the period 1933–66. The payments and program costs have been directed toward compensation of farmers, mainly commercial operators, for reduced revenues when greater production pours into a market of inelastic demand. This amount undoubtedly is much less than the gains to society generally, resulting from its investment in the improved technology of agriculture, in resource savings in agriculture, reduced real prices of food, and the annual net one-way transfer of human investment which moves from the rural community to urban society in the form of young people. However, in this large-scale attempt to bring equitable distributions of gains from farm technological advance to both farmers and consumers, the scope of the problem was formed too simply and narrowly. It left aside numerous groups in the rural community, and even on farms, who also suffer losses under progress of agriculture and subsequent decline in the number of farms and farm workers.

The question is not that this or other amounts were due the commercial farm sector in order that positive-sum distributions could be guaranteed it and consumers generally, but rather that the $60 billion did not solve the fundamentally important and basic long-run problems of agriculture and the rural community. These problems stem from economic progress and public investment therein. Neither did it erase all inequities in the distribution of outcomes from agricultural progress. The consequences were that certain programs more nearly adapted to solving the structural problems of agriculture were rejected by the rural community. These programs, either publicly discussed or initiated, did not have political acceptance because they also posed inequities in their distribution of gains and sacrifices.

POLITICAL ACCEPTABILITY
AND DISTRIBUTION OF GAINS

The free market was rejected in the past since rapid progress of agriculture within this framework brought gains to some farm families but losses to others. Active farmers with sufficient capital resources, able to extend output more rapidly than the decline of prices under a regime of inelastic demand, could gain under these conditions as they acquired more resources or applied new technology. Older farm families, young operators, and others whose capital and resource position restrained them from extending output as prices declined realized or expected losses under these conditions. One group championed free-market prices because it gained thus; another group resisted them because its reward from progress was then negative.

Free market prices were not the only policy proposal which was rejected due to its potentially inequitable distribution of benefits. Mandatory market quotas for some products also undoubtedly fell in this category. The distribution of quotas directly involves an allocation of future income streams and asset values among farmers. The effect on asset values has been obvious in the trend of land prices generally and especially those related to tobacco quotas. Future incomes and asset values are either augmented or restrained against what they would otherwise be. Farmers with scheduled growth plans for the future are faced with the prospect that their income stream will be reduced. While they may maintain this growth through the purchase of quotas, they must pay a greater price for this opportunity while those who sell the quotas realize a greater revenue.

But the distribution of gains and losses from public policy and economic reorganization of agriculture has impacts which extend far beyond farm groups. Major policies and proposals have been voted out or have failed to gain acceptance because the gains that they brought farmers were accompanied by losses to other groups in the rural community. An example was the Conservation Reserve and Soil Bank programs of the 1950's which paid the farmer for retiring his entire unit from production. The individual farm family could appraise its situation and decide if it gained from putting its entire farm into the program for a long period of time, then move to another location. Many did so to their own benefit and without losses to other farm families in the same or other communities. Yet this development brought supposed and actual losses to others in the rural community.

While farmers were rescued from a situation of depressed earnings, an income loss was transferred to merchants and others in the rural community who are part of the total farm complex. Their sales and revenues declined as farmers in concentrated areas retired their land on a "whole farm" basis and began moving to employment in other locations.

Consequently, sufficient pressure was put on Congress to change the format of acreage reduction programs. Supply control programs based on land withdrawal thus shifted to a different format in the 1960's. The Conservation Reserve and Soil Bank programs were stopped dead in their tracks and feed grain and other programs were initiated. These programs, based on retirement of the land on a partial farm basis, scattered land withdrawal more evenly over all rural communities and producing regions. The procedure better kept farm families in the community where they could gain from payments under the program, and local merchants could gain from their greater expenditures.

OTHER REORGANIZATIONS RELATING TO THE DISTRIBUTION OF COSTS AND BENEFITS

Other public policies and the market impacts of economic growth also have differential effects on income gains and losses. Almost typically, the major stream of the benefits is to the nonfarm economy and away from the rural community. However, others of these economic reorganizations do have their differential incident mainly within the farm community.

One distinct inequitable distribution, stemming from (a) past farm policies and (b) structural reorganization of agriculture, has been the differential trend in capital gains and losses among the different sectors of the rural community. Those two forces have facilitated a nice gain in asset values for farmers. Cochrane estimated that the capital gain to farmers, as a result of higher land and asset values, amounted to $87 billion between 1940 and 1964; a gain of about $3.5 billion per year (1, pp. 122–123). An increase in farm land values over the last decade has been characteristic of all major rural communities. But at the same time, asset values of local merchants and others have been evaporating in typical small rural towns and villages. As farm families and persons serving them have moved away, country towns are full of store buildings and dwellings whose value has dwindled from substantial amounts to nearly nothing.

An even broader impact of the same general phenomena has

been the export of capital invested in human resources as structural reorganization of farming has been speeded by national economic growth and policies. Taves has estimated that the net outflow in this form is $1 million annually from a rural community of 4,000 (5). The cost is quite heavy for the rural community, even though the gain in a trained labor force is equally great to the receiving community. The rural community thus resists exhortations and policies which would have it invest more in human resources to be exported in the form of better trained people for regions of rapid economic development.

The problem of the distribution of gains and sacrifices from farm advance and reorganization stretches complexly over all of society. While the effects are unleashed largely through the market, other public policies and private actions give rise to similar problems. American society has invested heavily in public research and education, providing new technology which changes the structure of agriculture. With farming now a highly capitalized industry, the private sector has reorganized similarly in order to sell more improved machines, chemicals, seeds, and other modern inputs to farmers. Although the outlay by both is still increasing, investment in the development and communication of new technologies by the private sector now surpasses that of the public sector. As a result of these investments by the public and private sectors, the real cost of food has declined markedly for the consumer at large, and we now need fewer farmers. But in this realm of benefits to consumers at large, innovating farmers, and firms which manufacture farm inputs, the rapid commercialization of farming denudes the countryside of farms and people. The growth of the modern input sector for agriculture causes the labor force of chemical, drug, and machinery plants to grow. But these increases in the labor force at urban or industrial centers serve as a substitute for laborers in the rural community. The volume of business in the rural community declines accordingly and progress of agriculture which brings gains to some groups brings decay to many country towns and sacrifice to their inhabitants.

National economic development itself distributes gains unequally over rural and other communities. Not only does it cause resource prices to change and bring a mammoth substitution of capital for labor in farming, with a further decline in the farm work force and the rural population, but also it seldom brings employment opportunities to the purely rural community. The gains in employment opportunities and income from national economic development fall largely to existing industrial centers favored by location and resource endowments. These development centers frequently have gained from their proximity to farm regions and the flow of human resources coming to them from agriculture. But the very nature of the rural community, dispersed over the countryside and apart from natural resource and locational advantages, makes it unable to offset losses from the change in agricultural structure by an advance in local industrialization and development. A few rural communities do have this opportunity, but the majority will hope in vain for it because the proper setting in location, resources, markets, and economic foundation is lacking.

Other examples would further illustrate policies and reorganizations which bring gains to one group but losses to another. Enough have been cited, however, to illustrate their broad impact over the rural community and their potential effect on the political acceptance of farm policies. Political acceptance and economic equity are not strangers. Where one is found the other also generally will be found. As we look to the future and wiser policies which might attach to the economic growth and structural dislocations in farming which thus occurs, we must consider all of the major groups whose income and welfare is affected by these changes and the farm programs which are developed to cope with them.

POSITIVE-SUM OUTCOMES AND UNANIMOUS CONSENT

If the alternative programs selected are to have political acceptance, a major task of public policy in the future is to develop and implement programs which are positive sum in their outcomes over all major groups which relate to agriculture. By positive sum, we refer to the need to be certain that the negative outcome to one group does not exceed the positive outcome to another group. But what quantitative measure are we to use—income, for example? If the comparison were that simple, we could roughly estimate the money loss to one group and the money gain to another group as a result of a particular policy or economic reorganization of agriculture. If the money gain of one group exceeded the money loss of another group, we could label the policy "positive." However, in the welfare context that is important, the summation is not this simple. The loss may fall on a person whose income is already low while the gain may accrue to one whose income is high. We would generally expect this to be true as a result of the major structural reorganization now taking place in commercial agriculture. The producers of chemicals and machines, for example, who distribute more inputs and prosper from a highly capitalized agriculture generally have higher incomes than the small-scale store owner of the rural community whose business dwindles as agriculture becomes commercialized into few farms and a smaller work force. Even aside from this difference, we cannot measure, or thus accurately compare, the utility or value of a unit of income to one person or group with that of another. Comparison of negative and positive money income changes thus serve inadequately to reflect balances in real income or welfare. Consequently, we generally can be certain that a policy has a positive-sum outcome only if it results in gains to one group without bringing losses to another; or, even better, if it brings positive gains to both. Intuitively, the sum of two positives is always positive. But under inability to express their magnitudes relative to each other, we have no way to know that the sum of a positive and a negative is positive.

One criterion for gauging the extent to which positive-sum outcomes result from economic development and a collection of agricultural policies might be unanimous consent or acceptance by all groups concerned; since each group then expresses a positive gain. Attainment of unanimous consent is not an easy matter, of course, because not all groups related to agricultural prices, outputs, inputs, income, and structure have consistent interests.

The many diverse groups surrounding agriculture have their incomes affected differently under initiation of a specific price policy or change in farm structure. Some dissent not because their incomes are reduced, but only because a particular policy prevents them from maximizing a gain at the expense of other groups. These potentially competing groups include consumers, small farmers, large-scale farmers, the young and old, farmers who buy or sell grain, firms which import or export commodities, companies who process inputs or outputs and store commodities, communities which are either the source or destination of migrants from agriculture, and the entire complex of the rural community mentioned earlier—including local merchants, churches, schools, and institutions generally.

While positive outcome for all groups under economic change might be possible, not all interested groups are satisfied with such a simple "equitable distribution." Instead, some groups may wish to optimize their individual position at the expense of others, and not just be "made better off." A means to this end is for one group to form a coalition with another, so that they have enough voting or political power to retain the gains while other or "outside" groups are left with negative outcomes. However, coalitions of this type will be unstable over time if the sacrifice falling on "outside" groups is substantial. Members of the coalition can easily eject one group, to take in another which now has gain but does not request "as large a slice" as the one ejected.

"Unanimous consent" among farm organization was attained in the United States in the 1930's during the Farm Bloc days when all joined together in obtaining major farm legislation to alleviate the depressed prices and incomes of that period. However, in postwar years, this unanimity has been absent. Diverse groups of farmers which make up the seperate farm organizations employ strategies more in the vein of zero-sum outcomes—"What our group gains, the other must lose or vice versa; but with the gain divided 'equitably' within the individual farm organization." Fluctuating policy in the United States over the last 20 years also suggests an instability of the coalitions formed, both among farm groups and between individual farm groups in correspondence with other economic and political groups.

The $60 billion mentioned earlier in this chapter could have been used equally for other types of policies which both provided positive gains from progress for farm families and resolved certain basic problems of the rural community. However, there were two reasons why it was not possible to use the funds for policies which might simultaneously accomplish these two ends: (a) Farm organizations either did not realize that they were playing the zero-sum game with each other and thus insisted on their own ends at the expense of income and welfare to competing farm organizations, or were inflexible in their attempts to do so. The result was a policy stalemate which prevented more realistic and efficient long-run programs than those used. Often these ends which farm and regional groups attained in farm policy included so many "side payments" and "trade offs," in the form of programs providing for flexibility to each farm and regional group, that the program had little content after legislation was finally completed. (b) They left other groups in the farm community, equally affected by adverse farm prices and structural changes in agriculture, entirely outside of the welfare accounting.

Improvement of policy and unanimous consent are not likely to arise until social conscience and legislation require the policy restraint: that no major group is left worse off as a result of further economic development and the policies which surround it. These "other groups" must be recognized and included, as a policy is being formulated. Hopefully, these conditions can be attained as farmers, farm organizations, and consumer groups become better educated on the consequences of the further economic development of agriculture and on the effect of alternative policy means among different economic groups over the rural community which relate to farm structural change. The possibility of policy selections among a set which is restrained to "make no group worse off" is not impossible where social choice is made under full information. Deeper analysis and greater information, especially through a restructured Cooperative Extension Service, thus is a requirement for creation of improved long-run policies which have broad political acceptance.

Actually, in societies as advanced as that of the United States, the gain from economic progress should be positive for all groups; not just "equal to or greater than before," but greater. It seems unrealistic and of doubtful political acceptance that some families and community sectors should be left "just as well off," with no gain from national economic progress, when other major sectors realize a large positive and absolute gain in real income. Hence, to be certain that the outcome is appropriately positive sum, we must provide conditions of economic progress so that the outcome for all major groups of farmers and farm communities, as well as the consumer in general, is positive. We must open up economic opportunity so that all have promise of increased income and welfare as national economic progress and the technical advance of farming proceeds further. Agricultural policies which compensate people who remain on farms but do nothing for persons displaced from agriculture through farm technological advance and without proper skills and training for the nonfarm economy do not meet these criteria. Neither do those thrusts in technology which benefit the manufacturers and distributors of farm inputs which have the second-round effect of curtailing the sales and reducing the values of capital assets for merchants of the rural community.

In this comparative sense, too, it is necessary to consider the cultural, recreational, welfare, and related activities which are available to different segments of society as economic progress and income growth occurs. In this set is that general mix of services to which societies attach high marginal urgency after those more fundamental and biological demands of adequate food, sufficient housing, and basic disease control have been attained. It includes recreational, general health, and other welfare services which are at a level consistent with the national level of consumer incomes. Because of the scattered nature of the population, rural communities have always had a sparse supply of these services. The further thinning of the rural population sometimes causes this set to decline absolutely, and typically to remain static or decline relatively. Advance from national economic progress is not likely to impress older citizens of rural communities who see their income base and cultural opportunities remain stable as both press rapidly upward for the nation at large. They are, in fact, likely to consider their welfare outcome to be negative and protest politically, even if in the mild form of negative ballots, for proposals and investments which extend the qualities and capabilities generally for the population.

EQUITY IN THE AGRICULTURAL COMMUNITY

The devolpmental forces underway in the national economy will further impinge on agriculture and farm communities. Relative real prices of resource and technology will continue to change. As a result, the massive injection of new technological forms of capital into agriculture also will continue. Capital will be further substituted for labor and land. The work force of agriculture will be halved again over the next two decades and the number of farms will be reduced similarly. The relative importance of land in production will decline in many regions and an interregional adaptation of crops will be needed accordingly.

These forces of economic growth will be reflected whether or not the United States tries to feed the world and domestic surpluses disappear. Most of them will occur regardless of the types of farm policies in force, particularly if they are of the nature of policies in effect over the last two decades. While they will have important impacts on farming, they will have even greater impacts on other persons of the rural community. The population of purely farm areas will continue to decline. Except in that minority of farming communities which is blessed with location, resources, or other unique advantages which favor local industrial development, there will be fewer patrons of local businesses, rural churches, schools, and other institutions.

It is important that we have policies in agriculture which bring equitable distributions of the gains from progress to all major groups of farmers—big or small, North or South, grain or livestock, or any allied category. It is important too, however, that we have policies equally for those forced to leave because of the progress of the industry as well as for those who remain in farming to receive the payments, higher prices, increments in land values, and other gains of policy and economic development. Too, it is equally important that our policies treat the problems, or offset the losses, of others in the rural community who are affected adversely by the changing structure and progress of agriculture. Even if the world food situation intensifies demand for U.S. farm products to the extent that major surplus problems disappear, the main problems stemming from agricultural change no longer will fall on operating farmers who remain in the industry. They will fall on those who are forced out of agriculture even more rapidly as the tempo of capital-labor substitution increases and the number of farms and workers declines further. They also fall on others of the rural community whose economic activities and capital values erode further as the rural community continues to decline in population.

Many rural communities are going to be faced with a halving of their population in the next two decades, even if farming becomes more profitable, or even as a result of this possibility. The mammoth change which is yet ahead in farm technology and agricultural structure will make the past appear mild and modest in many rural communities, because it will push the rural community below the "threshold level" in its ability to retain competent commercial services, maintain adequate incomes over all sectors of the population, and provide public services at needed levels. Thus, for the problems of the future, it is equally important that the policies stemming from agricultural change recognize those replaced from the industry and the persons of country towns as also part of the agricultural complex and changing society that relates to national economic progress and the general urbanization process. They must be brought into consideration when agricultural and related policies are fashioned. The intent is not to cut off all programs that will solve farm problems because they will upset obsolete economic, social, and political structures of rural communities. Instead, policy should be extended so that it provides appropriate opportunities and facilities to all people of rural communities in an urbanizing society.

The consequences of economic growth, including changes in factor prices and capital technology that give rise to extended scale economies, are repeated in all important economic and social sectors of rural communities separated geographically from major growth and industrial centers. They bite more deeply in these rural communities because industrial development is lacking at rates to absorb the labor and families released in the more general substitution of capital for human effort. Because of the scale economies in all types of enterprises, including the village grocery store or the country school, and because of the thinning of farm labor force and population, the rural community must itself expand in geographic spread and boundary. The rural community in geographically dispersed farm areas has the same developmental and adjustment problems as does the individual farm. Stranded in rural communities are nonfarm people whose income loss results from the same variables that cause depressing income of the farm and/or labor forces; they are no less important than farm people. Policy should be developed accordingly.

EQUITY IN ECONOMIC OPPORTUNITY

Agricultural policy which focuses only on compensation and market power for people who remain in agriculture is negative. It stands to constrain the future earning power and economic opportunity of important strata of the farm and country town population. It diverts attention from the many human resources which can be aided little or not at all by typical farm compensation policies and which have opportunity closed to them by price or production policy fixation. Many youth and other persons of agriculture need opportunity opened to them by means which are not apparent in conventional farm policies which focus only on support prices, marketing power, foreign aid, and similar devices. Even if demand and supply conditions change to bring high prosperity to the farm industry, the general problems of the rural community will remain.

There are many reasons why equality of economic opportunity does not prevail under economic progress where agriculture diminishes as a portion of the national economy. The geographic spread of farming puts people out of touch with job opportunities in urban centers and hinders their migration and relocation to other industries. Not only are costs of transportation and relocation involved but also the move from the rural community to a city is more complex than a shift between occupations while retaining the same domicile within the city. Skills used in farming have been quite typically found to be obsolete and of little transfer value for use in industry. This is in contrast to industrial skills which are more readily transferred among industries, although automation is giving rise to similar problems in industry. The cultural attachments to life in open farm country or farm villages also hinders migration to urban living conditions, as compared to a shift among occupations while retaining the same household in a city.

One important reason why farm people tend to end up in low-status and low-income jobs when they migrate to city employment is the scarcity of education and vocational training facilities in dispersed farming regions as compared to industrial communities. On the average, farm youth from these communities have had less selection in vocational training, have poorer quality educational facilities, and have an environment which is less inspiring in education.

Attention must be focused on the four strata of rural population if the major policy goal of equality of opportunity is to be applied impartially. For farm youth, equality of educational opportunity must be provided. For younger and middle-aged persons already established in farming with too few resources and greater economic opportunity elsewhere, opportunities for retraining, compensation during the training period, and some aid in relocation are desirable. This age group will increase relatively in size and have crucial problems throughout the decade ahead. Rapid technical advances and automation will increasingly cause previous skills to become obsolete and a large number of persons will be faced with underemployment or low incomes unless retraining opportunities are provided by the public. The need and justification of redevelopment of occupational skills for this group is a social problem of urgency equal to that of providing elementary education to children. Middle-aged workers must not only support themselves in the future, they also must provide an immediate and continuing livelihood for their families. For the third group—older farm persons with skills and cultural values tied to the farm community with little outlook for retraining and transfer to other industries and locations— equality of opportunity more nearly must be provided in the form of social and welfare services "on the spot." Appropriate levels of old age pensions, medical care, recreational opportunities, and similar facilities represent the requirement if they are to be given economic and social opportunities equal to their peer groups in growing urban and industrial centers. The fourth group—nonfarm persons in rural communities affected adversely by changes in agricultural structure—is faced with an extremely complex set of problems. Youth in this group are restrained in education and technical training for the same reasons as farm youth. Middle-aged persons of this group are faced with reduced earnings and lowered capital values unless many more of them move to urban centers. The old of this strata parallel those of the farm in their needs for income, security, and welfare measures.

IMPROVED EDUCATIONAL AND VOCATIONAL TRAINING FACILITIES FOR YOUTH

While economic growth and full employment is one element of an over-all policy to provide equity and economic opportunity for all people now in agriculture and the rural community, improved educational and vocational training facilities also are required elements. Youth in farm communities are at a great disadvantage, as opportunities to develop personal skills through education and vocational training are meager in rural areas in general and in low-income farm regions particularly. Places to learn nonfarm skills and trades have been almost completely lacking. Farm youth, and those of the rural community at large, thus have unequal opportunities in comparison with youth from urban areas in taking advantage of future economic growth.

Several aspects of education in rural communities lead to this disadvantage. First, the major method of financing education at the local level—property taxes within the local district—has crimped the rural community. It has less property to serve as a tax base in generating funds for education. The declining rural population and the method of financing has led to a greater cost per taxpayer, as compared to urban locations. The selective migration has left an older population in rural communities that has a shorter planning horizon and is less inclined to make large educational investments for the future. Too, the net flow of educational investment from the rural community is always outward. With declining numbers and opportunities in farming and a long-standing net outmigration, rural communities have consistently invested in the education of young people who end up in the urban economic sector. People do not flow into the farm communities, bringing educational investment from the urban sector. The net effect of these forces is lower quality, less inspiring, and a less complete educational program in the rural community.

While the figures are weighted somewhat heavily by the South, national data show that youth from rural communities rank much lower than urban youth in standard tests for reading, arithmetic, and other basic skills. They have a higher retardation rate (pupils one or more years behind their age group) than the urban schools. Too, the drop-out rate is about twice as great in rural communities as in urban communities. The proportion of rural youth who attend college is much smaller than for urban youth.

A further reflection of the relative quality of education in primary and secondary schools in rural communities is the outlay made for teachers and pupils. Over the recent past, salaries for teachers in counties where the population is 85 percent rural with 50 percent or more on farms have averaged only 55 percent of those in urban areas with 25,000 or more in population. The comparison is even much bleaker if it is made with cities having a population of 100,000 or more. Annual expenditure per pupil in the same rural areas has been less than two-thirds that of the urban areas. Equality in education, and hence in economic opportunity, cannot be provided without much more state and federal aid to education in the rural communities.

Funds through the Elementary and Secondary Education Act of 1965, and some of the Community Action programs of the Economic Opportunity Act of 1964 will provide modest aid in upgrading rural community schools. However, in the typically dispersed commercial farming regions that do not qualify as poverty centers, these provisions are still inadequate relative to the unique needs of an adjusting agriculture reducing its work force requirements. Finances and facilities must be increased to extend and enrich the school curriculum, to provide premium teacher salaries drawing equally competent personnel into the countryside, and to initiate adequate programs of vocational training and occupational guidance. The Vocational Education Act of 1963 will be an aid in bringing more training to the rural community. Yet it also is inadequate to meet the unique needs of an adjusting agriculture in dispersed commercial farming communities. It still requires that rural states, many of which will lose most of the skilled work force they train, must match society in investing in post-high school vocational training from which the latter reaps the major benefit. The area vocational-technical schools still won't put training at the disposal of enough youth. It does not overcome the inadequacy of insufficient and misdirected vocational training in high schools where the masses of students are encountered. Much larger efforts and extended federal aid is required before facilities in rural communities can be put on a par with those in urban centers and the ratio of benefit to cost is equalized between the rural community and the national society.

Rural areas have tended to be somewhat antagonistic towards federal aid to education. However, not only are they the groups most in need of it if their youth are to realize equality of opportunity, but also these communities were the first to have widespread federal aid to education. Since its very outset, through the Smith-Hughes Act in 1917, training in vocational agriculture has been financed through federal funds. So has a large part of the 4-H training programs initiated in 1900. Rural citizens seem to forget or overlook this facet of federal aid to education when they point with pride to their Future Farmers and 4-H Clubs and the vocational training they have thus attained. Without more federal aid, or state aid where the possibility exists, the quality of education in the typical rural communities will remain low. Too, a distortion in the distribution of costs and benefits will prevail as long as citizens of areas such as western Kansas pay the costs of education while Los Angeles, San Francisco, Portland, and similar cities reap the benefit of productivity from the youth who migrate. Less than a third of the high school graduates in typical rural counties have remained in the community; fewer may do so in the future.

To provide equality of economic opportunity over the next two decades for youth in rural communities, several steps are necessary. The geographic spread of the rural community must be further extended into a functional economic area so that it can realize the scale economies or cost advantages related to current capital technology. Under this revision, school districts must be made even larger and investment in education must be increased to: (a) provide a higher quality of education and a more comprehensive curriculum for basic education directed towards the employment needs in the national economy over the decades ahead; (b) extend investment and redirect technical education and vocational training in high schools of rural communities so that those displaced from farming will be trained to take employment in the faster growing industries of the economy; and (c) provide an appropriate number of vocational guidance and counseling personnel, both to keep more youth in school and to direct them better into occupations consistent with the nation's economic growth and manpower needs.

RETRAINING FACILITIES FOR LABOR REPLACED

To bring equity in opportunity, a particular need relates to those young and middle-aged persons already established in agriculture. A growing number of them will be replaced in the increased commercialization and capitalization of agriculture which is ahead. They have already become farm operators and invested in farm assets or they have become year-round farm workers. Some of them need to stay, and will, as they acquire the skill and resources to become successful farmers. Others do not have this opportunity. They simply drifted into farming because this was the tradition in the classic rural community, because their only training was in this direction, and because they lacked vocational guidance and counseling to direct them otherwise, or to allow them to compare their economic opportunities in farming and other pursuits. Many persons in this group will find, through bitter financial experience and after loss of several years of their life, that the rapid technical advance and the competition of agriculture does not provide them and their family with promising economic opportunities in farming.

Theirs is a hard decision, reflected in the extremely low migration rate from farms for persons in the 25–40 age bracket. The decision is difficult partly because they have little aid in making it. While they have ample public services at hand to advise them on the breed of hogs to raise or the place to market their cattle, they still get little organized advice on whether they are better off to stay with farming or shift to some other occupation. Nor can they get much help on which pursuit to follow if they were to transfer. Their decision also is difficult because of the costs involved. In liquidating their farming assets, they lose some time and income. Then there are the costs of moving and the time with earnings foregone while they seek other employment, or look around for jobs which match any flexible skills they still possess. Also, they are at an employment and income disadvantage with a person of the same age bracket who grew up in industrial employment.

These are people with families for whom, once their old jobs and skills in farming have been outmoded, the personal importance of vocational training and education can have even more meaning and immediate return than for a teen-ager still in high school. But given the difficulties surrounding decisions and the lack of skills for off-farm employment, many of them just don't leave agriculture; or they drift into low-paid employment in rural towns. It would seem to be only minimum compensation after they have been replaced by the advance of agriculture and the process of economic growth, to help to retool them for alternative occupational engagement.

Potentials for transfer in this group include many of the 19 percent, 665,000 full-time farmers whose gross sales are less than $5,000 and who produce only 6 percent of the nation's farm sales. Also, many of the 1.5 million farmers with sales of over $5,000 are candidates in this group. Many individuals in this age and occupational group are sufficiently young to be salvageable persons who can increase their income by moving from farming. While technical advance does away with the need for them in agriculture, we still fail to provide them with sufficient retraining opportunities so that they can profitably or easily transfer to other occupations.

This opportunity should be added as an element of policy to help solve the basic problems of agriculture, and not alone of poverty. We do have public evening classes for adult vocational education in farm communities, but again these are in vocational agriculture directed towards persons staying in agriculture. As the individual participates in them and improves his farming efficiency, he further speeds the decline in the number of persons required in farming. It is equally or more important, scattered widely over the broad stretches of farming regions, that education be aimed at retraining of persons displaced from agriculture or who would like to leave if they were given the opportunity to beef up their skills and capabilities. While recent federal legislation provides some retraining opportunities for alleviating obsolescence in poverty centers, it better relates to communities of larger towns and not enough will seep out to typical commercial farming regions to overcome disadvantages of displaced farmers. Also, funds for this purpose are yet too meager for sufficient coverage.

Accompanying a larger investment for retraining purposes should be counseling and guidance services which can help families decide when and whether they should remain in farming, and on the occupations and locations they should select as they make transfers. These facilities would upgrade their earning abilities and employment opportunities and lift many of the uncertainties which surround their transfer and moves. They would go far in helping relieve the misery in decision and change which face many families remaining in agriculture.

Not only should more retraining facilities be provided in

rural communities, but some type of in-schooling pay or unemployment compensation should be provided those farm operators who wish to cease farming and participate in retraining. This compensation would better allow them to support their families while they concentrate on acquiring new skills for off-farm employment. Without this element of the program, most farmers with families cannot take time out for adult retraining even if the necessary schools and facilities were available. A mechanism with experience behind it is the postwar G.I. on-the-job training. Some programs for distressed industrial or mining communities include these provisions. We mention these to indicate again that the means do not require any revolutionary social measures, but generally are represented in public legislation accepted in the present or past. The Netherlands now has this very combination of schools and in-training pay specifically for persons leaving agriculture.

SEVERANCE COMPENSATION FOR OLDER FARM PEOPLE

For older farm persons who lack flexibility in skills and have no prospect for retraining and relocation, current subsidies, paid if they remain in farming, might be reversed—given as payments if they terminated their farming operations. United States society has precedent in providing termination of severance payment to those released from particular employment. Such "mustering out" pay is traditional for armed services, as it is with many private firms. Its equivalent for technological unemployment or replacement in industry also is provided in unemployment compensation, possible between jobs, under the Social Security Act.

Severance payments actually might be used effectively with two groups of people: (a) For those who are still young enough for retraining and employment in other industries, the severance payment might be a substitute for, or be meshed with, transportation and retraining payments. Individuals could be given the choice of remaining in agriculture and receiving the existing small annual payments or leaving agriculture and receiving immediately in lump-sum form the amount that would otherwise accrue to them in the next several years. (b) For those too old to transfer and otherwise remain underemployed at low income in agriculture, severance pay could take the form of social security payments started at an earlier age. For example, if they ceased farming, their social security payments might be started at age 55. For an earlier reference to this possibility, and one now being exercised in Holland and England, see (3). Persons starting at 55 would have a lower payment, with the rate scaled up by years to 65. Hence, all would eventually graduate from the program. The Netherlands is using this plan for retiring older farmers in order that their small resource holdings might be recombined into adequate-sized units by farmers who remain. This kind of program could be on a voluntary basis so that only those who deem themselves to be made better off would participate.

AID IN THE RURAL COMMUNITY

For those communities where further thinning of the population is in sight and which do not qualify as strictly distressed poverty areas, the geographic spread of the individual community must be extended so that it provides a viable economic and civil unit. The typical rural county was laid out more than 100 years back, to mesh with distances and times for horse travel and a lower stage of capital technology. The same unit exists now but is too small and has too few persons to provide an area which is efficient in economic functions such as retailing and recreation, public services such as schools and churches, and civil services such as local government. Travel time no longer serves as the same restraint to extending the boundaries for these economic and public services. To accomplish these extensions to a scale allowing a sufficient supply and low cost of services, will require combining existing counties and trading areas into much larger units.

Changes of these magnitudes involve large costs and complex adjustments. As part of the minimum compensation to rural communities, with the need arising from structural reorganization of agriculture, society needs to provide them with the research and planning aids for reconstituting their communities and commercial public services. There are many alternatives for regrouping, with savings in some directions offsetting greater costs in other directions. If a Great Society is truly to be attained, these accomplishments are necessary as a social policy extending beyond pockets of rural poverty under programs of the Office of Economic Opportunity.

Other minimum compensation needs to be provided nonfarm persons in rural communities as the structural change of agriculture continues, farms become more specialized and fewer in number, and the farm labor is further reduced by substitution of capital technology. This minimum compensation might include in addition to the retraining and relocation or severance compensation for the farm population such measures as: (a) an extended or 10-year averaging of income tax payments, (b) federal aid to education designed specifically for these commercial farm regions and to offset reductions in the property tax base, (c) minimum income payments to bring income levels in line with what they would have been on Social Security or Workmen's Compensation, (d) an expanded and federalized employment service in rural areas, (e) "underemployment" compensation, (f) special college scholarships for eligible youth, and (g) perhaps some means for compensation of losses in asset values in rural towns as the farm population thins even more. Increase in economic opportunities to strengthen and aid the rural community, as it adjusts further to technological change in agriculture and national economic growth, must be given priority equal to that of compensation and aid for strengthening the agricultural economy.

Workable programs could be developed for rural communities affected most by the rapid structural changes of agriculture. Quantitative guides such as the rate of population decline, levels of per capita income, expenditures on education and training, or similar ones could be used to identify rural communities clearly in need of these compensation aids.

OPPORTUNITIES IN USE OF FREED FUNDS

In this chapter we have discussed programs and policies aimed at people—the people who sacrifice most from agricultural change. Largely, farm policies to date have focused on land, in controlling it as an input, on grain storage, and shipment of surplus food as foreign aid. Hence, they have been aimed at the people of farming and rural communities who suffer least from agricultural change. A main, long-run result of ongoing policies is that of higher land values, so that the income increment is cancelled for the next generation of farmers. What we need is a program that has the main long-run effect of broadening economic opportunity for the masses of the rural community. Some of the large funds now used for current farm programs should be shifted to these purposes. Hopefully, as wars can be brought to an end or as world food needs and commercial exports lessen the needs for public subsidies to commercial agriculture, funds will be freed to invest in those several groups in the rural community whose income position and economic opportunity will continue to decline even under a prosperous farming, but one which becomes much more capitalized and uses many fewer people. Whereas in the past, programs of agriculture were focused on people remaining on farms, the next phase of agriculturally related programs needs to be directed at qualified compensation of people who leave farms and the rural community generally.

LITERATURE CITED

1. Cochrane, W. W. The City Man's Guide to the Farm Problem. Minneapolis: Univ. of Minn. Press. 1965.
2. Griliches, Z. Research costs and social returns: Hybrid corn and related innovations. J. Pol. Econ. 56. 1958.
3. Heady, E. O. Adaptation of education and auxiliary aids to solution of the basic farm problem. J. Farm Econ. 39. 1956.
4. ———. Agricultural Policy Under Economic Development, Ames: Iowa State Univ. Press. 1962.
5. Taves, M. J. Impact of population decline and rural communities. In: Labor Mobility and Population in Agriculture. Ames: Iowa State Univ. Press. 1961.

CHAPTER TEN

The Rural Community and Its Relation to Farm Policies

RAYMOND J. PENN

RURAL AMERICA is, of course, changing very rapidly. New technology makes it possible for the farmer to supply food for more people every year, and still not produce at capacity. In 1960 each farm worker supplied 26 nonfarm people—five years later he produced enough food for 37 (1, p. 21).

Every year there are fewer farms, fewer farm workers, and fewer people living on farms. There were 6.1 million farms in the United States in 1940, 5.4 million in 1950, 3.7 million in 1960 (2, p. 434), and only 3.15 million in 1964 (3). The number of farm workers dropped from 9.9 million in 1950 to 7 million in 1960 and only 5.6 million in 1965 (3, p. 448). Professor Glenn Fuguitt estimates that the farm population decreased from 25 million in 1950 to 20.5 million in 1960. This means agriculture's share of the total population declined from 17 percent to only 11 percent in just ten years. (The latter data is from unpublished statistical estimates.)

The author is deeply indebted to Marion R. Brown, Assistant Professor of Agricultural Journalism, University of Wisconsin, for contributing major ideas to this topic.

This point will not be argued on the basis of principle. Community participation in policy decisions is important not only because it is democratic, but also because it is *essential* to an adequate formulation of goals and plans. The intent of this chapter is to show why it is essential. To do this, contextual material will be drawn upon and examples from experience and research both in the United States and in underdeveloped countries.

Technological change in other sectors of the economy have also affected rural communities. In addition to the continuous urban "pull" on rural people, there is constant and rapid change in rural industries, especially agricultural processing. Professor Hugh Cook gives us one illustration: On July 1, 1949, there were 2,250 dairy plants in Wisconsin. Fifteen years later more than half these plants had disappeared, leaving only 1,109. These trends will almost certainly continue. A recent projection of Wisconsin population predicts that most rural counties will probably lose population throughout the 1970's. The only counties expected to grow are those that are near an urban complex or that have industries or intensive recreation potential (4).

These few general illustrations serve only to demonstrate an obvious fact—U.S. farm economy is undergoing very rapid change. It is very important, of course, to analyze these changes and to understand the reasons for them—especially the part government agricultural policies have played in them. The primary burden of this chapter will not be to analyze the impact of past policies and impending issues on the rural community. Rather it will be to draw attention to the important role groups of people in local communities play in economic development. Rather than dealing with what is happening in the community, direction will be toward how the community can participate in resolving the issues we are all facing.

There is nothing new about the idea that "the people" should take part in public decisions and actions—it is an idea that most U.S. policy makers accept, at least in principle. However, it is an idea that enjoys precious little attention in practice. This is true in our domestic programs and doubly true in our attempts to help increase food production in other parts of the world.

First, the most pressing policy issue which we now face is the world food shortage. At the risk of repeating some of what is said in Chapter 1, this issue provides important contextual grounds for later points. Second, the present trend of thought regarding what to do about world food will be criticized on grounds that it ignores important institutional aspects of the issue. Thereby the problem is defined in such a way as to prelude an adequate solution. Third, we can go a long way toward eliminating this tendency to oversimplify the problem by giving local groups a larger part to play in the formulation of policy goals. Finally, it will be shown that communities can also play an important role in carrying out programs to meet policy goals.

FOOD AND POPULATION

Until very recently, the central issue in U.S. agricultural policy has been to hold farm production in line with effective demand. Programs to limit production were based primarily on federal inducements to the individual farmer to withdraw land from production. And land *was* withdrawn—more than 60 million acres of it. Since the fall of 1965, the United States has been reconsidering its production control policies in the framework of world food needs. Other food exporting countries, notably Canada, started modifying their agricultural programs in the light of world food needs several years before the United States. And, of course, increasing food production in the less developed countries has always been an important need. The present world food crisis has been developing for a long time, but is just now coming into sharp focus. According to FAO's preliminary estimates:

> World food production, excluding China (Mainland), was approximately the same in 1965–66 as the year before. Thus there was a fall of about 2 percent on a per capita basis.
> There were good harvests in North America, where food production rose by 4 percent. But Western Europe, with a rise of less than 1 percent, is the only other region where there was any increase in food production in 1965–66. . . . Food production fell slightly in Eastern Europe and in the U.S.S.R., and by 6 percent in Oceania. . . . In Africa, Latin America, and the Far East, excluding China (Mainland), food production is estimated to have fallen by about 2 percent in total and by 4 to 5 percent on a per capita basis. . . . Preliminary estimates for 1965–66 indicate that per capita food production in developing regions dropped back to the same level as in 1957–58, which in turn is the same as the inadequate prewar (World War II) level. In the Far East, Latin America, and Africa per capita food production in 1965–66 was a good deal less than before the war (14, p. 3).

Total world population is increasing faster than the food supply, and to make matters worse the food supply is not increasing at all in the countries where population growth is most rapid.

It seems clear that a worldwide program to reduce the rate of population growth—family planning—is most urgently needed. This goal will require much more consideration and investment than the nations of the world are now giving it.

However, even if such a program could immediately limit the birth rate to a level that would maintain a long-run balance of population with available food supplies, the need for substantially increased amounts of food in the short run would continue. Movement of the present large population through their fertile years will continue to increase over-all population and the labor force will continue to grow under any situation until the year 2000 (9).

United States policy makers have become increasingly aware of this problem, and new policy goals are coming into focus. President Johnson, in his 1967 State of the Union address referred briefly to the need for increased world food production (and also for family planning). Immediately following the President's address, former Undersecretary of State George Ball told a nation-wide TV audience that the President had, in his reference to world food production, spoken of the most critical problem the world now faces. The new policy focus, then, is on increasing food production somewhat in the United States and on doing much more to help increase it in other countries, especially those in the early stages of development.

HOW TO BRING ABOUT A SOLUTION

It will not be as easy as many economists would have us believe. Some economists even lead us to make the wrong kinds of observations by defining economics so as to exclude the most important aspects of economic development.

Earl Heady notes, "Theoretically we already have the framework or models for specifying the variables which result in economic development of agriculture." He further says, "What is less obvious is how to overcome the political, cultural, intellectual, and similar restraints, largely exogenous to the agricultural development process which prevents 'getting on with the job.'" (5, p. 1.) What is implied here is that an economist can look at the cost of physical inputs and the value of physical outputs (assuming market prices to put values on the inputs and the products) and determine highest profits or least cost combinations. This, of course, is very helpful and very important and it does place some limits on the alternative courses of action with regard to many policy goals. But it certainly is not sufficient by itself to define the policy goal or to fix the course of action. Whether or not the economist wants to admit them, the "political, cultural, intellectual, and similar restraints" will affect the outcome of any program. These factors don't fit into present econometric models— nor do they lend themselves to easy measurement and quantification. But they certainly are not, as Heady says, "exogenous to the agricultural development process." If we look closely at such catch-all labels ("social," "political," and "cultural") as they are used by economists, we find that they refer to what Commons and others have called "institutional factors." They are the working rules of society—the social inventions that govern relationships between people and affect their control over each other and over physical resources. They affect the power structure and the distribution of income and employment opportunities. They guide the actions of individuals, furnish the procedures for resolving conflicts between them, as well as the framework within which to plan and carry out public programs. An understanding of them is essential to any strategy for change.

Agricultural development programs must deal with questions about how local roads and schools can be built and maintained, how land and labor contracts are made and enforced, how local officials are selected, how local tax revenues are spent, how the local church serves in matters of finance and leadership, how merchants operate, and how local power holders support national officials and are in turn supported by them. These local structural factors are as important as physical inputs in determining agriculture's productivity. They dictate how farms wll be organized, what crops will be produced, what technology will be used, and how the products will be reinvested and consumed.

We will not get far into the matter of economic change as long as our attention is focused narrowly on questions of how to combine physical inputs and refuse to ask questions about these structural factors—about the rules people establish to control their mutual relations and their economic decisions. These rules may be noneconomic in somebody's definition of economics. But they certainly are part and parcel of the economic development problem, and this is true for the United States as well as for the underdeveloped countries. A majority of U.S. economists have felt secure in the belief that almost any amount of agricultural food products could be had simply by releasing the 60 million acres of diverted land and raising farm prices slightly. Some economists, including this author, doubt that it will be all that easy to get increased production. The diverted acres (in the Great Plains, on dairy farms, and in the Corn Belt) are considerably less productive than the land that is now in production. There are many fewer farmers and farm workers than there were 15 years ago—probably too few to bring those 60 million acres back quickly. More technology could be applied to existing farms, but technological change has been going on at a very rapid pace for many years. It may be hard to accelerate that pace. In short, it took a lot of changes in the working rules of our society and our economy to get that land out of production. It will take more institutional changes to bring it back.

Even if U.S. production could be increased very rapidly—and if we and other exporting nations were willing to pay enormous transportation and handling costs—we could not produce and distribute enough to bring world food supplies in balance with needs. Our exports have been at an all-time high level—more than $6 billion a year for three years, and nearly $7 billion last year—yet they have scarcely made a dent in the world food shortage.

When U.S. economists talk about increasing production in the underdeveloped nations, their prescriptions are similar to those they would apply in the United States—bring more land into production, develop new technology, and adjust prices. As has just been argued, these remedies don't work even in the United States without institutional adjustments to make them relevant and effective at the local level. In underdeveloped countries these conventional policy prescriptions are, by themselves, even less adequate. Without substantial institutional change, it is very doubtful that they can even be applied at all. And even if they can—if production can be increased sharply without any "reforms," the food problem will not really be solved. A very important part of the problem is "Food for Whom?" Without changes in the structure in these countries so as to distribute the increase more widely and to expand opportunities for secure economic employment, the result could still be instability and even violence. To illustrate this point, Professor Peter Dorner, Director of the University of Wisconsin Land Tenure Center, has cited the examples of Guatemala and Ecuador. In Guatemala, agricultural production in the sixties has been 17 percent higher than it was in the late fifties. In Ecuador there has been a 9 percent increase in the same period. Yet in both countries, political and economic instability have increased, and the possibility of massive violence is as great as ever.

Our own history is filled with examples of how structural factors, or working rules, affect economic growth. One of the most important things such rules do is to determine the incentives an individual has to increase his production. Line-fence laws, zoning ordinances, water laws, and property rights are all examples of the kinds of rules considered here—the kinds of rules that sometimes have to be changed before price adjustments, extension programs, and other conventional development tactics can have an effect.

Property rights are among the most important working rules of an economy because they control access to the use of resources. They determine whether people can actually make economic decisions on investments and use of land. Even more significant for change and economic development, property rights can give or take away a person's incentive to make an "economic" decision. If a person has a secure right to the future use of a resource and the returns from that use, he will be more likely to invest and otherwise improve or develop the resource.

In western South Dakota during the late 1930's, the rancher knew that it was profitable in the long run to limit grazing and practice other range management improvements. He knew it was profitable to develop stock water dams and that federal programs would give him financial assistance for their construction. Why didn't the rancher do these things? Because he did not have control of the resources. Owners of the land had let it become tax delinquent and had moved away. Some of this land was taken by the county on tax deed with intent to resell as soon as possible. Other land was in the tax delinquency "no man's land." It was neither private nor public. Taxes on the land were several times higher than its earning power. Research on the management of tax delinquent land was undertaken in an effort to develop procedures that would give operators enough security of tenure so they could make investment in range improvements (8).

In Wisconsin a farmer along the Black River was to lose his farm by foreclosure in two years. His soil consisted of a rather thin layer of productive top soil over a deep layer of sand. The farm could have been protected by a few investments to prevent deep gulley erosion. Did the farmer make those investments? No. He farmed to make the most profit in the current year even though the result was permanent destruction of the entire farm in two years.

Leonard Salter was prompted to do his research on land tenure by the Wisconsin Soil Conservation Service, which asked,

"Why do tenants invest less than owners in what we think are profitable soil erosion control practices?" (13.)

This insecurity of access to resources has a similar effect on farmers in other countries. Insecure subsistence farmers in Latin America should not be expected to take the risk of new technology. Neither should they be expected to respond to price when there is no assurance or knowledge of a place to sell the products profitably or of what products will be available to buy and at what price.

So in the less developed countries of the world, even more than in the United States, it is not enough to know how to produce more and what inputs are needed. We need to look at how people control their resources—property, tenure, working rules, and institutions.

LOCAL PARTICIPATION

It is with respect to these institutional factors that groups of people representing local communities make their greatest contribution to public policy and programs. Working rules and institutions are formed in many ways and at all levels of government. However, a rule governing relations between people generally must be accepted and even enforced by local groups, local government, and local communities. The best way for policy makers to avoid overly technocratic and irrelevant solutions is to involve such groups in the planning process.

It is necessary, of course, that policy planning be based on research and technical appraisal of the consequences of alternative action. This is where the skilled economist can play a key role—especially if he understands how local institutions function. The role of the local community is emphasized in the planning process because it is too often overlooked by economic technicians or planners. It seems to be too common, perhaps because it is easier and more natural, for the technician to use only cost-benefit analysis to arrive at a judgment as to what is the better course of action. The person who disagrees often is considered to lack knowledge and understanding. Actually he may have very useful information that the technician lacks.

More often than not, people in the local community have a vital interest in the outcome of the analysis because they must live with the consequences of the plan. These people have actual experience and insights which should be taken into account in the planning process. They may have very different values. And,

perhaps most important, they are familiar with the local structure and they know how it operates. They may not know it
analytically and they may have difficulty articulating their understanding of it. But they do understand it functionally. That is,
they know how to live and work and survive within it. Therefore, their experiences have important bearing on any issue which
involves institutional change.

An adequate planning or policy-making procedure requires
integration of: (a) technicians from several disciplines, (b) program administration officials, (c) legislative representatives, and
(d) the people affected. The Land Use Planning Program of the
USDA and Land Grant Colleges from 1937–42 contained many
fundamental ideas and procedures needed to accomplish this integration. An attempt was made to reorganize the USDA so that
all programs—research, extension, and action—would carry out the
results of the integrated planning process (11). In many major
program reorganizations, personal and bureaucratic frictions develop. The Land Use Planning Program was no exception. Frictions at the Washington agency level and with the American
Farm Bureau Federation were particularly severe. Unfortunately
we remember the frictions and problems rather than the value of
the ideas. Actually it was not so much the frictions as the outbreak of World War II that prevented this program from being
tested.

Many examples in our history show the value of having
people in local communities participate in policy and program
formulation.

1. In the late 1930's, U.S. agricultural programs included
one in the Great Plains described as the Restoration Program
under which the rancher was paid to re-grass certain lands that
should never have been planted to wheat. An evaluation of this
program in two South Dakota counties suggested several changes
which came largely from the advice of local people. For one
thing, it became clear that a regulation to require seeding was not
desirable. There wasn't enough seed, the seed didn't grow, and
it cost nearly as much as the land was worth. When left to use
their own judgment as to what land should be in the program
and returned to grass, local people made better decisions than
were made later when each county was given an acreage quota
with pressure on the local people to fill it.

2. Zoning is a use of public power to enforce a plan. But
many communities do not want to use such force for regulating
land use in their areas. Where this power is used it is nearly

always carried out by local governments and based on locally formulated plans. In the period when rural zoning was beginning in Wisconsin (1934), Professor W. A. Rowlands conducted an extension program in 27 northern counties. In addition to helping with the legal steps for adopting a zoning ordinance (two actions by the county board of supervisors, public hearing, and approval by the town board) Professor Rowlands met with local people including town board officials. At these meetings they discussed such questions as what changes in land use might be desirable, and what rural zoning could do. The local people made the decision to proceed with a zoning ordinance and set district boundaries. With these "extralegal" steps, as they were called by Professor Rowlands, rural zoning ordinances were passed in 27 counties with a total of only 22 dissenting votes.

On one occasion, a group of technicians from Madison drew up the boundaries for a forest district (in which year-round settlement was restricted). They made this district as large as they thought local people would accept. However, local people, without seeing the work of the technicians, placed more land in the forest district. The technicians agreed that the larger area more nearly represented what should be in the forest district.

More recently local people in Wisconsin have taken the initiative to develop three new types of use districts. One county has a district which limits the use of the flood plain. Another has a lake-shore protection district and a third has a highway interchange district.

3. In another Wisconsin illustration, the State Highway Commission planned a highway through a county which would bisect the best land in the county. Local people prepared an alternative route. The Highway Commission considered the alternate route and found that it was less costly if the state left the good farm land unmolested, and it resulted in a much more scenic highway.

These three illustrations can be expanded by anyone's experiences from all parts of the country. It is enough, however, to demonstrate that the local community can contribute and should be an integral part of any formulation of policy goals or planning.

PROGRAM ADMINISTRATION AT THE LOCAL LEVEL

Communities also have an important role in the administration of programs.

Planning and administration cannot, of course, be completely separated. USDA officials in the late 1930's anticipated that the soil conservation district would be an action device to put land use plans into effect. This use of the local soil conservation districts has not really been tested, however, since only a few districts in the United States have ever applied land use regulations. But soil conservation districts have become the local unit and sponsor of the Soil Conservation Service (see also, 10, and 6).

In the United States, local groups, when given authority, have actively organized and carried out development programs. In the late 1920's, grazing districts managed by local people were attempting to get greater security of land use in order to develop programs for better range use. Montana grazing districts were given more authority and actually developed the idea of grazing districts to the extent that they were incorporated in the federal Taylor Grazing Act of 1934 (7).

In 1965, the Wisconsin State Legislature passed a major water law. One part of the law authorized counties to zone shorelands. This was done to permit counties not only to guide shoreland development, but also to protect the lakes and streams against uses that cause pollution.

Wisconsin communities are also using the town sanitary district as a device to organize themselves and protect against pollution. With increased concern over water pollution, we may expect communities to expand these types of efforts.

Currently in Wisconsin, local governments and a state agency are at odds as to how to set priorities for use of some forest land. About 2.5 million acres are in the cooperative forest crop program of the state. The land is owned by the counties but managed in partnership with the state and with technical guidance from the state.

It was intended that land needed for "a higher use" could be withdrawn from the program by mutual agreement. The local government feels that some of the land put into irrigation would have a value of $400 an acre when developed and that this is a higher use since it is more than the $6 to $10 assessed valuation of other comparable land. The issue has been drawn when the state agency not only said that this would *not* be a higher use, but also claimed to have authority to make the final decision without county approval. As expected, local governments have introduced legislation to get the state laws changed so they can withdraw lands in their counties at will. If the basic partnership idea, so necessary for the continuation of the program, is maintained, law and procedures must be modified so this decision remains a joint one.

One part of the Soil Bank program could have been much improved if recognition had been given to local group action. The Conservation Reserve section of the Soil Bank was designed to permanently shift cropland to other than agricultural uses. One provision was a rental contract with other cost-sharing features which permitted the farmer to shift at least 2 acres of land to forest use. The rental contract could run for 15 years.

Emphasis on price policy programs with the individual farmer as the decision maker made this forestry program much less effective than it could have been.

Obviously if the goal is a 200-acre forest, 100 farmers selecting the 2 acres they want in trees is a very unsatisfactory method. The decision unit was not appropriate. Instead, the community should have made some plans and decided whether a 200-acre forest would be desirable. Then the tract best suited with respect to soil, topography, and location should be decided on. The community could have performed a major function in this program. If it had been given the opportunity, I suspect more permanent forests would have resulted from less expenditure.

Up to this point, the attempt has been to demonstrate that the effectiveness of any program depends upon local support and participation. Only U.S. illustrations have been used.

We also have evidence to indicate that the structure and functioning of the local community is vital in the economic development programs of the less developed countries. Without some changes in the local structure so that more people become involved in the community and have income and employment opportunities, all our efforts to increase production may increase conflicts within the less developed country without making any permanent friends for the United States.

Research by the Land Tenure Center in Latin America indicates that where responsible local organizations exist, development programs are more effective (12). The local organization can give the individual some incentive by giving him more secure access to resources. It can give him a device to improve his community (schools, water, and health). It can give him someone to talk to and a vehicle for two-way communication with his government and the "outside world." And by no means least important, there is some evidence, particularly in Venezuela, that local organization can actually help maintain political stability.

Research done by the LTC has focused on land tenure and

the economic and social structure of rural communities in Latin America. (The Land Tenure Center does research and training in Latin American land tenure. It is financed in a large part by U.S. AID. The research is done in partnership with host country research institutions and professionals, and most of it has been done in rural communities.) FAO and CIDA have been conducting similar research in Latin America. Until recently, however, not much attention was given to rural community organizations in less developed countries. Even now we are giving it much too little consideration as we make an all-out effort to increase world food production.

LITERATURE CITED

1. Agr. Handbook No. 325. USDA. 1966.
2. Agr. Statistics 1966. USDA. 1966.
3. Census of Agriculture, 1964. Prelim. Rpt., Bur. of Census, Washington, D.C.
4. Fuchs, Z., R. B. Kearl, and D. G. Marshall. Population Changes and Forecasts in Wisconsin Counties 1960–1980. No. 11, Population Series, Wisconsin's Population. Dec., 1966.
5. Heady, E. O. Processes and Priorities in Agricultural Development. Paper presented at the Univ. of Florida Developmental Seminar. 1966.
6. Hardin, C. W. Soil Conservation. Glencoe, Ill.: Free Press. 1952.
7. Loomer, C. W. and V. W. Johnson. Group tenure in administration of public lands. USDA Cir. 829. Dec., 1949.
8. ———— and R. J. Penn. County Land Management in Northwestern Dakota. S.D. Agr. Exp. Sta. Bul. 326. S.D. State College, Brookings. 1938.
9. Myrdahl, G. Opening address at the Second World Land Reform Conference, FAO, Rome. June 20, 1966.
10. Parks, R. W. Soil Conservation Districts in Action. Ames: Iowa State Univ. Press. 1952.
11. Planning for Permanent Agriculture. USDA Misc. Publ. No. 351. 1939; Land Use Planning Underway. USDA. July, 1940; Gaus, J. and L. Wolcott. In: Public Administration and the U.S. Chicago: Donnelley and Sons. 1940.
12. Powell, J. Campesina Federation of Venezuela. Univ. of Wis. Ph.D. Thesis, 1966, supported by the Land Tenure Center. (To be published as a book.)
13. Salter, L. A. Land Tenure in Process. Res. Bul. 46, Wis. Agr. Exp. Sta., Madison. Feb., 1943.
14. The State of Food and Agriculture, 1966. FAO of the United Nations, Rome. 1966.

CHAPTER ELEVEN

Policies To Meet the Needs
of Commercial Farms
in the Next Two Decades

DONALD R. KALDOR, WALLACE OGG, and
WILLIAM E. SAUPE

THE GOAL of this chapter is to discuss long-range economic policy for commercial agriculture. It is assumed that the primary objective is to improve the economic performance of commercial agriculture. The point of view accepted is that the need for policy and for modifications in policy arises because of differences (gaps) between actual performance and desired (preferred) performance of the industry. The view is also accepted that policy instruments for eliminating performance gaps should be selected on the basis of benefits or contributions to improved performance in relation to costs or value of the alternatives foregone.

The discussion is divided into four main parts. The first focuses on performance goals, followed by an evaluation of the industry's recent performance, then future adjustment needs, and the final section is concerned with program direction. The emphasis throughout is on long-range considerations. It is recognized that in achieving longer-run goals there must be a transition from the current situation to the preferred long-run situation. In this transition, short-run needs must be taken into account.

The important impact that commercial farm policy will have on the rural community will not be discussed here. Commercial farms are defined to exclude noncommercial farmers as discussed by Tolley in Chapter 12. Commercial farmers are defined as those that have adequate human and physical resources so that if they are organized effectively their income will exceed the poverty level. Their output is produced primarily for the market, and farm production is the major income generating activity. Commercial farmers may be grouped several ways. For policy purposes one such grouping is on the basis of age. This in turn is associated with job mobility.

Estimates based on Census of Agriculture data indicate that about one-half of the 1964 population of commercial farm operators will die or reach retirement age by 1980. The older commercial farmers are relatively immobile. Few will leave the farm for nonfarm employment in the interim.

A second relevant category of commercial farmers are those that are now below age 50. They are relatively more mobile than the older group. They can adjust their farm business or they can leave farming. A recent Iowa study found the median age of farmers who quit farming and took nonfarm jobs in the 1959–61 period was 39 years (7).

The third category of farm people toward which agricultural policies will have a decisive impact is the potential entry group. This group is made up largely of young people who are considering the alternatives of farming and nonfarm employment. With more farming entrants, less land will be available for existing farmers to add to their units through consolidation.

The definition of commercial farmer used in this chapter does not coincide with the Census of Agriculture definition. The definition used here would likely include all Census Class I and II farms, most Class III and IV farms, and smaller proportions of Classes V and VI farms. This definition excludes the part-time farmer and semiretired farmers as defined by the Census. It also excludes a farmer in Census Commercial Class V or VI, if his resources would not allow him to generate an income greater than the "poverty level."

Some farmers are able to rationally decide to be part-time

farmers. They can fit their farming enterprises around a non-farm job. Their farms may be organized in a way that meets economic efficiency criteria with comparable returns to the resources that are used. These efficiently organized part-time farms may provide a fourth relevant category of farms.

PERFORMANCE GOALS

People in general have an interest in the economic performance of the farm industry. Nonfarm people are especially interested in the industry's performance as a supplier of food and fiber. Likewise, they are interested in the demand for purchased farming inputs and consumer products the industry provides. Farm people are particularly interested in its performance as a source of income and as a means of using their labor and management skills and investment capital.

There are varied interests, even among farm people. Although both the corn farmer and the livestock feeder may be interested in the industry's income-generating performance, the corn farmer's interest may focus on income from feed production. The feeder's interest may emphasize income from livestock.

Because of economic interdependence, all of these interests are related, but not always compatible, particularly in the short run. As a result, individual performance goals vary and this variation gives rise to policy disagreements.

It would be useful to have an unambiguous specification of the performance goals which reflect the public or social interest, that is, the weighted interests of all people. But such a precise specification is not available. Without it, some assumptions have to be made about performance goals for the farm industry. If these goals are to have political realism, they should be reasonably consistent with the broader goals of the American people. Farm people are a minority group and their political power is waning as a result of reapportionment. Industry goals which have strong justification on grounds of complementarity with national goals and equality of treatment are likely to have the widest acceptance.

There are four broad social goals that appear to be most relevant to the selection of performance goals for commercial agriculture: growth, efficiency, equity, and stability (4, 10). The industry goals that follow were selected with these social goals in mind.

GROWTH

1. *A rising trend in the productivity (output per unit of total input) of farm resources consistent with the general scarcity of investment goods and the relative opportunities offered by the farm industry to contribute to national economic growth* is the first goal.

Opportunities to increase resource productivity will be offered the farm industry by public and private investment in agricultural research, the production of new, more productive reproducible inputs, and general and agricultural education. Exploitation of these opportunities implies appropriate farmer motivation, cost-price relationships, credit facilities, and other conditions. This goal implies that people in their roles as consumers would continue to experience a decline in the real price of food and fiber.

PRODUCTION EFFICIENCY

The next three goals regard production efficiency.

2. *Supply an adequate total quantity of food and fiber for domestic and export needs.*

An adequate total quantity is defined as an amount of current production plus stocks which will persistently clear markets (that is, meet domestic and export demands, including public and private inventory demands) at prices that permit comparable returns for labor and capital on well-organized farms.

3. *Produce a mix of farm products reasonably well geared to relative demands for different kinds of food and fiber.*

4. *Supply the needed quantity of each product at the lowest cost consistent with available technical know-how and the prices of farm inputs.*

EQUITY

Following are four goals dealing with equity.

5. *Income-earning opportunities for labor and capital on commercial farms equal to those offered by other industries, allowing for any differential amenities. Further allowance is made for the preferences of people for different kinds of work.*

To be consistent with production efficiency, this goal would need to be achieved by adjusting the structure and organization of the industry. It is recognized that this requirement may have to be compromised in the short run. Current programs which reduce income-earning disparities by encouraging a less efficient use of resources are not likely to be overhauled all at once. A transitional period seems essential.

6. *Equality of opportunity for commercial farm people to participate in public welfare programs and public services, including education.*

7. *Equality of treatment of resource ownership and control arrangements in commercial agriculture.*

There appear to be no strong logical or factual grounds for discriminatory treatment of ownership and control arrangements in the farm industry. This goal implies that arrangements in all industries would be subject to evaluation and modification on the basis of uniform criteria related to social goals.

8. *A degree of income inequality within commercial agriculture consistent with the national concept of distributive justice.*

Income differences arising in the pursuit of economic growth and efficiency goals under our mixed enterprise system are restrained by national policy instruments such as the progressive income tax, "free" education, and welfare programs. These actions imply a social goal of greater income equality. As applied to commercial agriculture, this means that programs designed to change the distribution of income should reduce, not increase, income differences among families.

STABILITY

The final two goals consist of stability considerations.

9. *Provide a stability in the year-to-year flow of farm products into the channels of trade and consumption consistent with the efficient production and use of farm products over time.*

10. *Achieve a degree of farm price and income stability reasonably consistent with the adjustment needs of the industry arising in the process of growth and development.*

These performance goals for commercial agriculture provide the basis for this appraisal of recent economic performance and for identifying policy needs and directions. It should be recognized that use of a significantly different set of goals would produce a change in the appraisal of the problem. Identification of policy needs and programs also would change.

APPRAISAL OF RECENT PERFORMANCE

How well has the commercial farm industry been meeting these performance goals? A reasonably complete and refined answer to this question would require a major research effort. Offered here are some tentative judgments based in part on recent studies relating to certain aspects of the question.

GROWTH IN RESOURCE PRODUCTIVITY

The farm industry's productivity growth performance since World War II may be categorized as excellent or moderately good, depending on the standard used in making the judgment. The rating is excellent if one compares the farm industry of the United States with that of other countries. The U.S. farm industry has had one of the highest, if not *the* highest, rates of secular growth in farm resource productivity (output per unit of measured total input) in the world.

The high growth rate in the United States can be explained largely by considerations relating to the creation and exploitation of new opportunities for raising productivity. Large investments have been made in: (a) agricultural research and development activities; (b) general and agricultural education; and (c) facilities to produce new, more productive reproducible inputs arising from research and development activities. Thus, new opportunities have been created for commercial farmers to increase resource productivity. Conditions also have been conducive to exploitation of these opportunities by commercial farmers. Farmer motivation, price-cost relationships, and credit facilities, among other things, have been relatively favorable. As a result the measured productivity of resources on many commercial farms has risen rapidly.

If one compares actual productivity increase with the potential productivity increase permitted by the rising stock of technological and managerial knowledge, the performance rating is not as high. The exploitation of the opportunities for raising resource productivity has been highly uneven among farms. Moreover, the industry has not been able to fully adapt its resource structure and organization to the impact of improved technology, the changing pattern of input prices, and a relatively slow growth in the demand for farm products. As a consequence the potential increase in resource productivity has not been fully realized. Thus, there exists a gap in meeting the minimum-cost goal for production efficiency.

PRODUCTION EFFICIENCY

Regarding the goal of adequate food and fiber, it is clear that until recently the farm industry has been producing more than enough to meet domestic and export demands at prices that would permit comparable returns for labor and capital on well-organized farms. During most of the 1950's, the excess supply probably was upwards of 8 percent of total output.

For a time, much of the surplus was simply removed from markets under the government loan and purchase programs. As excessive stocks accumulated, production controls were instituted. The early control programs, however, had little effect on total farm output, although they did change the mix of products produced. Farmers shifted resources from controlled crops to uncontrolled crops and this resulted in increased feed grain production.

The failure of these programs to reduce total output prompted a more generalized control effort with features that limited substitution among crops. The newer control programs were based on the withdrawal of land from current production. In the 1962–65 period, the land withdrawal programs removed upwards of 60 million acres. This effort has had a substantial output-decreasing effect, helping to reduce the imbalance in the level of total output.

Since the early 1960's, commercial export demand for U.S. foodstuffs has expanded at a fairly rapid pace. Although cotton exports declined, the dollar value of all commercial farm exports more than doubled between 1959 and 1965. Exports under government foreign assistance and surplus disposal programs rose about 30 percent in the same period.

The combined effects of increased exports and land retirement permitted a large reduction in surplus stocks without appreciable decline in the level of farm prices until 1967. During 1967, however, there was a substantial decline in prices received and a continued increase in prices paid. Between 1961 and 1965, wheat stocks dropped 42 percent and feed grain stocks dropped 36 percent. Meanwhile cotton stocks rose about 96 percent. But in 1967, cotton production dropped sharply as a result both of lower yields and reduced acreage. At the end of the 1967 crop year, cotton stocks were down 27 percent from the 1966 level. In contrast, 1967 year-end stocks of wheat and feed grain were higher.

The ratio of prices received by farmers to prices paid by farmers (1910–14 = 100) stood at 79 in 1961, 77 in 1965, and 80 in 1966. In 1967, this had dropped to a level of about 73. In the Midwest, a ratio in the neighborhood of 78, with relative prices at recent historical levels, appears to be high enough to permit opportunity cost returns on well-organized farms but not on other farms. This judgment is based on a study of 1959 factor earnings on well-organized farms in the North Central states and on the likely effects of more recent technological and economic developments (8).

The mix of products in total farm output has shown some imbalance in recent years, but this has not been as serious as other production imbalances. Although wheat was the major problem product in this respect in the 1950's, its relative balance position has been greatly improved as a result of production controls and export expansion. More recently, cotton has been the main problem product. Imbalances in the product mix are relatively easy to correct, since farmers are quite responsive in the short run to changes in differential returns offered by the production of different products.

How has the farm industry scored with respect to the minimum cost goal? In a long-run context, this undoubtedly has been the most serious production imbalance of all, even though it has not received much public attention. It is reflected in interfarm variation in the difference between gross return and the long-run opportunity cost of the resources used on individual farms. With a given set of product prices, there are wide interfarm differences in the long-run earnings of labor and capital that cannot be accounted for by inherent qualitative differences. This imbalance has its origin in the changing pattern of resource productivities and input prices associated with technological advance and economic growth. These developments have been modifying the resource characteristics of the well-organized farm. But the changes have been reflected very unevenly in the organization of individual farms. Some have made the adjustments in size and in the mix of land, labor, and capital enabling production at near minimum costs. On the vast majority of farms, however, adjustments have lagged. Some have fallen behind badly.

In a recent study of an income-efficient farm industry in the North Central states, it was estimated that in 1959, if all farms had been as efficiently organized as the most efficient farms, total output would have nearly doubled and at the same time total resource costs would have declined 10 percent (8). This points to a large gap between actual cost and the goal of minimum cost. Another recent study also indicates that there has been a serious imbalance in the total cost of producing the output of farm products (13).

Under recent control programs, substantial amounts of land have been withdrawn from current production. The opportunity cost of using this land in producing farm commodities has been near zero. Insofar as this land could be substituted for labor and capital, inputs with relatively high opportunity costs, the total opportunity cost of producing the control level of farm output could be reduced. In a long-run context, it is clear that reducing output by land retirement increases the real cost of producing the nation's food and fiber supply.

EQUITY

The performance goals relating to equity involve (a) equality of income-earning opportunities for labor and capital, (b) equality of opportunity to participate in public welfare programs and public services, (c) equality of treatment of resource ownership and control arrangements, and (d) distributive justice in income redistribution programs.

With respect to the first, there is substantial evidence that for many years the income-generating efficiency (the terms on which resource services are rewarded) of the farm industry has compared unfavorably with that of most other industries. For example, estimates for 1959 indicate that the typical commercial farm in the North Central states paid a reward for labor and investment capital which was only about one-third as large as that paid "comparable" resources in the nonfarm economy (8). And this reward included the income effects of the support programs.

The reward to labor has shown the greatest disparity, and the reasons are fairly clear. Advances in farm technology have raised the productivity of new forms of capital more than the productivity of labor. At the same time, labor has become relatively more expensive than capital inputs. As a result, the minimum cost-mix has moved in the direction of more capital and less labor, inducing a relative redundancy of labor. Since the input of labor has not declined in accordance with the decline in demand, labor earnings have been depressed relative to capital earnings.

It needs to be recognized, however, that returns to labor and investment capital have varied widely among farms. During much of the period since 1950, rewards on well-organized farms have been fairly well in line with those in nonfarm employments.

This probably would not have been true without the support programs. But only a small proportion of all commercial farms have been in the well-organized category. In general, farm prices under the support programs have been high enough to permit comparable returns, but relatively few farms have been organized to earn such returns. The disparity in returns among farms producing similar products has reflected the gap in minimum-cost performance.

How have farm people fared with respect to equality of opportunity to participate in welfare programs and public services? The evidence is not very clear for some programs and services; it is more adequate for others.

There is some presumption, but sketchy evidence, that farm people have been at some disadvantage in participating in welfare programs when the need arises. Certainly farmers made real progress toward equality on a major front when they were included a few years ago for participation in social security. A recent study of retired farmers in Iowa indicated that 95 percent of those in a statewide sample were receiving social security payments (3).

There also is some presumption, supported by very little evidence, that farmers may be at some disadvantage in using the federal-state cooperative employment service. Available evidence does clearly suggest that employment aspirations are lower among rural people than among urban people of comparable ability (2). This may or may not be related to availability of information about employment requirements and opportunities.

The area of clearest inequality of opportunity for public services is in education. While the research evidence does not sharply focus on the gaps and especially on the size of the differential opportunities, it all seems to point in one direction: children and young people from farms and small rural communities are at a decided disadvantage.

Schools in these areas have not been supported as adequately as in urban areas and the poorer the area the less adequate has been the support. Schools for Negroes and poor white children in farm areas of the South are an example, but the same holds for schools in areas of low-asset values in the Midwest.

By all widely accepted standards of judgment, rural elementary and secondary education in the rural South, Midwest, and the Great Plains has been inferior to that available in urban and metropolitan areas. Elementary teacher quality seems to have been a critical variable. Evidence indicates that teacher quality is closely associated with teacher salary levels. In many farm areas, elementary teacher salaries have been low and have not been competitive in the national market for well-trained personnel (1).

Research on pupil preparation for college indicates that graduates from small rural high schools have not been as well prepared for college entrance as those from urban and metropolitan schools (5). A smaller proportion of young farm people go to college, which probably reflects not only poorer preparation but also differences in incomes, occupational preferences, and values attached to higher education. Vocational and technical education beyond high school has been less available for young people on farms than for young people from urban areas; although this difference now seems to be diminishing. The evidence strongly suggests that in the area of public education, farm people have not had equality of opportunity. Since investment in education plays a critical role in economic growth, in agricultural adjustment, and in providing equality of income opportunities and distributive justice, the elimination of the educational gap is of paramount importance.

What has been the performance with respect to the income distribution goal? During the period following World War II, the price and income support programs have provided substantial income benefits for commercial agriculture. Historically, the justification for these programs has been based largely on income needs. Allegedly, the free market would not provide farm people with a fair share of the nation's income and so programs were needed to redistribute income in favor of agriculture. The income benefits have been induced partly by maintaining prices persistently above uncontrolled free-market levels and partly by direct government payments to producers.

In both cases, the amount of income benefit received by the individual participating producer has been related directly to the size of his farming operation. This has meant that the dollar benefit received by the large-scale producer has been much greater than that received by the small-scale producer. Since larger producers tend to have higher incomes than smaller, the effect has been to widen absolute income differences among farm families. Moreover, many of the larger producers receiving program benefits have had higher incomes than people who have contributed to these benefits through higher prices and/or higher taxes. As a result of the methods used to redistribute income, there has been a strong tendency toward greater inequality rather than less.

It needs to be recognized that efforts to encourage growth and efficiency may also have unequalizing effects on the distribution of income. For example, it is highly likely that public investment in agricultural research and extension activities has increased income differences within agriculture. Of course this has not been the objective of these activities, rather a side effect. In this case the tendency toward greater income inequality has been generated in pursuing the goal of economic growth. In the case of the price and income support programs, the main objective has been to redistribute income, but the income distribution effects generated have been inconsistent with available indicators of the national concept of distributive justice.

STABILITY

The short-run stability performance of the industry seems to have been relatively good, particularly as related to instability induced by weather fluctuations and emergency demands. Of course the success of general economic stability policy has minimized sharp shifts in domestic demands for farm products. Farm prices have shown only moderate year-to-year fluctuations under the support programs. Storage policy has helped to stabilize the flow of feed grains into animal production.

In the 1950's and early 1960's stocks were permitted to grow to levels higher than needed for stabilization purposes with attendant heavy carrying charges. And because support programs did not fully recognize the product and resource allocation functions of prices, the cost of additional price stability has been unnecessarily high. Some parts of the industry still experience self-generating cycles of over- and underproduction accompanied by inverse price movements. Past support programs have done little to temper this kind of instability.

ADJUSTMENT NEEDS

The performance gaps relating to production efficiency and equal income-earning opportunities reflect a serious lag in the adaptation of the industry's resource structure and organization to the forces associated with economic growth. These forces have been especially strong during the past two decades. Even though the industry has been adjusting rapidly in terms of historical standards, the rate has not kept pace with the forces inducing a need for adaptation. In many areas, the annual rate of decline in the number of farms increased between 1945 and 1959. Preliminary data from the 1965 Census of Agriculture indicate that the rate of decline continued to increase in many areas between 1959 and 1964.

A rough indication of the extent of the adjustment lag is provided by a study of what the commercial farm industry (Census definition of commercial farms) of the North Central states would have looked like in 1959 if it had been meeting the goals of production efficiency and equal income-earning opportunities (8). The results show that the number of commercial farms would have dropped from 1,171,000 to 306,000. The input of labor would have declined 66 percent. And total investment in land and operating capital per farm would have increased from $63,000 to $212,000. Although some of the estimated change reflected an adjustment to eliminate the overproduction of farm products that existed in 1959, most of it reflected an adjustment to meet the minimum cost goal.

But what are likely to be the adjustment needs of the future? For the next decade or so, they are likely to be much the same kind as those of the recent past but perhaps with some decrease in magnitude. The adjustment lag, particularly with respect to the number and organization of individual farms, is so large that even changes in the direction of some of the determinants are unlikely to reverse the pattern.

Recent developments abroad have brightened the export prospects for U.S. farm products. It now seems likely that commercial export demand will continue to grow, although probably at a much slower rate than it did in the 1961–65 period. It is also likely that most of the increase will be in foodstuffs, especially feed grains and soybeans. United States cotton faces increasing competition abroad from synthetics and expanded foreign production and the longer-run export prospects are not as favorable.

Perhaps the biggest uncertainty in the export picture is food aid. If recent developments are indicative of future trends, greater emphasis in assistance programs on population control and building food production capacity in underdeveloped countries will restrain aid expansion in the form of food. But even if future food aid were to be geared largely to meeting emergency famine conditions abroad, the volume of such aid might be as large as that of recent years. On balance, it appears that total export demand will show some increase over the next decade. Domestic demand will continue to grow as a result of increases in population and rising per capita income. But a decreasing rate of increase in population growth and a declining income elasticity of demand may hold the increase in domestic demand to less than that suggested by earlier projections.

Development and introduction of new opportunities to increase the productivity of farm resources probably will continue unabated. There seems to be no indication that public and private investment in agricultural research and development activities will decline. Investment in general education is increasing rapidly and signs of any substantial reduction in agricultural education seem to be absent. Moreover, there appears to be a large current "technological gap." Consequently, farm resource productivity is likely to grow at least as fast over the next decade as over the past decade, probably faster if the minimum cost gap is reduced.

Under these circumstances, the farm industry will still require a lot of resource adjustment to meet the performance goals relating to production efficiency and equal income-earning opportunities. Keeping market supply in line with demand at prices permitting comparable income-earning opportunities for labor and capital on well-organized farms may not be as big a problem. But to get this job done and at the same time approximate the goals of minimum cost and equality of income-earning opportunity on all commercial farms will likely involve a large transfer of resources out of farming over the next two decades, particularly human resources.

Some indication of the adjustments needed to meet these goals in the North Central states is provided by a recent study projecting the characteristics of an income-efficient commercial farm industry (census definition) in 1980 (8). On the basis of projections of domestic and export demands, technological conditions, and resource supply conditions, estimates were made of the resource and organizational characteristics which would be consistent with the goals of production efficiency and equal income-earning opportunities for labor and capital on commercial farms (no allowance for nonincome preferences). Total output was adjusted to meet projected demands at prices covering the opportunity costs (returns in alternative employments) of resources used. And individual farms were reorganized (on paper) to produce this output at the lowest possible cost permitted by the stock of technical knowledge and input prices. Estimates were based on data from the 1960 Census of Agriculture and records covering nearly 9,000 individual farms throughout the region.

A comparison of the results with the existing commercial farm situation in 1959 showed large differences. Under the income-efficient organization (2 percent factor productivity growth assumption), total labor input was down 74 percent. Total capital input was 45 percent less, and total land input was projected to decline 3 percent. There was a 71 percent reduction in the number of commercial farms. In line with the assumed rise in resource productivity and the clearing of markets at efficiency prices, the ratio of prices received by farmers to prices paid by farmers (1910–14 = 100) was down to 56 compared with an actual ratio of 81 in 1959.

On a per farm basis, the differences were even more extreme. For the income-efficient organization, the input of land and buildings was up 238 percent. Operating capital per farm was 97 percent higher. Total investment (constant prices) in operating capital and land and buildings per farm was projected at $188,000 compared with $63,000 in 1959. But labor input per farm was only 9 percent greater. Output per farm was 262 percent higher. Earnings of labor and investment capital were equated with projected opportunity costs and were 475 percent greater than in 1959. Most of the difference between the projected values and the 1959 actual values reflected an adaptation to the adjustment lag which existed in 1959.

These projections, of course, are subject to substantial errors. Some of the underlying assumptions were not completely realistic at the time the study was undertaken. Certain technical estimation problems were not solved satisfactorily. Since 1959, there has been a sizeable additional adjustment in the number and organization of individual farms. Also, the projections took no account of the nonincome employment preferences of people. For these and other reasons, the projected adjustments undoubtedly are on the high side. But even after liberal allowance for these considerations, the conclusion still emerges that large adjustments in the structure and organization of North Central regional agriculture will be needed to meet performance goals by 1980.

Inasmuch as the North Central states contribute about 45 percent of the nation's farm output and since the number and organization of farms in this region is probably in better adjustment than in most regions, the above conclusion may be generalized to the commercial farm industry as a whole. It appears, however, that the rates of adjustment needed to approximate the performance goals by 1980 are well within the range of feasibility, considering past accomplishments and future potentialities.

FUTURE POLICY DIRECTION

In the foregoing discussion, we have identified four major kinds of performance gaps suggesting future policy needs for commercial agriculture: (a) the gap in production efficiency relating particularly to the goals of supply adequacy and minimum cost, (b) the gap in income-earning opportunities for labor and capital on commercial farms, (c) the gap in participation in public services, and (d) the gap in distributive justice.

Because of a heavy concentration of farmers in the older age groups, there will be a large opportunity to adjust the structure and organization of the farm industry over the next two decades. And this opportunity will involve a minimum of adjustment costs. Even without major modification of present agricultural legislation, the farm industry could show a large improvement in economic performance over the next 15 years. Much of the opportunity, however, could be lost by inappropriate short-run program decisions within the current legislative framework.

In the main, the policy instruments and programs needed to reduce the size of these gaps and improve (in terms of the specified goals) the over-all performance of the industry are at hand. Some are already being applied, although in certain instances the level and mix of program activities probably need major modification. Others are available for use if and when they become politically acceptable. Some of the more important program needs can be met by the appropriate application of general programs to the farming sector. This is especially true in the area of human resource policies.

FULL EMPLOYMENT

One of the necessary conditions for improving the over-all performance of the farm industry is a high and stable level of nonfarm economic activity. Over the long pull, improved efficiency and a reduction in the disparity in income-earning opportunities for commercial agriculture are heavily dependent on a further decline in the input of labor.

If this adjustment is to proceed smoothly and rapidly, alternative employment opportunities must be available for potential farm entrants and for existing farm workers who may wish to obtain nonfarm jobs. A high level of nonfarm economic activity also is conducive to a strong domestic demand for farm products. Consequently, the farm industry has a large stake in the appropriate application of monetary and fiscal instruments to achieve over-all economic stability.

TRADE POLICY

Commercial agriculture also has an important stake in the nation's foreign trade policy. Much of the expansion in farm exports to Japan, now number-one dollar buyer of U.S. farm products, has been made possible by the growing volume of U.S. imports of Japanese manufactured goods. Tighter restrictions on Japanese imports would have undermined this development. Liberalization of trade on the basis of comparative advantage and equal treatment can provide larger farm markets in Western Europe and some of the underdeveloped countries. Although the removal of import restrictions may adversely affect some domestic farm commodities, it appears that on balance U.S. agriculture has much more to gain than to lose by a more liberal trade policy.

LABOR MARKET

If the adjustment in manpower on farms is to be as consistent as possible with the needs of a growing economy, monopolistic restrictions on entry into particular fields of employment must be minimized. In some occupations, long periods of apprenticeships unrelated to the time needed to acquire essential skills, recruiting methods, and licensing requirements far beyond what can be justified on grounds of public health and safety operate to limit entry and discriminate among prospective employees. These restrictions induce an imbalance in the allocation of manpower among occupations and close opportunities for qualified people to maximize their personal income and their contribution to the national product.

RESOURCE OWNERSHIP AND CONTROL

The performance goal relating to resource ownership and control arrangements specifies that there should be no discriminatory treatment for or against such arrangements in commercial agriculture. Ownership and control arrangements in the farm industry would meet the same criteria for social acceptance as those in other industries. A goal of owner-operated family farms was not specified because such a goal has become increasingly competitive with other goals and there is little evidence that a majority of people would be willing to pay the price (sacrifice of other goals) needed to achieve it.

The era of the "agricultural ladder," on which an enterprising rural youth could climb from farm hand to renter to owner-operatorship, has ended. Wages paid hired men are not generally conducive to the level of saving needed to accumulate the necessary capital to enter farming with an adequate farm unit. In some Midwest areas, farming entrants are almost all sons of farmers that are buying into the family business.

In response to price changes relative to productivity, American farmers have substituted capital inputs for labor. Cost economies of size have emerged, and farms have grown larger. The value of land, improvements, farm machinery, and livestock on a well-organized farm in the Midwest today is upwards of $200,000. Sole ownership of this bundle of resources may not be a relevant farmer goal, given the competition with other farm family goals.

In most types of farming, however, the typical well-organized farm of the foreseeable future is likely to be a unit in which management and most of the labor is provided by the farm family. But because of the high level of investment required, the ownership of land and capital resources is likely to become more diffused among relatives and other people. The corporate form of ownership may well become the principal device for the intergeneration transfer of well-organized family farms (6).

HUMAN RESOURCES

The key to long-run improvement in the industry's economic performance is to be found in the developments which influence human resource investment and utilization. And the most critical kind of human resource in this context is the farm operator and potential farm operator. Over the next two decades, operator entry and operator withdrawal for nonfarm employment will play highly significant roles in determining the pace at which the industry can adjust its structure and organization to eliminate the performance gaps in production efficiency and comparable income-earning opportunities. A lower rate of entry and a higher rate of withdrawal for nonfarm employment would mean more opportunities for existing farmers to enlarge their land base and organize more efficient units.

On the basis of data from the Census Bureau and the Public Health Service, we estimate that about one-half of the 1964 population of commercial farm operators (Census of Agriculture definition) will die or reach retirement age by 1980. This large natural withdrawal of farm operators offers a unique opportunity to adjust the number and organization of farms with a minimum of stress and strain. Projections for the North Central states suggest that if in the interim the rate of operator entry were somewhat less than the rate of operator withdrawal for nonfarm employment, the number of farms and the number of farmers in 1980 would be in moderately good balance with performance goal requirements (8).

There is evidence that the decision to enter farming is strongly influenced by the following factors: (a) preferences and aspirations regarding income, work, and living conditions, (b) expectations about what farming and alternative occupations have to offer in the way of income, work, and living advantages and disadvantages, and (c) the set of resources (e.g. skills, initiative, personality, innate ability, and financial backing) possessed in relation to entrance requirements (9). Many of the same factors also are likely to influence the decisions of younger operators to withdraw from farming and accept nonfarm jobs. Developments which affect these factors will, in turn, influence the rates of entry and operator withdrawal for nonfarm employment.

To maximize its contribution toward achieving the performance goals, human resource policy for agriculture probably should emphasize (a) increased educational investment, (b) more information of the kind needed in making rational occupation and employment choices, and (c) educational and adjustment incentives.

A relative increase in educational investment in farm youth can contribute to national economic growth. At the same time, it can contribute to the performance goals of production efficiency, comparable income-earning opportunities, and equal opportunity to participate in public services. A decline in the rate of entry into farming is likely to result if farm boys are exposed to more and better educational opportunities. Equalizing the quantity and quality of elementary and secondary education available in rural areas can induce higher student aspirations, improved vocational guidance, and more adequate preparation for post-high school training. Equalizing the opportunities available for vocational and college training can provide the skills needed to open up a wider range of nonfarm job opportunities and can redress the competitive advantage held by nonfarm youth in the urban labor market. A number of studies suggest that the income return from investment in education is high compared with the return offered by most other forms of investment (12). In view of the lower investment per farm pupil, the return may be even higher in rural areas.

The increased emphasis in recent years on federal educational investment is having some impact on farm people. But much of the new effort seems to be heavily oriented toward the needs of urban and metropolitan centers. It is not clear at the the moment whether these programs will reduce or increase the disparity in educational opportunities for farm youth. In many areas, increased state aid may offer the best chance of eliminating the disparity.

Because of less exposure to employment alternatives, farm youth typically need a heavier dose of vocational and occupational guidance and counseling than youth from urban areas. They need more and higher quality information about occupational alternatives—the advantages and disadvantages that may be expected when employed in each and the requirements and opportunities for gaining entrance. They also need more understanding of the adjustment problems of the farm industry and more reliable information on the incomes that can be expected on farms having different size and organizational characteristics. In the past, vocational agricultural teachers in high schools have not concentrated on providing this information. Their contact with potential entrants should be an excellent opportunity to provide such counseling.

The farm industry's performance could be improved if more opportunity to utilize a better federal-state employment service were made available to young farm operators who may wish to leave farming and farm youth who have completed their formal education. This would require a greater effort on the part of local employment service offices to establish working relationships in rural areas and a more effective and fuller orientation of these offices to the national labor market. Recent efforts at computerizing labor market information hold promise of future improvements in the operation of the employment service.

Reducing the disparity in educational investment per farm pupil undoubtedly will require a larger allocation of public educational funds to schools serving farm youth. It also is likely to mean continued consolidation of rural schools, a widening and deepening of curricula, increased emphasis on vocational and technical subjects, higher salaries to attract more qualified teachers, and school integration. Whereas federal and state aid can pave the way for these changes, much of the job will rest with local communities, school boards, and educational administrators.

Providing greater educational opportunities for farm people will contribute to other performance goals only if the opportunities are utilized. For maximum utilization, more research is needed on understanding educational motivation and the kinds of incentives that induce educational response. There also is a need for more research on the dropout problem and how best to cope with it.

Human resource policy for agriculture might include special monetary and nonmonetary incentives to encourage participation in educational and job information programs and to induce greater labor mobility. For example, a payment to defray the cost of moving, or T. W. Schultz's suggestion of "homesteads in reverse," could lessen the obstacles to a smooth and rapid movement of labor from small farms (11). Such incentives might best be offered in a "lump sum" tied to specific performances.

If human resource policy in agriculture is to make its maximum contribution to the performance goals, short-run price and income programs should be reasonably well tuned to underlying economic conditions. In other words, these programs should not operate in a way that creates more favorable long-run income expectations than those warranted by long-run, supply-demand developments. For example, if farm prices were increased appreciably before all retired land was brought back into production, it would likely encourage higher longer-run income expectations and induce an increase in the rate of operator entry. There is some evidence that the number of entrants is highly responsive to changes in relative income-earning opportunities in farming (9). Price and production control programs may help to determine if effective structural adjustment will take place.

FARM STORAGE PROGRAMS

Storage is a device for changing the distribution of a commodity over time. To be most consistent with the performance goals, a storage program should attempt to accumulate and deaccumulate stocks in a way that makes the intertemporal differences in the value of a commodity equal to the marginal cost of storage. Storage programs are viewed as a method of encouraging farm price stability and a more efficient use of farm products over time.

Storage is not an appropriate tool for persistently raising farm prices above free market levels, since stocks will ultimately increase to an unmanageable and costly level. Storage is an appropriate tool for tempering the effects of year-to-year weather fluctuations (domestic and foreign), seasonal variations in production, and changes in demand due to national emergencies.

Weather fluctuations generate large risks on the domestic production side. Probabilities of the occurrence and degree of adverse crop production weather are determinable and the cost of maintaining reserve stocks can be weighed against the likelihood of these occurrences and their effects on product values.

Alternatively, levels of exports could be reduced in a season of short domestic production, in lieu of maintaining storage stocks. The opportunity cost of this alternative in terms of other national goals foregone, e.g. food aid for a developing country, may be too costly, however.

Besides domestic weather risk, our storage program could also insure against weather risk in foreign countries which were dependent on our efforts. Private trade may find it profitable to hold some reserves to sell in years of reduced domestic supply. It is unlikely, however, that the commodity trade would view as profitable private storage to meet crisis shortages in underdeveloped countries without resources to purchase imports.

FARM PRODUCTION AND PRICE SUPPORT PROGRAMS

Excess output capacity has been and continues to be a pressing problem in American agriculture. The optimistic expectations of 1965 and 1966, which in their extreme form implied an unlimited export market, have been exploded by developments restraining export demand and expanding farm output. Until structural adjustment has proceeded much beyond where it is today, there will be continued need to control farm production to prevent excess supplies at current prices or prices offering comparable returns on well-organized farms.

Programs of recent years have relied on land retirement spread over all farms as the tool for this control. If and when structural adjustment proceeds to the place where diverted land may be returned to production, crop control achieved by voluntary land retirement with its wasteful use of high quality crop production land may become a transitional program. After adjustment is achieved it could be used only as a standby program to meet short-run excess supply problems.

It must be recognized that continued use of the voluntary land retirement program as the transitional means to achieve a balance of supply and demand at price support levels would continue to redistribute farm income in a way which favors large-scale prosperous farmers. This, of course, would mean continued compromise of the distributive justice goal for the duration of the transitional period.

Stability of prices and the flow of products implies a fairly narrow range of price fluctuation but not a fixed price. If there is to be some fluctuation, the price targets should be somewhat above the minimum support levels or price floors and average prices should approximate the target level. If the above production and adjustment goals are to be achieved, the price targets should be low enough to avoid bidding up the price of land and also making entry too attractive. Even so, an average price which provides comparable returns to resources on well-organized farms could make entry too attractive to achieve the intergeneration adjustment in farm size and output. If this were true either the important opportunity for relatively painless adjustment would be missed or some additional restriction on entry would be necessary.

The restriction on entry such as is practiced in some European countries would be an alternative. The limitation requires that certain efficiency criteria be met before entry into farming is permitted. Restriction on entry would make the level of prices somewhat less critically important to production adjustment policy. It should be recognized that there will be constant political pressure from farmers and especially farmers who are land owners to raise the price targets.

How should price support levels be set? Congress has given the Secretary of Agriculture considerable discretionary authority within general guidelines. If more specific guidelines are to be used, action by Congress might be required. An alternative to the present discretionary authority would be a legal price formula. Some years ago there was some consideration given to a system of moving average market prices.

If support and control programs are to make the largest possible contribution toward achieving the long-run performance goals, they should meet certain conditions.

Price supports should achieve price targets which approach but do not exceed these implied by the equal returns criterion. Higher prices would be likely to bid up land prices and encourage too much entry into farming.

A storage program should provide sufficient stocks to stabilize prices against short-run supply shortages and short-run shifts in emergency demands which could bid prices up and create unjustified expectations about long-term resource returns. If prices are to have a firm floor, the agricultural industry and consumers need tools to prevent instability on the high price side also. Price supports can serve as a protection to farmers, and storage stocks as a protection to consumers.

As this paper has viewed the goals Americans have for commercial agriculture and the present situation, a unique opportunity now exists for greatly improving the performance of the commercial farm industry. This opportunity involves a relatively painless adjustment of the number and organization of commercial farms. Price, production control, and storage programs become tools to this end rather than just short-run means to higher current income. The opportunity could be missed.

LITERATURE CITED

1. Ackerman, J. and W. E. Ogg. The Challenge of Educational Reform. In: Working Papers From a Seminar on Adopting Institutions to the Conditions of Economic Growth, the Center for Agr. and Econ. Dev., Iowa State Univ. 1966.
2. Burchinal, L. G. Differences in educational and occupational aspirations of farm, small town, and city boys. Rural Soc. 26: 107–21. 1961.
3. Christensen, L. A. Characteristics and Experiences of Operators Retiring From Iowa Farms, 1959–61. M.S. Thesis, Unpubl. Iowa State Univ. Lib., Ames. 1966.
4. Dahl, R. A. and C. E. Tindblom. Politics, Economics and Welfare. New York: Harper and Row. 1953.
5. Folkman, W. S. Progress of Rural and Urban Students Entering Iowa State University, Fall, 1955. Agr. Econ. Rpt. 12, Econ. Res. Serv. USDA. July, 1962.

6. Harl, N. E. Public Policy Aspects of Farm Incorporation. Jour. Paper No. J-5083, Iowa Agr. Exp. Sta., Ames. July, 1965.
7. Iowa Agr. and Home Econ. Exp. Sta. Post Adjustment Experiences of Iowa Farm Operators Who Quit Farming To Take Nonfarm Jobs. Unpubl. Project 1477, Ames, 1965.
8. Kaldor, D. R. and W. E. Saupe. Estimates and projections of an income-efficient commercial farm industry in the North Central States. J. Farm Econ. 48:578–96. 1966.
9. —— et al. Occupational Plans of Iowa Farm Boys. Res. Bul. 508, Agr. Exp. Sta., Iowa State Univ., Ames. Sept., 1962.
10. Report of the President's Commission on National Goals. Goals for Americans. (A Spectrum book.) Englewood Cliffs, N.J.: Prentice-Hall, Inc. 1960.
11. Schultz, T. W. Homesteads in reverse. Farm Policy Forum, Vol. 8, No. 5. 1956.
12. ——. Economic Value of Education. New York: Columbia Univ. Press. 1963.
13. Tyner, F. H. and L. G. Tweeten. Optimum Resource Allocation in U.S. Agriculture. J. Farm Econ. 48:613–31. 1966.

CHAPTER TWELVE

Combating Income Problems of Noncommercial Farmers and Other Rural Groups

GEORGE S. TOLLEY

FOR YEARS it has been recognized that farm commodity programs can lead to adequate incomes for only a fraction of those rural persons facing serious income problems. Success in dealing with rural income problems does not go much beyond improving conditions of commercial farmers since World War II. Other measures have as yet been relatively minor and relatively ineffective.

THE JOB TO BE DONE

This chapter is concerned with the 15 million rural residents estimated to be poor by poverty standards in 1965. Of this total, 5 million lived on farms and 10 million were nonfarm rural residents. Many additional persons are operating well below their potential though not in poverty by technical standards. Conservatively, only one farmer in three has any prospect of earning a living comparable to those of similar age and education in nonfarm occupations. The other two out of three are helped to some extent by farm commodity programs. Numerous adjustment studies show that even the most favorable circumstances imaginable would not bring these others to an income level comparable to their nonfarm peers. Including the families of these two-thirds of farmers, with at best dim prospects, would add another 5 million farm persons to the above figures.

Among the nonfarm rural labor force, earnings of younger persons who have completed high school are quite similar to what they could expect to earn as nonrural residents. However, the rural population is heavily weighted with middle-aged and older persons who have little education. Their incomes are very low compared to urban earnings for the same age and education levels. About half of the nonfarm rural men in 1960 had earnings 25 percent or more below earnings of urban men of the same age and education level. Recognizing that these persons and their families face serious income problems would add another 10 million, bringing to *30 million* the number of persons of concern in this chapter.

The variety of rural income problem situations is impressive. Lower income farmers include whites in scattered concentrations throughout the South where upland cotton is still grown on small farms not amenable to up-to-date techniques. Included also are the hill farmers of Appalachia and the Ozarks, those in the cutover area of the upper Great Lakes region, and others in concentrated pockets. Many live in the same neighborhoods as farmers earning adequate incomes throughout the country. Hired farm laborers, who have a high incidence of poverty, number over 3 million. Nearly one in ten rural residents is a Negro—most live in the South, and many are sharecroppers in cotton and tobacco whose numbers have been declining rapidly due to labor-saving changes. Rural Indians and Spanish-speaking people are concentrated in the Southwest. Each of these two groups numbers less than a million, but they contain some of the highest incidences of poverty.

The varied circumstances of farm persons with income problems are easier to visualize than are those of the more numerous nonfarm rural persons with income problems. Many nonfarm rural residents have in the past farmed enough to be defined as living on farms but are not doing so now because of retirement or partial retirement. Many nonfarm rural persons rely on income sources in areas of very low wage rates. But the income problems of nonfarm rural persons remain less well understood than for those whose livelihood is related to a census-defined farm.

For the most part, rural income problems appear to be the backwash of the nation's rapid economic progress. They stem from the very fact that rapid gains in agricultural efficiency have had uneven effects and have contributed to the situation that productive job opportunities have grown more rapidly in urban than in rural parts of the economy. It will be assumed in this chapter that efforts should be directed at rural income problems comprehensively. The assumption is that helping persons earn nearer to their potential makes a contribution to national income and that efforts are justifiable to provide more equal income and opportunities to persons.

Attempts to combat rural income problems comprehensively have encountered a double barrier. First, after the maximum contribution by farm commodity programs, the problems that remain are harder to solve even with unlimited effort. Second, a way has yet to be found for policy-making processes to bring about a strong effort for an effective attack on the broad rural income problem. This policy search seeks for means of overcoming this double barrier.

Too often a reaction is to conclude pessimistically that little can be done effectively. Yet, in addition to more gradual changes affecting rural areas, there have been recent sharp changes in national attitudes which lead to contemplating a wider range of alternatives. Changes *are* underway that will help ameliorate these problems even more than in the past.

LESS PROMISING APPROACHES

Some suggest simply moving people to where current job opportunities are. Government directed "resettlement" was tried and rejected long ago. Subsidized migration has more to recommend it. Opposition to migration subsidies reflects more than congressmen's selfish opposition to presiding over the liquidation of their own constituencies. Subsidized migration is only one step removed from active central direction of the location of persons and of economic activity. Attempts to influence location of activity are implied by several government policies. There is a preference for making the influence as indirect as possible. Perhaps this is because we are in the era of the carrot, one of the few genuine consensuses being on the manner in which the federal government shall be used to foster goals. The taxing resources of the federal government and the focusing there of effort and interest on national problems mean that federal measures are likely to be used. The measures must be of a voluntary nature insofar as the communities and individuals participating are concerned. This fundamental direction in policy making does not show signs of changing.

If migration subsidies were modest, they might be paid largely to persons who would move anyway. To induce persons really attached to where they live to pull up stakes could be prohibitively expensive. Furthermore, deliberate depopulation of areas increases the problems of providing services and opportunities to the persons who are left. If we could turn Appalachia into a reserve or national park which people only visited and was not used for anyone's residence, a deliberate depopulation policy might warrant more consideration.

Regardless of government measures, outmigration of younger persons from rural areas will continue at a rapid rate, particularly those plagued by low-income problems. One would, of course, not want to directly subsidize people to stay in areas, either. A corollary of the probable continued outmigration is that time will eventually do something to solve rural income problems. However, it is not a satisfactory cure by itself. Middle-aged rural persons locked into unproductive careers will within a few decades pass from the scene. Fewer young people will enter into similar unproductive situations. In the meantime, those already locked in need to be made somewhat better off than they presently are. This can at best be only partially corrective. Few would argue seriously for programs that would completely succeed in bringing the income of middle-aged and older rural persons to a par with what persons of the same age and education are receiving in the rest of the economy. Of those locked into poverty, the most directly affected persons are the children who are not provided with necessary food, health, education, and cultural opportunities. The entire community is affected because low incomes lower the tax base available to supply all kinds of public services. Finally, attitudinal problems permeate the local environment when whole communities are left outside the mainstream of American life.

Policies that do not go beyond consideration of movement of people fail to meet these needs.

POTENTIALS AND PROBLEMS OF PERSON-TO-PERSON PROGRAMS

There is a tradition in agricultural programs of a person-to-person approach. It has not, however, extended as helpfully as it might to persons with more difficult income problems. Extension and credit agencies find it difficult to reach lower income people. Intensive, comprehensive career counselling oriented to a person's needs suggests itself as an approach. Low interest rate credit is a traditional approach which may be viewed partly as a means of transferring income contingent on the borrower carrying out certain activities. It might be helpful to try to guide these loans to older persons so as to avoid the possibility that they would attract young persons into unproductive situations. This would most wisely be done in the context of having loans contingent on approval of career choice rather than any outright age limits. A most important need is for credit programs to contain larger accompaniment of technical assistance. The fundamental needs of low-income rural people are not so much credit as counselling and teaching.

Outreach is a term now heard much of, particularly in reference to broad government programs such as medicare and vocational education. For the most part, efforts have been made to tack the mission of reaching low-income persons onto existing agency activities. The federal agencies have their own traditional jobs and sources of political support. Extension, with funds granted automatically, is little subject to direction. No wonder, then, that it is difficult to secure significant redirections.

Three constructive suggestions may be made, all of which would entail only modest outlays. First, regardless of what agencies are responsible, training for the personnel is needed. Large-scale, three-to-six month training in special courses at full pay, either by agencies or institutions such as land-grant universities, would be appropriate. Special emphasis might be placed on the problems of lower income persons and how to work with them. Personnel without previous orientation cannot be expected either to be sympathetic to or have the know-how to work with lower income persons.

Second, in view of all the difficulties of redirection, would it not be more fruitful to add personnel with clearly lodged new responsibilities? Most preferably, this would be done in new agencies, since the structure and leadership of traditional agencies is not sufficiently geared to serving lower income groups. For less than $100 million, an agent can be placed in every county in the United States. This is not enough, but it indicates the feasibility. An entire new USDA agency or new state agencies—but in either case funded through the Office of Economic Opportunity rather than the Senate and House agricultural channels—would be appropriate.

While the new effort would not need to be carried out through institutions with any previous rural concern, to do so appears the most likely way to reach to the grass roots and would be consistent with a heritage of enthusiastic liaison between the people and public service institutions which is one of the best legacies of past agricultural programs.

Third, the 4-H movement can be a more powerful weapon if rebuilt to larger scale with directions to lower income youth. One of the strongest indications of research on poverty is that the earlier people are reached, the likelier it is they will be served effectively. Most of us know of persons who have escaped from poverty, many because they fell into fortunate influences in school. Perhaps some person outside the home took an interest in them. Studies of aspiration formation verify that this can be important.

MEASURES FOR SPECIAL RURAL GROUPS

Farm labor, another group mentioned earlier, has received more attention than any other very low-income rural group. It has just come under minimum wage coverage, and some programs of the Office of Economic Opportunity provide funds for improving living conditions for the migrant part of the hired farm working force. It remains to fund out the OEO programs more fully so that good housing and day care will be available wherever the migrant streams go. Thus will be minimized the adverse effects on the children moved hither and thither with their parents. The impact of the new minimum wage legislation is not yet clear. It will certainly improve the lot of some of those who remain as farm laborers. Some workers will be displaced by more rapid introduction of laborsaving practices. A portion of those displaced—housewives and school children who find local seasonal employment—will lose a source of income. Migrant and full-time resident laborers displaced will be better off if they find alternative, higher paying jobs where living conditions are more desirable. One of the social bonuses of continued farm mechanization will be to further reduce hired farm laboring as a way of life. In a fully employed economy where displaced persons are likely to find a reasonably good alternative income accompanied by a more stable life and better social services, the case for hastening the demise of hired farm labor is strong.

The same indignation brought by public concern for the living conditions of some farm laborers should also be brought to ensure that employment services find the best jobs and facilitate occupational mobility. Every effort is needed to avoid using information to monopsonize through covering a narrow range of jobs, which can give the appearance of serving the interests primarily of farm employers.

A logical case can be made for arranging for income transfers to the middle-aged and older rural persons mentioned at the outset who form the large heart of the rural income problem. Provisions for early retirement in recent legislation are in this direction. Earlier beginning of social security and enlarged payments might be a way to carry out such transfers. Measures along these lines can have more impact on lower income groups than past commodity programs. In some areas, they can facilitate resource adjustments by inducing older operators with smaller farms to make their land available for expansion of more efficient farms. However, if tied to farming, these measures miss the more numerous nonfarm, rural low-income families. Especially with broader coverage, there would be a significant amount of added U.S. Treasury expense. It is difficult to see how in policy making, this approach would be arrived at to be vigorously pushed as a purely rural program.

AREA IMPROVEMENT

Rural Development

At one extreme is the view that rural industrialization efforts are largely hot air activities. This view presumes only a fraction of the meager local benefits trickle down to lower income persons. A view at the other extreme is that promotion on the part of a few people can successfully have leverage through changing the climate of opinion. This leads to more jobs, to a will to supply better public services, to an expanded tax base, and to new leadership energies from technical and managerial persons coming into the area in connection with new plants. One reason the answers are in doubt is that the effects of the promotion of local development are difficult to measure. There have been some outstanding local successes where development efforts have paid off. In other cases results are less dramatic, but one is not sure what would happen in the absence of the efforts. It will be possible to make a better assessment in the future if systematic comparisons are attempted for all or many counties to measure how much relation there is between promotional inputs and development indicators such as job growth.

While agencies of the USDA with field staffs have devoted time of their personnel to the promotion of rural industrialization, a hindrance to evaluation is that the extent of the local promotion is not accurately known. There are needs for good estimates of how much energy goes into the activity and for appraisal of effectiveness of persons hired and given responsibility for traditional agency missions, with rural industrialization promotion a part-time added activity.

The general part-time efforts of USDA agency persons should be sharply distinguished from two more highly focused endeavors. These are Resource Conservation and Development carried out by the Soil Conservation Service, and Rural Renewal carried out by the Farmers Home Administration. They have so far been limited to pilot areas. Planning is done for an area of perhaps four to six counties. There are some special loan authorities, but the most important impact may be the placing of personnel in an area to spend full time catalyzing local activity and bringing to bear the variety of state and federal programs now available. The approach of having full-time persons in an area concerned with action for development is probably more effective by several orders of magnitude than the more diffuse approach where agency employees are expected to devote some portion of their time to community development in addition to their other responsibilities. Furthermore, this approach is likely to be even more effective if the action is oriented to the needs of the community and not to traditional agency mission. It remains moot whether this can be done within the traditional agencies. In building on the valuable experience gained so far, consideration could be given to centering the multicounty action programs for area economic development in a separate agency. An alternative would be to set up a grant program leaving implementation to state or local organizations.

The Increasing Federal Involvement in Local Economic Development

The more important teeth, newly grown, for fostering economic growth of areas are for the most part not rurally oriented programs. They are a rural concern because income and welfare improvements at the local level take place in an area context. The destinies of town and rural residents are tied together. People travel to jobs, whether city or rural residents, in a multicounty area. Public services including roads, school systems, and hospitals are most efficiently planned to serve such an area. One of the major pieces of legislation aimed at areas with prevalence of lower incomes is the Appalachian Act. It provides for road systems, water resource development, and other over-all development measures, many of which foster growth around central towns and cities within subregions. The Public Works and Economic Development Act (PWEDA) is potentially more sweeping. Not only does it provide for the possibility of commissions for additional regions similar to what was set up for Appalachia; other major parts of PWEDA provide for planning, loan and grant funds for areas that (a) are distressed according to economic indicators and (b) have been willing to organize themselves into multicounty entities containing a center which can logically serve as a nucleus for growth.

A proposed Community Development District Act has received widespread support which has a more distinctly rural orientation. If enacted, it would provide funds for integrated planning for any multicounty area which appears to be a logical economic entity on the basis of commuting patterns and similar criteria. Without attempting to do away with county governments, one of its main purposes is to secure cooperation between local governments. It would provide them with more planning resources than they individually would feel they could afford and encourage more efficient, nonduplicating provision of public facilities. The proposed Act clearly visualizes an emphasis on sparser, more rural areas.

It is to be hoped that, as time goes by and experience is accumulated, yet more effective approaches will be pushed. Roads and dams, central in the Appalachian development effort, give costly but physically visible evidence of development. It is questionable whether they are highly effective in terms of amount of permanent increase in employment and income achieved in an area per dollar of federal expenditure. Improvements in labor supply through general education, vocational education, and manpower training would probably attract much more industry per federal dollar spent. Labor supply is the main resource most areas have to offer. As another alternative, saturation level of industrial promotion activity could probably be carried on for the costs of the roads and dams.

General planning funds together with loans and grants for specific types of facilities may hit close but just miss what would have far greater payoff: provision for full-time efforts of able men of action who can promote development, stir others to it, and help mobilize all the programs of the federal government that are of particular benefit to the area. Personnel engaged in planning can do this only in part. There should be a major responsibility for action, not just planning; and those involved in action should have responsibilities for bringing together all needed measures. This would avoid an orientation toward certain funds for public facilities provided by the Public Works and Economic Development Act.

Even with general economic development measures at their best, the trickle-down question remains. That is, to what extent will increasing the general level of activity in an area affect the lower income rural people? It is they who contribute so importantly to the poor showing in terms of economic indicators of most depressed areas. The new jobs that are created in an area will give employment to only a few of the older, less educated persons who are the heart of the problem. These persons are almost as immobile job-wise as they are immobile geographically. Most new jobs are likely to be taken by younger persons who otherwise would have migrated away and by persons attracted to the area from elsewhere. More likely, any very significant effects on lower income rural people will be the indirect ones that come from an enlarged tax base. More enlightened leadership would make possible improvements in education and other services provided by local government.

Furthermore, the general economic development activities discussed above are relevant only for viable areas with prospects of economic growth. Realistically, many rural areas of the country do not have this prospect. Past outmigration has already gone too far. They have lost their former attractive labor pools and the population is weighted so heavily with older people that the people of working age are no longer being replaced. There is no prospect for a future labor pool of sufficient size to support industrialization. There cannot be realistic hope that economic development will help these areas. Yet for the disadvantaged citizens already there, measures to upgrade local government are particularly needed. Emphasis should be placed on hospital and other services important to the aged and on education to prepare the children still there for occupations in other parts of the country. The existence of essentially nondevelopable areas, then, further strengthens the case for special measures to upgrade local government services apart from general economic development efforts.

Improving Local Government

Improving governmentally supplied services in local areas entails increasing the resources available to local governments. It also involves increasing the quality of local government decision making. Increases in the quality of decision making will come in part automatically with increased resources. They also can come through insisting on minimum standards accompanying federally supplied funds. And, finally, direct approaches such as education and extension activities for local leadership and government personnel can be effective.

Federal transfers to nonfederal government entities are already sizeable. The newer view gaining adherents is the idea of making general purpose grants. A reason given in support of this view is that there is a general tendency for the tax revenues of the federal government to rise faster than the demand for federal government activities. However, the revenues of nonfederal government have not been growing as rapidly as the demand for their services.

Rural people will be greatly affected by the way arrangements for such transfers are made. Transfers should be attractive enough not to be turned down by any one. At the same time, some incentives should be included that will result in the upgrading of quality of services for at least those areas seriously below the nation. The incentives should concern professional standards to some extent and also program content. One of the worst arrangements would be to make the transfers strictly proportional to population. The more the transfers are based on need, as measured by amounts required to more nearly equalize government services between areas, the more are lower income rural people likely to gain.

Compared to the nation at large, they receive relatively poor public services—devoting a higher than average proportion of income to these services out of a low per capita income. There are many precedents for grant formulas based on need. Formulas could be based on explicit requirements to raise local government services to specified norms, or on indicators such as taxable income in the area and sparsity of population as a factor which increases the cost of supplying a given level of public services. There is precedent for the latter in the extra payments made by some states to their counties whose costs of education per pupil are unusually high. High transportation costs and high fixed plant costs per pupil result in schools of small enrollment which serve a sparsely populated area.

Federal funds could be supplied to greatly increase the education of local government personnel, making sure that such training reaches people both in and out of government who are influential in local decision making. Land-grant universities, could participate by taking responsibility for needed rural emphasis. A part of the endeavor can be to increase technical competence in the major activities of local government—education, roads, health and welfare, and protection. Persons from all localities should be encouraged to participate in educational activities already going on in each of the technical areas. This could be done by making travel and scholarship funds available virtually free, thus expanding already existing means for the dissemination of improvement.

The development of newer, broader programs is needed for local leaders and planners for local areas, aimed at providing both enlightenment and know-how for action. An example, would be found in the activities of the Office of Economic Opportunity. It is well known that the various poverty programs reach rural participants with relatively low frequency, even though one-half the nation's poor are in rural areas, and one in four rural persons lives in poverty. The prime candidate may be the Community Action Program, whereby local areas mobilize themselves for attacking a range of their own particular poverty problems. Education is needed, ranging from giving information on the mechanics of formulating plans and applying for participation, to imparting a deeper understanding of what poverty programs can mean to the people served. The latter procedures present serious obstacles to rural communities because of the relative scarcity of people with organizational experience. Because the effective size of a program may encompass several communities, the extra barrier of getting different leadership groups to work together is encountered.

In addition to imparting this kind of specific know-how on how to participate effectively in available programs, there is a need for more general enlightenment activities aimed at the key people in rural communities. One aim of enlightenment should be to help communities establish meaningful over-all goals. Another aim should be to show how to go about achieving the over-all goals. Four subject matter prongs of planning could be emphasized in this enlightenment activity: (a) how to find out what the promising economic potentials of an area are so that these can be fostered and other policies made consistent with them, (b) planning for investments in physical resources and facilities, (c) planning human resource investments encompassing a variety of education and manpower approaches as suited to the economic potentials of the area and the needs of the residents, and (d) meeting the needs of special groups such as the aged or particular poverty groups.

A great part of needed enlightenment could be accomplished through greater dissemination of existing knowledge. Because knowledge about how to plan is not completely adequate, an important accompaniment should be research aimed at improving the ability to plan. The social scientists of the land-grant universities could make fundamental contributions by turning their sophisticated powers with as much energy toward optimizing for the four planning prongs as they have toward optimizing for the farm firm.

THE DISPROPORTIONATE STAKE OF RURAL PEOPLE IN ECONOMIC POLICIES OF THE NATION AT LARGE

One reason the benefit to rural people of general economic measures is larger than commonly realized is that rural people stand relatively low in most indicators of well-being. Programs which aim at a target audience using a criterion of need will tend to make a larger proportion of rural than urban persons eligible for participation. Even more important, rural people as a whole do not form an effective lobby for obtaining special measures for themselves. In spite of population declines, their numbers probably are still great enough to secure special programs if they would be active as a group for themselves. But, among other complications, the most needy ones are not articulate enough to make their needs known effectively. A result is that there is more prospect of their being helped by general measures than by measures aimed specifically at them.

The list of general policies which can importantly aid rural people is long. Monetary-fiscal policies maintaining national employment and buoyant prices are often pointed out as being important to farmers. That these policies are important to the economic development of rural areas has more recently been shown by the finding that growth in nonfarm employment in rural areas speeds up markedly during periods of national business expansion. Rural youth of an age to enter the labor force can find jobs more easily—whether they go to work in rural or urban areas—when there is full employment in the nation.

Recent federal general and vocational education legislation are steps in the direction of bringing equality of educational opportunity, particularly the more liberal payments to low-income states that may benefit rural children. Extension of social security has already benefitted many farmers and other rural elderly persons. If payments were liberalized, perhaps the worst of the poverty of the rural aged would be eliminated. Expansion of medicare to a health insurance program for all age groups would benefit rural people, whose health is poorer than for the nation as a whole due to their lower incomes and the relative scarcity of medical services in sparse areas. The costs of providing every school child with a free nutritious breakfast and lunch are probably small compared to the sheer economic benefits of having a more productive population. More frequent health examinations, health service, and health education in the public schools would also be a good investment. The schools remain the most effective institutions for reaching children in homes lacking basic culture. To do so effectively may require funds for intensive extracurricular efforts woven inextricably into student programs.

These general measures, rather than being utopian, will probably be contemplated more and more seriously as the country grows richer. Rural people have incentives to push these in favor of other activities which compete for the federal dollar. Of major importance may be the attempt to ensure that these general measures are not neglected in the feeling that pressing income and social problems are best fought only through slum clearance, the job corps, and other measures primarily directed to the inner cores of metropolises.

EMPLOYMENT APPROACHES WORTH CONSIDERING

Up to this point, measures considered have been those under discussion for some time. In closing, two less conventional approaches may be mentioned. One of these is among the most general of all, the negative income tax. This measure well exemplifies what a general approach can mean. If instituted, a significant portion of the payments would be to rural people. It would then become more important to estimate with care the rural-urban differences in the income below which a family is considered to be in poverty. Estimates of rural-urban differences in this poverty-line income have so far not had much effect on policies. With a negative income tax, the estimates could determine the distribution of many million dollars.

While a negative income tax might benefit rural people greatly, other general income measures should be considered either to complement or to substitute in the event a negative income tax is not enacted. Without attempting to detract from the merits of a negative income tax, one should remember that any measure along these lines with much impact would be quite expensive to the U.S. Treasury. Furthermore, both givers and receivers of money feel better if the receiver does something in return for the money. Any supposed moral fiber problems arising from aiding people are more severe if there is the idea of giving money as a right than if the health, education, and poverty programs discussed earlier are carried out.

Through contracts of the federal government with state and local governments and with private firms, unskilled labor could be employed in useful activities. A proviso would be that a certain proportion of funds be spent in the employment of unskilled labor. The work could include beautification, unskilled help for health occupations, and cottage industry activities.

One might complain about economic efficiency in relation to this approach. Yet tried as an alternative to a negative income tax, some product is obtained as contrasted to no product. Unskilled workers would be paid at the floor specified by actual or recommended minimum wage legislation. This, plus efforts of the program not to contract in labor short areas, would help minimize the competing of employment away from other activities. The germ of the approach being suggested here is contained in the work-experience payments of the Office of Economic Opportunity; these take the form of paying a part of the wages when certain chronically unemployed persons are hired. By sponsoring useful work indirectly through contracting as suggested here, the opprobrium that used to be cast toward employing persons in government make-work projects would be avoided. A general program of this type could be effective against the major income problems of rural people and of other problem groups such as urban unemployed Negro teenagers.

CONCLUSION

Two major points that have emerged from this chapter are as follows: First, the importance has been stressed of recognizing that this is a time when programs are likely to be geared to voluntary participation with initiatives at the local level. Therefore, the discussion has emphasized the possibility of a vitalization effort to spur rapid improvement in the local decision making through which measures affecting rural people are channelled.

Second, rural people have more prospects of being benefitted by possible legislation aimed at lower income persons *generally* than by legislation with little chance of passage aimed at rural persons *specifically*. This suggests that greater energies in attempting to solve rural problems should be directed toward securing the enactment of general programs that would have a major impact on rural people and further toward securing the effective participation of rural people in these programs. Results could be dramatic if the many individuals and institutions with special concern for rural well-being would agree on this approach and push it vigorously.

CHAPTER THIRTEEN

Rural Communities for the Future

MARION CLAWSON

FARM PEOPLE, no less than their city cousins, have economic, social, and political lives—lives which are intertwined in their various aspects, not neatly separated according to our academic disciplines. Farm people are concerned not merely with personal income, but also with a complex range of human relationships. The latter affect their content and level of living, in the sociological sense of those terms; and their standard of living, or what they aspire to, involves these social and other aspects as well as purely economic ones.

In the current American scene, the small city and rural town are perhaps the most neglected segment. In addition to the extensive and expensive farm programs, there is an increasing array of programs for the city. The latter may still be incomplete and there is considerable dissatisfaction with results obtained to date; but major programs exist and will probably be extended. But there are almost no programs aimed at the small cities and rural towns, as such; and many of the serious problems of such communities have gone unaided by society as a whole.

271

POPULATION REDISTRIBUTION OF THE
LATTER TWENTIETH CENTURY

The people of the United States in the latter 20th century are engaged in a large-scale population redistribution. It is as dramatic as, although different from, the population redistribution of western migration across the country which so dominated the 19th century. It is also as dramatic as the technological and economic revolutions currently under way, but of course differs greatly from them.

Many people are leaving rural areas. Migration from farm to city has always characterized American economic development; but such migration was only part of the natural increase until comparatively recently. Now, the farm-to-city migration is drastically reducing the size of the farm population. Half of all counties in the United States lost population in the decade of the 1950's; some of them had also lost population in earlier decades, and there is good reason to believe that most of them continue to lose population. In many other counties, rural areas also lost population during the 1950's, but the major small town or towns gained enough that the whole county at least held its own.

National statistics on population by farm, rural nonfarm, and other major categories are misleading; they show the rural nonfarm population rising fast enough to offset the decline in farm population. One must disaggregate such data, on a geographic basis, to understand what is really happening. The rising rural nonfarm population is largely a remotely located part of the urban population—located beyond the more closely built-up suburbs, but economically and socially just as much a part of the city as are the suburbs. If one omits the rural nonfarm areas lying within commuting distance of urban employment centers, then rural nonfarm areas are also losing population.

At the same time that people are concentrating in urban agglomerations, on one scale of measurement, they are also moving away from older centers of population, on another scale. City centers have generally lost population also partly because land in city centers has been taken for nonresidential uses, and also because central residential location is no longer as attractive as it once was. The suburbs around cities are growing; if "suburbs" is broadly defined, then virtually all the population increase is occurring here. These are the frontiers of the latter 20th century; it is no longer the Indians, but the real estate promoters, who scalp the unwary migrants; the "welcome wagon" has taken the place of the community roof raising or barn raising.

The modern migration from rural areas to urban agglomerations and from city centers to suburbs is selective as to race, income, age, and other personal characteristics—as was the 19th century westward migration and as have been most human migrations in world history. The city centers are rapidly becoming exclusively settled by racial minorities—Negroes in most cities, but Puerto Ricans and others in some. These, plus the higher income, childless white couples, either relatively old or relatively young, living in luxury apartments, are coming to dominate many central cities. The newer suburbs are typically middle- to upper-income whites, from white collar and professional occupations, young married couples with children. The sharp demographic differences entail major economic, social, and political consequences. Important as these are from a national viewpoint, they cannot be explored in this book on food and agricultural policy.

But these demographic changes are profoundly modifying the urban communities, considering the latter in their sociological sense. They are also markedly affecting farm and rural people. Migration always involves some destruction of the old community and the necessity to form some kind of a new community. People break old ties, personal, human, and group, as well as old economic ties; and they must find or make new ones in the new locations. In our view, these sociological changes in the modern era are fully as sweeping and dramatic as the more frequently remarked technological and economic changes now under way—granted the difficulty of a precise comparison of basically unlike factors or processes.

Farm and other rural people have been caught up in this migration and relocation process, and indeed have contributed to it. By and large, they must adjust to it—they are more affected by it than they are affecting it. In the process of adjusting to these broad social changes, farm people are rapidly destroying the older rural communities; professional workers and social servants can help them form new and different ones.

DEFINITION OF RURAL COMMUNITY

In this chapter, "community" is used in the sociological sense, of a series of relationships among people. But there is also a physical community—more visible and about which we have somewhat more, though still seriously limited, information—which often may be used as an index to the sociological or human community. Typically, a rural community in a spatial sense is a small city or town together with surrounding farm and nonfarm population. Today, the latter may utilize more than one town or city for their services of various kinds.

It is important to distinguish, and to define as far as data permit, the kind of rural towns used in this discussion, especially since some of the more readily accessible sources of data often confuse rural farm towns with other small towns. Through the 1940 census, the Bureau of the Census classified all incorporated towns and cities of 2500 and more as urban, and all smaller places as rural; beginning with 1950, some unincorporated and smaller places have been classified as urban, depending upon additional criteria. Throughout, there have been relatively large numbers of smaller "places," some unnamed and ill-defined yet congregations of people in somewhat nucleated fashion, and some incorporated or otherwise rather clearly defined towns, some rather old and well known, at least locally, all of which have been classified in the census statistics as "rural nonfarm."

Although classification systems have been developed to group cities of generally similar characteristics, there has never been developed, as far as we can learn, a system of classifying small towns and "places."[1] There would be a good many difficult problems in getting data about all such places, and their very numbers would make the classification somewhat difficult. These smaller towns and places could be classified according to their function: bedroom towns, where a substantial proportion (perhaps 30 percent or more) of the labor force regularly worked in a larger town elsewhere; resource extraction towns, such as mining or lumbering or fishing towns; the resort and tourist towns, the main functions of which are to provide services to visitors who come and stay for longer or shorter time periods; service places, along transportation routes, who serve the traveling public which is passing through; primarily farm service towns; and perhaps others. Or

---

[1] See the following: Harris, Chauncy D., "A Functional Classification of Cities in the United States," *Geographical Review*, XXXIII, January, 1943; Jones, Victor, and Andrew Collver, "Economic Classification of Cities and Metropolitan Areas," *The Municipal Year Book, 1959*, The International City Managers' Association, Chicago, 1959; Nelson, Howard J., "A Service Classification of American Cities," *Economic Geography*, XXXI, July, 1955; and Alexandersson, Gunnar, *The Industrial Structure of American Cities*, Univ. of Nebr. Press, Lincoln, 1956.

these smaller towns and places could be classified according to their distance from larger towns of various sizes, as this distance affects opportunities for employment and also the kind of commercial and trade services that the local population will seek from the smaller place. Or the smaller towns and places could be classified according to the population growth trends in the general region; the economic health of a small place in a region of growing population and economic activity is likely to be much better than a similar place located in a region of declining population and economic activity. Still other bases of classification might be employed, or combination classifications, using two or more kinds of considerations. These suggested factors are likely to be somewhat interrelated in a particular situation; that is, small, bedroom places are likely to be relatively close to larger cities and to be located in regions of growing population, while the farm service towns are mostly located further away and are in regions of declining population.

Karl Fox has shown that there is a hierarchy of towns and cities, from the smallest to the largest, with complex interrelationships among towns and cities of different sizes (4).

"Rural towns" will be considered as any towns of 2500 or less, and sometimes those of 5000 or less, which lie more than 30 miles distant from a city of 10,000 or more, and whose major economic support is not mining or lumbering. Hart and Salisbury found a sharp difference in growth rate between small towns located within 30 miles of such larger cities, and similar towns more distantly located (6). There is nothing magical about the figure 30, of course; the effective distance may be somewhat more or less. Certainly some people are willing to commute somewhat further than this, and yet within this range there may well be much agriculture and a social structure based upon agriculture. The essential thing is to distinguish between the largely independent rural town, primarily dependent upon agriculture, and equally small towns largely dependent upon a larger city or upon other economic activities.

A number of studies show that rural small towns of the general type have been declining in recent years. Fuguitt has found that in Wisconsin the smaller the small town, the more likely it is to be declining in population; the farther it is from cities of 25,000 and over, the more likely it is to be declining; and its chances of decline are greater if it is located in a region where total population is declining (5). By and large, small towns in southeastern Wisconsin have grown, especially if they were already over 1000 in population, whereas, with limited exceptions, small towns in other parts of the state have declined.

Antonides has shown that large numbers of small towns in the eastern half of South Dakota have been declining in population, especially when they were already small and performed only a limited trade function (1). This is a primarily agricultural region and many of these small towns were first established under the influence of horse-drawn transportation. In Nebraska there is a clear correlation between town size and rate of population change; the very smallest towns have lost heavily, those of 500 to 2000 population have lost somewhat, and those of over 2000 have generally gained (7). These population changes are related to diversity of commercial and trade services provided in towns of these sizes; the larger the town, the greater the variety of services and the greater the likelihood of future growth. These Nebraska towns are primarily agricultural. Hart and Salisbury, in the study previously referred to, found that village growth in nine midwestern states was also related to size of village; most villages with less than 250 people lost during the 1950–60 decade, about half of those with 250 to 500 lost, whereas more than two-thirds of those with over 750 people gained during this decade. Their study included all types of villages but many were agricultural.

The rural town, whatever its exact population, is economically dependent upon agriculture. Its economic, social, and political rationale lies in the services which it can provide to agricultural people, for their living and their productive activities. In turn, agriculture sustains their income.

It is not possible to present a map which shows clearly and accurately where these primarily rural towns are located. In the heavily urbanized area from Boston to Washington—the "megalopolis"; in the not-quite-so-heavily urbanized area from Pittsburgh across northern Ohio to Detroit, across southern Michigan and northern Indiana to Chicago, and up to Milwaukee; in the heavily urbanized areas of California; within the 30-mile zone around some other urban centers such as Atlanta, Birmingham, New Orleans, St. Louis, Cincinnati, Dallas-Fort Worth, Houston, Kansas City, Denver, Phoenix, Seattle, Portland, and other centers. Even in all these, some small towns and villages are to some degree agricultural. Outside these regions, a large part of the small towns and villages are farm oriented, although there are exceptions in the vacation country of New England and of the northern Lake States, and in mining and lumbering territory in several states. Although it is impossible to identify exactly which towns and areas are primarily farm oriented, it can be assumed that they are numerous and include considerable numbers of people. Most of the poor people to whom Tolley refers in Chapter 12 live in such small towns or in open country or on farms, in dominantly agricultural regions.

FORMER ROLE OF RURAL SMALL TOWNS

Small rural towns and intervening open-country business and social establishments of all kinds, arising in the age of horse-drawn equipment, provided places where the farmer bought goods and services for his home and his farm, where he marketed his output, where his children went to school, where he and his family attended church, where they usually buried their dead in the country church yard, and where he found other social and political services necessary to his life. Animal-drawn transportation on country roads averaged four miles per hour or less, and distances between farms and service establishments of all kinds were geared to this rate of speed. It was desirable that distances be short enough for towns to be visited, goods and services obtained, and the return trip made to the farm in less than a day. This resulted in rural towns that were small, in spite of the fact that farms often averaged smaller in area than is true today and a farm population density that was higher than now.

The average county in the United States, until the 11 western states were settled, was less than one-half million acres in extent; if square, its sides would average 26 miles. The most remote resident, even if he had to travel north-south and east-west roads running only at right angles, was only 26 miles from the center of the county; most were far closer. For most farmers, it was possible to travel to the county seat, conduct business, and return in one day, although a long one in some instances. For most shopping, smaller towns more closely located could be visited in still less time. Grade schools were typically on a township or other local district basis; a substantial proportion of the children could walk to school.

The rural community, using that term in the sociological sense, under these conditions was very much a face-to-face one. People knew their neighbors and nearly everyone they might see, even when they went to town. It had the virtues of humaneness and of small-scale personalness. These virtues have often been lauded or glorified. But such localized communities had another side also. They were frequently dictatorial, in terms of social or group domination over the individual. Everyone not only knew everyone else; he also knew all about everyone's personal life. There was little privacy; indiscretions did not go unnoticed nor unremarked. Gossiping was a major activity of many persons.

Whatever the virtues and limitations of the highly localized rural community of more than a generation ago in the United States—and of somewhat similar rural communities in many other parts of the world today—such communities have largely ceased to exist in the United States, although some of their aspects may yet be found.

CHANGES IN THE ROLE
OF THE RURAL SMALL TOWN

As transportation methods changed, the rural towns and communities have perforce changed also. By the early 1920's, the predominantly dirt and gravel rural roads of that day and the autos then available had raised the average speed of rural travel to perhaps 25 miles per hour, as contrasted with the four miles per hour of horse-drawn equipment. Today, with most rural roads paved, trucks and autos probably have an average speed in rural areas of close to 50 miles per hour. Traffic densities are typically low, and delays due to traffic are small. Multiplying by ten or more the average speed per mile on rural roads in 60 years or so has enormously widened the service area of any particular town. By the same token, it has equally widened the area from which the farm family can secure the goods and services it needs, and in the process has exposed the small towns to a degree of competition, one with another, which formerly was lacking.

Farm and other people today are not content with the old-time distance relationships for economic, social, and political services. If they were, there could be 160 counties in the United States today, instead of 3000, for instance. As a nation, we have taken some of our rise in real income, or in productivity, in the form of more conveniently located services, so that less time is spent per trip. At the same time, major changes in life style have made people much more dependent upon frequent purchases of goods and services, so that it may well be that more, not less, total travel time is involved. But farmers can and do travel today far beyond the town which served their fathers and grandfathers.

As part of the change in life styles, some kinds of services have now been brought to the farm. In particular, most farms today are electrified, with all that this means in terms of radio and TV, of kitchen appliances, and of living generally. Farm people today are demanding much better services of many kinds. They are no longer satisfied with the small grocery or general store with its limited choice of goods, which were frequently stale, and with its all too often generally dirty appearance that was so common a generation or more ago in many rural areas. Instead, today's farm family wants grocery supermarkets, good furniture and clothing stores, and other retail establishments that compare favorably with those in the larger cities. Likewise, the typical rural church, with its small congregation and its part-time and poorly trained preacher, is completely outmoded.

Changes that have taken place in public services in rural areas have been, on the whole, less marked than the changes in buying habits. Many schools have been consolidated, and children taken by bus to more distant schools, but county government and many other aspects of rural life have remained much less changed.

In addition to these changes in rural living patterns other changes have had their impact on the rural towns. In particular, farm numbers have been shrinking rapidly until at present they are down to less than half their peak, on a national scale, with somewhat greater adjustments in some areas balancing smaller adjustments elsewhere. The predominant part of the reduction in number of farms has been by young men not entering farming; withdrawals of older men in farming have not been accelerated.[2] The remaining farmers are getting older, and indications are that the average age of farmers will rise considerably further by 1980, after which it may decline somewhat.

At the same time, farm technology is changing rapidly. Farmers today purchase far more of their inputs for production than once was the case. Farm machines of all kinds must be purchased, and their servicing and repair is frequently hired also. These advances have changed the kinds and quantities of goods and services which the farmer buys from a town supplier, and the point of purchase has shifted away from the small village toward the larger towns and cities.

In the provision of goods and services which the farmer buys today for his family living and for his farm production processes,

---

[2] See articles by Jackson V. McElveen, "Farm Numbers, Farm Size and Farm Income"; by Marion Clawson, "Aging Farmers and Agricultural Policy"; G. S. Tolley and H. W. Hjort, "Age-Mobility and Southern Farmer Skill—Looking Ahead for Area Development"; and Don Kanel, "Farm Adjustments by Age Groups, North Central States 1950–1959," *J. Farm Econ.*, Vol. 45, No. 1, Feb., 1963.

there are important economies of scale. These are less evident in the prices he pays for particular commodities or services than they are in the quality of the goods or services. That is, the large grocery supermarket may not sell particular items much cheaper than the small grocery store, but it may have a vastly wider range of goods and a better quality of each. Likewise, the larger farm supply town is likely to have a much better stock of spare parts for the farm tractor than does the smaller town, although the price for a particular part may be identical in each. Medical services may actually be cheaper in the small town, but facilities may be inadequate for dealing with many illnesses in a completely modern way. Many other examples could be cited.

It has become customary to refer to the agricultural changes as an agricultural revolution; the combination of a doubling in output, with half the labor input, with somewhat less cropland, and with a changed capital input but not a much greater one, all in one generation, can properly be called a revolution. Brewster has pointed out that farmers have been eager to adopt new, more productive, and often more efficient methods of farm production, which have had the indirect effect of destroying the economic base upon which the rural towns rested (2). At the same time, farmers have generally opposed changes in the social and institutional structure to meet these new life styles and new productive processes. They have shown a marked preference for rural living as it was, while at the same time busily dismantling the rationale for that pattern of rural life. The incongruity of their actions seems not to have been apparent to them and, with few exceptions, to agricultural professional workers.

As a result of all these factors, the rural small towns as defined here have been declining somewhat in population and much more in volume of business and in economic health. Unfortunately, the available statistics are not in a form to measure this readily. It is not an exaggeration to say that rural towns are sick.

Although precise data seem to be lacking, it seems highly probable that the rural small towns are suffering the same adverse changes in age distribution that farmers are suffering, and for the same reason. Young people can more readily move away from a location where their economic and social ties are less binding, and they can more readily get a job and adjust to a new environment, than can older people from the same towns. In some degree, the population of rural small towns has been bolstered because farmers have retired to live in them; but this has only aggravated the age imbalance of such towns. The decline of small rural towns since World War II may be but the prelude to a much greater and swifter decline in a few years, when the present older people pass out of the picture and there are few young ones to replace them.

NEED FOR RESEARCH

An essential requisite for healthy rural communities of the future is vastly more research on how farm and rural town people can best use economic, social, and political services of all kinds. There has been some limited research done to date, but in general, it has been too fragmentary in outlook, too inclined to study only one aspect of rural life, and too unimaginative in dealing with the needs of the future.

What population and spatial structure would provide the best economic, social, and political services for rural people, at reasonable costs? (3.) In my view, such research can best start with the farm. In view of production and living requirements where should the farmstead be located and the farm family live in the future? Need the farmer live on his land at all? Might he not live in town and commute to the farm, just as urban workers live in one spot and commute to work? Might we not create a new type of farm village where farmers live and from which they drive their pickup trucks or autos a good many miles, if necessary, to their fields and barns? Needless to say, such farm villages of the future would not house the farm livestock nor store the farm crops nor be the source of the farm manure, as have farm villages traditionally been around the world. Might not the whole pattern of rural roads be changed in the direction of fewer but better roads at wider intervals? Could not the homes of farmers who did live on their farms be clustered along such major roads?

In considering an optimum pattern of rural communities for the future, scale-cost relations and, even more, scale-quality relations are highly important. That is, most retail establishments serving rural people operate in the declining cost range of the scale-cost curves, but in the rising phase of the scale-quality curves. A larger grocery store will have lower costs per unit, but fresher vegetables and fruits, a wider range of more durable commodities, and generally be a better place to shop. The same is true of almost all other retail establishments; it is also generally true for social services of all kinds. Moreover, the rural town with a larger volume of business may be able to support two or more efficient firms providing similar services, thus bringing the advantages of competition. The larger schools are much likelier to have good libraries, good teachers, good laboratories, lower costs per pupil, a wider range of subject matter classes, and such cultural activities as drama. County and other local government is also likely to show similar scale-cost and scale-quality relations. Costs per unit may indeed rise for any or all of these aspects of living, beyond some volume of business, and quality may indeed fall beyond some size; but the point or the range at which increasing cost and/or declining quality begins is usually far above the size likely to be found in the rural community of the future, even if it is vastly larger than the rural community of today. The small number of people per square mile or other unit of area inevitably limits potential volume of customers.

The scale-cost and scale-quality relations for the services at the point of service are, however, only part of the story. In order to get volume, it will be necessary for some users to travel farther, either from their homes on the land to the town or city where the services are provided, or from their farm village homes to their farms. Travel involves both money costs and time; the travel-cost curve generally rises steadily as numbers of customers increase. A falling scale-cost curve for services at the point of service and a rising scale-cost curve for travel to get to that point of service obviously results in some form of U-shaped curve. The research problem is to locate it vertically, in terms of probable costs per unit, and to show its general shape—in particular, how wide and flat is its valley? Similar considerations apply to scale-quality relations also.

In research on these matters, it will be the interactions between different kinds of business, social, and governmental services which is especially important, and which has been most neglected in the past. The farmer and his family are interested not only in buying good quality groceries at reasonable prices, but also furniture, clothing, household appliances, and a host of other goods for modern living, and for each of these the scale-cost and scale-quality considerations are important; likewise for farm machines of all types, fertilizer and feed, and many other goods and services for use in the farm productive process. Also of concern for both cost and quality are general business services such as banks, social services such as entertainment in its broadest scope, health services of all kinds, schools, and other matters. As suburban residents go to different shopping districts, the farm family might go to one rural town for one kind of goods or services and to another town for another type, yet it is also true that there are very great advantages in a wide variety of goods and services obtainable at one center. Modern suburban shopping districts have found enormous advantages in having a wide variety of services, with some degree of competition for at least some of them, at each center or individual shopping district. Each kind of business or other establishment tends to strengthen the others in what might well be called a community scale-cost and community scale-quality relationship, which may overshadow that at the enterprise level.

Research in this general field might, of course, study experience in towns and establishments of different sizes and types. Studies have indeed been made which establish some optimum range of volume of business for modern grocery supermarkets, or for furniture or clothing stores, or which show per pupil costs and quality of education with size of school, or general county costs in relation to population or county area. But small-scale enterprises in practice often have high costs because they are poorly designed—are really partly larger scale enterprises used at only partial capacity. More importantly, studies which focus on only one aspect of total living necessarily must take "as a given" the actual kinds and qualities of the other aspects of living.

A more fruitful approach might be to construct essentially engineering models of rural communities of different sizes and different volumes of customers, perhaps with different patterns of location of the rural customers. Such a model-building approach would utilize all available information on scale-cost and scale-quality relationships, of course; but its focus should be on the interactions between different kinds of business, social, and political units. It would surely include school, health, library, entertainment, and other aspects as well as provision of consumption and production goods.

All aspects of life considered, what would be the optimum scale—considering not only cost but also quality and use of time by customers for travel—of the rural community? This might necessarily involve some kinds of business or of social services operating at a less than optimum scale. The answer would not necessarily involve rural communities with only one town or other service point; they might be multinucleated and with different areas for different aspects of rural life.

Such research should also explore explicitly the relationship between different but nearby small towns. That is, how far might one kind of function be performed in one town, and another function in another town? Might, for instance, the grade schools be in one town and the high school in another? Or the farm machinery dealer in one town and the furniture store in another? Intuitively, I suspect that such division of functions between towns, except as an interim measure in an adjustment process, is not practical; but careful research might yield a different answer.

Such research should also consider the social and political power structure of small towns, and how far existing structures would be disrupted by any shift toward fewer but larger and more viable rural towns. Some persons now occupy positions of economic, social, or political power and strength in each town; would they regard as a threat to their personal position any effort to build toward a more effective rural community structure? If so, could their opposition be reduced or minimized in some way? Questions of costs of economic and social services and of their quality, while highly important, are rarely the only or even the major considerations in motivating people to act. Research on human attitudes and actions is as possible as research on strictly economic or cost relationships.

Such essentially engineering models of future rural communities obviously should try to deal with anticipated conditions in the future, not with present conditions. The longer the time horizon, the more difficult to estimate all the factors involved; yet if any effort is made to implement the research findings, they must be forward looking.

Research on this general problem must surely be interdisciplinary if it is to be really successful. The reference to engineering models has been primarily to distinguish them from purely economic models. The space relationships of these models would have major importance; many economic models do not explicitly deal with spatial relationships. Transportation engineers or planners might indeed well be involved, but so would the farm management specialist, the business management researcher, the sociologist, and many others. The need to deal with the full range of economic, social, and political aspects of rural life, and to include quality as well as cost considerations, would surely require a broad and comprehensive approach.

Research of the type outlined here could properly be undertaken by the land-grant colleges and the USDA, as well as by other organizations. Very little such research has been undertaken in the past—one factor may have been a fear that rural people would resent any study which implied that the rural community was not healthy and vigorous. However, evidence that all is not well with rural communities is now so overwhelming that many people might welcome research which seemed to offer some hope of improvement. Some means will have to be found to put some steam behind such research, if a significant volume of it is to be done in time to be of real help in meeting the problems of the presently decadent rural communities. The federal government might help strengthen the rural communities which appear most viable, and a later section outlines how that help might be extended in a way which would greatly encourage research within each state.

NEED FOR PLANNING

Although more incisive and inclusive research on the organization of the future rural community is necessary, it alone will not be sufficient if material progress is to be made. Organized planning for rural community betterment will also be necessary. Research results will presumably have rather general applicability—the relationships established between various factors should apply under a considerable variety of circumstances. Actual change in a rural community will depend upon circumstances in that community; change must begin from the existing situation and lead toward some defined end, if not actually achieving the latter. Railroad lines and major through highways exist and presumably will remain more or less indefinitely. Present town structure will persist for some time, even under the most effective planning and operations. For the longer future, many towns may decline and disappear, while a few others might grow considerably.

Planning for rural community betterment must start with present facts. In particular, economic investments in buildings and physical works of all kinds provide an opportunity for their further use; such capital is sunk, and therefore costless as long as the works involved are usable. New investment is a different story, of course; but the fact that the latter is ordinarily incremental, with the decision at each point being based upon existing structure of other buildings and services, as well as upon future outlook, tends to perpetuate present patterns which would never arise anew if the slate were clean.

More important than the physical plant, however, are the present attitudes of the residents of the area. Their willingness to face change may be critical. In any event, planning would focus on an optimum plan or structure of each rural community for 1980 or the year 2000 or some other future date, with "optimum" being defined to include as wide or as narrow a range of subject matter as the resident and nonresident decision makers were willing to consider.

The first and most basic consideration in any improvement in rural communities for the future is to face facts honestly and courageously, not to live in a dream world of what is hoped for but mostly unlikely of realization. The typical rural community is not merely decaying; it is doomed. Retention as it now exists is not a real alternative for the future. The assumption that something like the past or present rural community could be rebuilt by some future date seems most unlikely, but is attainable, if at all, only by substantial effort and cost. A drastically different rural community is in process of evolution, its form is still subject to modification, but it is possible to achieve one that will not evolve "naturally."

In this connection, it may be useful to distinguish between a rural community structure that is viable, in the sense that it can survive, and one that is optimum. The distinction is analogous to that between statisfying and optimizing, in the conventional economic analysis. Farmers and other rural people might seek to establish a rural community for the future which resembles those of the past as far as possible, and yet be sufficiently viable to persist and function; this would be a minimum change compatible with survival. The considerable investment in present physical works and the strong attitudes toward certain kinds of change would be forces leading toward such a minimum-change plan. A truly optimum rural community, one which might evolve were the slate clean and were present forces to continue operative unchanged indefinitely into the future, might be very different.

At any rate, any plan for future rural communities must have major local citizen participation, not be simply an "expert" plan. One need not accept local judgments as infallible or even as always informed, and yet one might recognize that local attitudes will be strongly influential if not dominant in decisions taken to implement any plan. The informed expert, without deep emotional commitment to a particular local situation, will almost certainly be an essential member of any effective planning group. Local participation should not be limited to farm people; the small town and nonfarm rural people have an equal stake in the structure and functioning of the rural community. The territorial extent of planning for future rural communities should ordinarily not be limited to a single county; even if one assumes that county government and county boundaries are sacrosanct—which we do not—yet any informed person will realize that the future service area of many economic and social services will not be confined to a present county.

Effective citizen participation in planning always means slower evolvement of the formal plan than does expert planning; it is less clear that it means delay in actual achievement of results. Planning for social services and structure of the rural community may be touchy business; local defenders of the status quo or of the status ante may resent outside advice and help and be suspicious of motives. Yet it is also true that in most rural areas both farmers and townspeople are capable of intelligent and far-sighted decisions if they are fully informed of the relevant facts. If a major effort were to be made to improve the rural community of the future along the lines outlined above or in any other way, there would probably be a noticeable reluctance to face up to these facts—there would be a natural inclination to hope that the present decay of the rural community would come to an end, that a new form of stability would arise, that a new social and economic structure would arise which would prove viable and tolerable if not better, and in general to avoid the hard choices that the foregoing analysis regards as inevitable. On the other hand, the signs of decay in the rural community are, or soon will be, obvious to almost everyone, and it is altogether possible that farmers and townspeople from rural towns might seek to build substantially better rural communities for the future. The duty of the expert is to show them as clearly as possible what their real alternatives are.

Questions might be raised about the criteria for this type of rural community planning. One obvious criterion might be the minimization of cost of business and personal services and the maximization of personal gains. For instance, it is sometimes said that a town must have a trade population of 6500 in order to support an automobile agency, or of 50,000 to support a modern department store, or that it must have a high school graduating class of at least 100 in order to provide adequate instructional opportunity to its young people. Such statements of standards have some value in indicating general scales of size; but they can also be quite misleading, because costs per unit of output fall over a wide range, while quality of service often increases over the same range, and one cannot reasonably say that a high school with 99 graduates is inadequate while one with 100 is adequate or that an automobile agency can be supported with 6500 population but not with 6400. There are falling cost curves and rising quality curves for most ranges of size in small towns for most services; the minimum-cost point for one service may not be the same as the minimum-cost point for another. While it is true that a minimum-cost point could be calculated for all economic and social services combined, it may well be that the people concerned would make their choices on other factors as well. For instance, the degree of school consolidation that would produce lowest costs per pupil and/or highest quality of education per pupil might involve more transportation of students than most parents would choose. While we think cost and quality considerations—however the latter might be measured—are highly important for all economic and social services, yet we think it both probable and desirable that some decisions include other factors as well; if the people who bear the costs and who receive the results prefer some other alternative, when they are aware of all the facts, we think they should be allowed that choice.

MEASURES TO STRENGTHEN
VIABLE FUTURE RURAL COMMUNITIES

Assuming that a plan or plans for a future rural community—hopefully solidly based and capable of realization—have been drawn up and have strong public support within the area as well as elsewhere, the next major step would seem to be to strengthen those rural towns which seem to have a viable or prosperous future or which can be made to have one. This assumption that any plans must inevitably strive to strengthen some towns while allowing or helping others to decline and eventually to fold up presents special problems.

A well-thought-out and factually supported plan for a rural community would contain within itself some of the force for its realization. New businesses would tend to locate, or existing businesses to expand, in towns marked for survival or expansion, and not in other towns. Some new building or rebuilding takes place at intervals, and over a period of time a good deal could be accomplished toward building up a particular viable rural community. To the extent that this was successful for the stronger community or communities, it would tend further to weaken those already weak, and this in turn would strengthen the development of the stronger ones. The town or city growth process is often cumulative, as is the decline process.

Perhaps more force could be put into the plans for rural community development through various public programs. To the extent that hospitals, schools, parks, cultural activities, and other public programs could be concentrated in the town or towns planned for development or retention, this would be a powerful element in itself and even more in terms of the other activities it would attract. Various state and federal programs operate through local offices, and their existence can be a strong force in developing some towns, just as their absence or their removal would be a major factor in the decline of others. Federal and state financing of locally run programs is also important, and may become more so. The establishment of standards as to size and quality of facilities, size of service area, and the like could go far toward concentrating activities in the stronger rural towns. All of this would have much greater force if some programs were to operate on regional bases, with regions composed of several counties, rather than to operate on a county basis. The direction of state and federal programs and financial support to some towns or cities and not to others always has some political overtones, and might be hard to support as an administrative action of the higher level of government. However, if taken to help implement a plan developed locally, such actions would have a very different appearance to the local people.

The possibilities along this line may be dramatized by a suggestion, which might or might not be feasible in execution. Suppose that the federal government were to locate its own offices and to limit the implementation of its grants in aid, in agriculture, education, health, housing, and other fields to small cities which were the trade center for a total population of 30,000 people. This might be modified, by permitting smaller centers if the total population within a radius of perhaps 50 miles were less than 30,000, in order to meet some of the problems of the thinly settled plains and the West. Or it might be modified to meet any locally developed community plan, if it could be shown by careful research and planning that substantially the same economies in cost and in quality of service could be attained by the alternate plan. Direct federal specification would be enormously influential in strengthening the rural community centers to which the programs applied; permitting alternate local plans that were based upon research and planning would equally stimulate the latter. We do not wish to make too much of this specific proposal; the point is that public policy, including policy of the federal government, can be effective in producing action in local community planning.

To those who think that this use of the powers of central government is undesirable, it should be pointed out that the powers of that same government are now used to influence local community structure and inevitably will be as long as any federal programs provide funds for local programs. The real policy issue is: to what ends or purpose should those powers of federal government be directed?

MEASURES TO CONSOLIDATE NONVIABLE RURAL TOWNS

The foregoing may be described as a policy to "accentuate the positive"—to put primary emphasis on building up rural towns and rural communities which can have viable futures. It is based on the assumption that a substantial proportion of all present rural towns are nonviable in the absence of some special programs and that not all of them could be made viable with any programs for their help. By definition, a nonviable rural town will not endure and prosper in any event; it is going downhill now, will go faster in the next couple of decades, until it reaches a very low level or expires completely. Some people who live in such towns as well as some others may feel that this picture has been overdrawn, that the future of the average rural town is not as black as we have painted it. The evidence seems clear that the situation will grow more marked, perhaps at an accelerating rate. If this is right, then preservation of many existing rural towns as functioning rural communities is impossible in any case. Further study would help to make a better supported judgment in this area, but a full test of rural town viability could only come over a period of years, as towns died or lived or prospered.

Assuming that a policy of drift toward small rural towns would eventually result in a great many of them becoming no longer functional, this policy seems unacceptable because its costs would be too high. Some of the costs could easily be measurable in terms of greater cash expenditures or in terms of smaller cash incomes, but much would come in more human terms of wasted lives spent in a declining local society. We consider it socially irresponsible to allow rural people to commit several years of their lives to situations where failure is ultimately inevitable, without at least advising and warning them of the outlook. A "drift" policy may be rational if one challenges the facts upon which the decline of such towns is based, but it seems doubtful as a desirable policy if such facts are accepted.

If an effort were made to help the people of declining rural towns deal more directly with their problems, a number of measures seem practical:

1. Public aid might be extended to help employable people migrate and get established elsewhere—including within the rural town planned for retention and expansion. Such aid might take the form of paying moving expenses, retraining the workers involved, payment of some re-establishment costs, and perhaps limited-income support during the early period in the new location. Such aid obviously would be most helpful to those persons best qualified by reason of age or training for new jobs elsewhere.

2. Public aid might be extended through subsidized early retirement of workers in the declining rural towns; for instance, workers might be helped to retire at 55 by providing the same retirement income they would have normally received at 65. If the workers in the declining rural towns are as old as we think they are, and if the migration away from such towns continues, then a substantial proportion are, or will be within a decade, over 55 years of age. By and large, it would be better if such early retired workers moved elsewhere—frequently to relatively nearby rural towns planned for strengthening—rather than to continue to live in their old locations. It is true that they often have housing where they are and personal ties of many kinds; but it is also true that such towns will increasingly become poor locations for elderly people, as public services decline and as young people increasingly leave. By their relocation, the dying towns could gradually be adjusted out of the picture and the growing towns could be aided.

3. Homes, businesses, and other privately owned properties in the dying towns might be purchased, either as part of the two foregoing programs or separately for those who wished to move on their own. The salvage value of an unneeded small rural town is enormously less than the salvage value of an unnecessary farm; the land and livestock of the latter, sometimes its machinery and some of its buildings, have a value for the farm to which it is added. But the homes and businesses of a small town whose economic rationale is disappearing have little value. Their purchase—and presumably their demolition or salvage for other use—would have some similarities to the purchase of submarginal farms in the 1930's, when one purpose was to ease the departure of stranded farm families. Payments for such individual proper-

ties would, for the most part, be subsidy; the chances of salvaging much from them would be low.

4. Financial aid might be extended to pay for public facilities such as schools or municipal water supply or sewage disposal plants. These, too, would have very little value indeed as the rural town drifted downhill. However, if some payment were to be made for such public property it should not be made to the local town where it is located, but rather to the towns or other units of local government where these people will relocate. If the purpose is to help ease the liquidation of a dying rural town, it would be a contrary action to give that town a subsidy for its unneeded property; but the money could materially strengthen the same services in the growing towns.

In the case of both individual and public property, the question of payment of creditors would arise. Some property would have mortgages or would have bonded indebtedness. If subsidy from federal or state sources were used to pay only part of the former market value of such structures, the help would be more to the lenders than to the nominal property owners. It might be necessary to insist upon some scale-down of debt. If the rural community is really dying, then the loans are of dubious value in any case.

CONCLUDING COMMENT

Although the sociological and community problems of farm and rural small town people have had comparatively little attention in the past, we would argue that these problems have been fully as important as the farm income problems which have had so much attention and so much public funds. If our goal is healthy rural and farm living, satisfying to those who live there and able to hold some proportion of its young people, then more attention must be paid to these problems. Research, planning, and action programs are needed.

LITERATURE CITED

1. Antonides, R. J. Some Guidelines for Organizing Economic Development Efforts in South Dakota Along Trade Area Lines. Ext. Cir. 651. S.D. State Univ., Brookings. Aug. 1966.
2. Brewster, J. M. What Kind of Social and Economic Order Do We Want in the Plains? Proc. of Great Plains Agricultural Council. Published by Great Plains Agr. Council, Univ. of Nebr., Lincoln. 1964.

3. Clawson, M. Factors and forces affecting the optimum rural settlement pattern in the United States. Econ. Geog., Oct., 1966.
4. Fox, K. A. The study of interactions between agriculture and the nonfarm economy: local, regional and national. J. Farm Econ., 44:1–34. 1962.
5. Fuguitt, G. V. Growing and Declining Villages in Wisconsin, 1950–1960. No. 8, Population Series, Dept. of Rural Soc., Univ. of Wis., Madison. The small town in rural America. J. of Coop. Ext., Spring, 1965; Trends in unincorporated places, 1950–60. Demography, Vol. 2. 1965; and, with D. R. Field. The Social Characteristics of Villages Differentiated by Size, Location, and Growth. (Undated mimeo.)
6. Hart, J. F. and N. E. Salisbury. Population change in middlewestern villages: a statistical approach. Annals of the Assoc. of Amer. Geographers, 55: No. 1. March, 1965.
7. Ottoson, H. W. et al. Land and People in the Northern Plains Transition Area. Lincoln: Univ. of Nebr. Press. 1966.

CHAPTER FOURTEEN

Implications of Export Policy Choices for American Agriculture

A. A. MONTGOMERY and E. E. WEEKS

HISTORICAL BACKGROUND

THE INTERDEPENDENCY of American agriculture and the world economy long has been of prominent importance to the welfare of the farmer and the nation. Historically, the foreign demand for American farm products gave impetus to the westward expansion of agriculture and it supported capital investment that helped make possible the nation's subsequent development into a continental industrial power. Except for brief war periods in the present century, however, America's economic development and the history of agriculture itself until recently have been less perceptibly influenced by agriculture's relation to the world economy. Having built an immense and largely self-sustaining industrial economy upon its agricultural base, 20th-century America became its own best customer for its food and fiber production. Because of this development and introspective farm policy outlook engendered by the depression of international trade throughout most of the first half of the century, the course of agriculture has been largely insulated from world affairs.

But events of the past decade promise that agriculture's

history in the remainder of the century will, as stated in Chapter Two, depend importantly upon the volume of exports. One of the key developments has been the accelerated growth of agricultural productivity. Despite, and partly because of, the continued exodus of labor from agriculture it became clear in the 1950's and 1960's that agriculture has the capacity to increase production more rapidly than warranted by the prospective growth of domestic demand over the coming decades. At the same time, much of this recent growth in capacity has been utilized to produce for foreign markets.

The number of the nation's cropland acres harvested for export purposes has more than doubled from the 1952–54 level to the present total of approximately 78 million acres. Correspondingly, the share of the nation's total harvested acres attributable to exports increased from approximately 10 percent to 26 percent. Public policy has encouraged agriculture's growing relative dependence upon exports, but the recent growth trend is almost wholly the result of a dramatic increase in commercial farm exports. Because of this resurgence in commercial exports, agriculture has once again assumed importance in the nation's economic relations with the world. Farm exports remain small in relation to the national economy but they now comprise about one-fourth of the nation's exports.

Significant as the growth of commercial exports has been, the growth in productivity would have weighed heavily upon farm prices and income had it not been for the recent success of government efforts to divert cropland from production. In 1966, some 60 million acres were diverted, an amount equivalent to about four-fifths of the cropland currently harvested for both commercial and concessional exports. For the most part, these acres were diverted under a program that offers the farmer as much income for his diverted acreage as he could net from its output. Because of farmer response to this incentive, the government has achieved much greater control over the volume of production. At the same time, the cost to the taxpayers is far less than if the government had attempted to support farm income by purchasing the output of the diverted acreage.

A related development or set of developments was set in motion by the public decision in the mid-1950's to make available agricultural surpluses to nations too poor to be effectively in the world market for these commodities. It is well remembered that P.L. 480 was passed as a means to help us rid ourselves of a stockpile of commodities that was embarrassing to the price support program and costly to store. This objective has been achieved without major disturbance to world markets and food production in recipient nations. More than this, because of the acreage diversion alternative that now exists, food aid is no longer needed to help support the level of farm income. However, in the process of this disposal operation, food aid has come to serve broader purposes than the support of farm income.

For one thing, food aid has become a tool of our foreign economic policy. Chapter One discussed and evaluated the contribution food aid has or may make to the stability and development of the world's emerging nations, and examples could be cited where our foreign policy interests have been served by this means. At this point, the value of food aid as a tool of development and diplomacy is subject to debate. But there are other considerations. In light of the sense of urgency given the age-old world food problem by the postwar growth of population, few would argue that human welfare demands a continuation, if not expansion, of food aid until the agricultural self-help efforts of food-deficit nations become effective.

On a less altruistic plane, some who have been encouraged by the fact that former recipients of our aid have become important commercial customers, see food aid as a device to stimulate future markets for American farm products in the largely tropical and subtropical developing nations. Others point to the fact that the foreign currency earned by concessional shipments help support U.S. activities in recipient countries that would otherwise require tax support and a drain upon our balance of payments. Similarly, the nation's merchant marine and other shipping and storage interests as well as industries supplying inputs to and processing the output of agriculture may argue that they need the business directly and indirectly generated by food aid. For that matter, as will be seen, even the nation's consumers may have an interest in the continuation of food aid.

EXPORT POLICY CHOICES

If agriculture's productive capacity continues to grow more rapidly than domestic demand, analyses demonstrate that the key determinant of agriculture's history over the remainder of the century will be the rate of growth in farm exports. Agricultural policy, in turn, will importantly determine export growth. At least recent legislation and statements by agricultural officials indicate this will be the case over the near future. Taking a long-term view, there will be a continuing choice between a policy in which exports are considered as an exogenous variable in the deliberations of those who manage the farm program mechanism and a policy which attempts to make exports a management variable itself and seeks to serve broader social interests than the support of farm income.

The former policy choice would imply an attempt to meet the income requirements of agriculture by balancing the growth of domestic and foreign commercial demand against a supply constrained well within limits of growing productive capacity and by subsidizing farmers for unused capacity. This has been the policy direction of recent years, notwithstanding continued concessional exports of commodities from surplus stocks. The alternative policy would promote reasonably full use of agriculture's growing capacity for various social purposes as well as for commercial demand. To be more specific, this policy would not only attempt to stimulate commercial exports, but it would augment them with concessional shipments of commodities from land presently diverted from production or, possibly in the long run, with shipments from land brought into production by public and private investment. Circumstances have tended to reorient our policy outlook in this direction so it is our intention here to examine its implications. A full analysis of the question of whether and how far to pursue this policy would entail consideration of the value of concessional shipments to recipient nations as well as the domestic benefits and costs. In focusing upon the latter, we run the risk of seeming to advocate expanding food aid to the neglect of policy alternatives. It should be made clear that cash aid, technical assistance, adjustments in raw material import policies, assistance in the penetration of our markets by manufacturers of developing nations, and other actions deserve national consideration as well as the food aid alternative.

ASSESSMENT OF THE SITUATION

REORIENTATION OF FARM POLICY

The transition from an introspective farm policy, principally concerned with the support of farm income as such, to one in which the nation's world responsibilities will influence the allocation of agricultural resources has already begun. The broad outline of this policy reorientation is plainly discernible in recent legislative statements by agricultural officials. In his appearance at the Committee Hearings for the Food for Peace

(Freedom) Act of 1966 and a companion measure to establish commodity reserves, Secretary of Agriculture Orville L. Freeman succinctly outlined the direction of the new policy:

> Food for Freedom needs would be taken into account by the Secretary when he exercises his responsibilities under domestic farm programs. These programs are flexible enough so that production can now be geared to potential use. They will be administered so that American agriculture will produce enough food and fiber to meet domestic needs, commercial exports, food aid for those developing nations that are determined to help themselves, and reserves adequate to meet any emergency and to insure price stability. Commodities available to food recipient countries will no longer be as limited as they have been in the past. The commodity "mix" sent abroad under concessional programs will be geared to the kind needed rather than circumscribed by the kinds held in stocks. We can expect the trend to be in the direction of commodities with special nutritional values.[1]

An elaboration of the objectives and procedures of the new farm policy is to be found in the Food and Agriculture Act of 1965 and the Food for Peace Act of 1966. Among the set of general policy objectives affirmed by this legislation are several that are relevant for this discussion. Of course, a high ranking purpose will be to support the economic progress and welfare of commercial agriculture through maintenance of adequate income levels. At the same time, in the interest of consumers as well as farmers, it will be policy to promote stability of commodity prices. National farm policy will continue to encourage farm exports and, more generally, international trade in agricultural commodities. Finally, food aid will continue, but the new policy stress will be upon the economic development of the recipient nations. To facilitate these objectives, Congress has given the Department of Agriculture considerable authority for the year-to-year management of the national policy for commercial agriculture. In particular the Secretary of Agriculture has been provided with authority to react immediately to situational change.

FOOD FOR PEACE ACT OF 1966

The Food for Peace Act of 1966 reflects an almost complete reversal in policy maker attitudes concerning the relation between American commercial agriculture and the millions of hungry people abroad. The letter of the law now commits us to use our

---

[1] From Hearings before the Committee on Agriculture and Forestry, U.S. Senate, 89th Congress, p. 37.

agricultural capacity and expertise in agriculture to promote the economic growth of the emerging countries. This new turn in policy, it should be emphasized, is not motivated merely by moral consideration or, for that matter, the nation's foreign policy interests. The plain fact is the developing nations comprise an immense potential market for our commercial farm exports that can be successfully exploited only if they achieve significantly higher levels of income. It is equally plain that their economic growth cannot be sustained if they rely upon our food aid to the neglect of their problems of food production and population control.

For this reason and because there simply isn't enough capacity to make up the food deficits of these nations in the long run if present trends in population and agricultural productivity continue, it is the intent of the new legislation that food aid recipients must demonstrate a willingness to help themselves. More than this, it seems clear that Congress intends that the United States provide food aid in the short run only. At the same time, the legislation reflects a genuine desire to accommodate the food needs of the developing nations. The Secretary of Agriculture no longer has to declare commodities in surplus before they can be shipped under this program to recipient countries. Thus, he has the power to commit productive capacity as well as commodity stocks to their use. We have also committed ourselves to giving more weight to the preferences and nutritional needs of receiving nations in determining the profile or mix of commodities offered them.

There are other aspects of the new legislation that may have greater significance than the publicity they have received. While concessional sales for foreign currency will continue, it is intended to shift the terms of sale to long-term dollar credits by 1970. One reason for this is that the unused balances of foreign currency have been an object of criticism in recipient nations and at home. The announcement of this intention also gives our aid negotiators greater leverage in the meanwhile to encourage long-term dollar sales when this would be to the advantage of our balance of payments.[2] Another reason is that this will place food aid on the same financial terms as our general economic assistance. Recipient nations should thereby be encouraged to fully assess the value and cost of food aid to their development

---

[2] For a discussion of this subject, see Warrick E. Elrod, Jr., Monetary Effects of Financing Agricultural Exports. USDA, FAO Rpt. No. 12, Nov., 1963.

programs. The Food for Freedom Act also contains a provision which formalizes the relations between the U.S. Departments of Agriculture and State. The two departments have always cooperated in the administration of food aid, but this provision underscores the fact that foreign policy considerations will continue to determine to some extent the purpose, geographical direction, and, therefore, the volume and composition of food aid. Finally, the authors believe that it is the intention of the new policy to find ways and means of helping these nations improve their trading relations with other countries, so they can earn the foreign exchange with which to purchase our food through commercial channels.

FOOD AND AGRICULTURE ACT

In anticipating the procedural requirements of the 1966 Food for Peace Act, it almost seems as if Congress were clairvoyant in 1965 when it passed the Food and Agriculture Act. This Act gave the Secretary of Agriculture more authority and charged him with more responsibility in the management of land output relations at the margin than he has ever had in the past. For most of the commodities with relevance to this discussion, he has the authority, within limits, to set national allotments and program participation reimbursement levels. Furthermore, he has the authority to attempt to induce farmers to divert acreages voluntarily from specific crop production, even below national allotment levels.

The Secretary of Agriculture can now reduce acreages of many of these crops even more than they are reduced presently. He can also restore to production or cause incentives to be put into effect that would encourage restoration to production of nearly all the cropland now diverted. Because of substitution provisions between wheat and feed grains in the present legislation and because he has authority to establish financial incentives, the Secretary of Agriculture is in a position of critical importance in adjusting both the level of total output and the composition of the output mix. It is a declared intention of domestic policy for commercial agriculture to orient agriculture toward commercial markets and to lessen commodity credit corporation activity as a purchaser and handler of agricultural commodities. Nevertheless, the Commodity Credit Corporation does have the authority to enter commercial domestic markets for some commodities in order to meet national commitments abroad, even though no surplus exists.

DIMENSIONS OF THE FREE WORLD FOOD GAP

In his appearances at congressional hearings for the Food for Peace Act, Secretary Freeman depicted the potential magnitude of the Free World food gap over the next two decades in relation to the availability of U.S. grain in excess of amounts needed for domestic consumption and commercial exports. In estimating the food aid requirements of 66 developing nations it was assumed that food production in these countries would increase 2.6 percent annually, a rate approximating the recent trend in their grain production. The projection of aggregate consumption needs assumes that population will continue to grow almost as rapidly as their food production. Furthermore, the consumption projection recognizes the existing caloric deficiency in the average diet of many of these nations and projects growth in per capita consumption that would meet minimum caloric standards by 1975. Given these assumptions, the physical magnitude of the potential need for food aid is shown in the first column of Table 14.1. The second column represents the amount of feed grains and wheat that could be produced by the United States in excess of its estimated domestic needs and commercial exports if the 60 million acres now diverted from production were reemployed by 1970. Bringing these acres back into production would make available some 69 million metric tons of grain for food aid by 1970, 44 million tons more than would be needed by developing nations in that year. With the expected growth in yields, grain that could be produced for food aid is projected to increase to 76 million tons by 1985. Meanwhile, the food aid requirements of the developing nations are projected to increase from 25 million tons in 1970 to 88 million tons by 1985. Thus, in less than 20 years the food gap of developing nations in the free world

TABLE 14.1. Availability of U.S. grain for food aid and food aid needs to 1985*

Year	Food Aid Needs	Available U.S. Grain Production	Excess of Available Grain Over Need
		(Millions of metric tons)	
1965	18.4	. . .	. . .
1970	25.0	69.0	+44.0
1975	42.0	72.0	+30.0
1980	62.0	74.0	+12.0
1985	88.0	76.0	−12.0

* Source: Food for Peace Hearings before the Committee on Agriculture and Forestry, U.S. Senate, 89th Congress.

could reach such disastrous proportions that the United States would be unable to fill it.

In making these projections, Secretary Freeman was not urging that the United States should make available all the grain it can produce in excess of commercial needs as food aid. Rather his intention was to dramatize the need for developing nations to greatly accelerate growth in their agricultural productivity and, it goes without saying, to curb the growth in their populations. Nevertheless, the projections indicate that there is a near term need for food aid considerably in excess of that given in the past. Under the P.L. 480 program, some 13 million metric tons of food were shipped abroad annually. In less than five years, it is probable that the annual food gap will be twice this much even if developing nations make determined efforts to increase food production. Moreover, there is a qualitative dimension of the food problem that demands the highest priority of concern in the near term.

In the judgment of many observers of the world food and population problem, nutritional deficiencies, particularly that of protein, constitute a more serious threat to the welfare of developing nations than deficiencies in the bulk and caloric content of the diet. This is because infants and small children are vulnerable to death from childhood diseases and to permanent mental and physical retardation, if not disability, when they do not receive a diet with balanced protein. While there is room for optimism that the doleful projections of population growth in the coming decades will not be realized, and hope, too, that with our help developing nations will eventually be able to increase agricultural yields markedly, there is no consolation in this hopeful future for the 171 million children under 6 years of age and 98 million children between the ages of 6 and 14 who at this moment are suffering from serious malnutrition in the developing nations of the free world.[3]

Apart from the inhumanity of this malnutrition, it can have large and lasting effects upon the social and economic development of these nations. Children, particularly infants, comprise a much larger proportion of the population in developing nations than in the United States, even after the postwar surge in its births. Americans, who are by now well acquainted with the personal and social burden of preparing the 30 percent of the population that is less than 15 years of age for a healthy and

---

[3] From *Food for Freedom* Hearings before the Committee on Agriculture, House of Representatives, 89th Congress, p. 194.

productive life, can well appreciate the urgent need of the low-income nations for help in feeding the 40 to 45 percent of their population that are children.

The *World Food Budget* for 1970, a 1964 USDA study that provided much of the data for Secretary Freeman's projections, gives rough and probably too conservative estimates of the quantities and costs of various foods that might fill the free world's nutritional deficit of that year. Excluding Communist Asia, developing nations with an indicated deficit in their average diet would require 16 million tons of wheat, rice, and other grains to fill that year's energy deficit. This is 36 percent more than the annual volume of grain shipped under P.L. 480.[4] To fill the animal protein deficits of these nations either 1.2 million metric tons of fish concentrates or 2.6 million tons of nonfat dry milk would be required. The dry milk requirement for one year is virtually as much as was shipped in the first 12 years of the P.L. 480 program and it is more than eight times the annual volume of all dairy products shipped under the program.

The annual pulse or other protein deficit would require 6.7 million metric tons of dry peas and beans or 3.2 million tons of defatted soygrits. Again, there is an enormous discrepancy between the needs of developing nations and the amounts shipped as food aid in the past. Since the inception of P.L. 480, only 233,000 metric tons of pulses have been shipped abroad. Finally, the fat deficit estimated for 1970 would require 1.5 million tons of vegetable oil. Although substantial quantities of vegetable oil have been shipped under the present program, the volume of need is four times the average of annual shipments in the past.

The *World Food Budget* provides estimates of the cost of filling the food gap by valuing these physical quantities at 1963 U.S. export prices. Table 14.2 is a version of these estimates that illustrates a profile of food aid that would be geared to the nutritional needs of the developing nations. The total physical volume shown is several million tons less than Secretary Freeman's estimate of the developing nations' need for food aid in that year. Among the reasons for the discrepancy is that the *World Food Budget* estimate does not include several nations that might receive concessional shipments even though their average diet meets the study's minimum nutritional standards. Moreover, this estimate of the food gap does not include the

[4] Data taken from: Tables 14 to 17 of the World Food Budget in 1970 and Table 2 for House of Representatives Rpt. No. 1558.

TABLE 14.2.   Quantities and cost of food to fill the free world nutritional deficit of 1970*

Food Item	Quantity	Quantity Profile	Export Value	Value Profile
	(1,000 metric tons)	*(percent)*	*(millions)*	*(percent)*
Wheat	12,019	51.5	$ 781.2	34.3
Rice	673	2.9	67.3	3.0
Other Grain	3,367	14.4	168.3	7.4
Defatted Soygrits	3,174	13.6	428.5	18.8
Nonfat Dry Milk	2,575	11.0	463.5	20.4
Vegetable Oil	1,528	6.5	366.7	16.1
Total	23,336	100.0	$2,275.5	100.0

* Source: World Food Budget for 1970, Table 18.

study's projection of food aid that would have been made under past programs.

Assuming that this would be an economically feasible profile of food aid, it is seen that grain would continue to dominate the physical quantity shipped. But the quantities of other foods would comprise a much larger share of the total volume than in past programs and their total value would exceed that of grain. Which is to say the developing nations will continue to need large quantities of cheap grain to fill their energy requirements, but their need for more expensive foods containing fat and various proteins is relatively greater. The need for animal protein alone would require 20 percent of the budget, and this illustration assumes that it would be possible to ship the large quantities of nonfat dry milk required at the low price of the recent past.

SOCIAL COST CONSIDERATIONS

To inquire into the implications of the export policy choices for American agriculture is to raise broad questions concerning the social cost of food aid. This complex subject has been well discussed in past evaluations of the surplus disposal program (1). A few years ago it was generally agreed that the costs of food aid were but a small fraction of the billions of dollars that were appropriated by Congress for P.L. 480 and other concessional programs. Indeed it was argued that the marginal treasury costs of the concessional shipments might well have been more than offset by the saving in storage costs and by the program's small returns to the nation from recipient countries. The basis for these assertions was simply that the bulk of the program's cost to the nation had been incurred already as a result of the domestic agricultural programs. To put it more bluntly, the surpluses shipped abroad were generally regarded as an embarrassing, if not unwanted, by-product of government programs to support the level of farm income. For this reason, perhaps the most fundamental criticism of the surplus disposal program was that it was a release valve for public pressure that might otherwise result in needed changes in domestic farm programs.

If there was disagreement about the proper remedies, the broad outlines of the so-called American farm problem were generally agreed upon. The costly and unwanted government surpluses were the obvious result of an imbalance between agricultural demand and supply. High support prices coupled with advancing technology were bringing more output to the market than could be cleared at those prices for domestic and foreign consumption, even though exports were subsidized for the difference between domestic and world prices. Thus, consumers incurred the real cost of paying more and consuming less than they would if prices had been at an equilibrium level. And as taxpayers, they were bearing the obvious burden of the surpluses and subsidies.

A less obvious cost was the loss of the economy of goods that could have been produced by the resources that were retained in agriculture to produce the unwanted surpluses. At the same time, because of this resource retention, the income of individual farmers remained depressed even with the forced redistribution of income from other sectors of the economy. In sum, the argument was the consumers, taxpayers, and the farmers themselves were paying the real cost of too many resources being employed in agriculture.

In the few years since the nation was so exercised with this problem the agricultural situation has changed. While agricultural productivity has continued to increase, adjustments in the farm program mechanism have resulted in improved program control of the volume of production. With some 60 million acres diverted from production and a continued decline in farm operator population, farm policy has become less vulnerable to the charge that it retains resources in agriculture that could be better used elsewhere in the economy. Moreover, the nation's recent interest in and understanding of the causes of rural poverty has done much to relieve agricultural policy of this particular onus. Contemporaneously with these developments, the volume of commercial farm exports has grown much more rapidly than thought possible a few years ago, in part because of the demands of former recipients of our commodity assistance. With continued concessional shipments, the government's commodity stocks consequently have been reduced to levels that are politically acceptable, and it is expected that export subsidies on major commodities will continue to diminish over the foreseeable future.

In all, it would appear that agriculture has at last achieved a social equilibrium. After decades of controversy and experimentation, it seems that the current situation is acceptable to farmers, consumers, and taxpayers, if not all economists. The present farm programs may exact taxpayer and social costs, but these costs seem justifiable when we look to the future and consider the nation's food needs and world responsibilities. In context of this social equilibrium, therefore, the distinction between the taxpayer and social costs attributable to the domestic farm program and those to food aid would no longer seem to be so important. The relevant question concerning the expansion of food aid would simply seem to be whether the marginal treasury and social costs of such an expansion are justified by the additional benefits to the recipient nations and ourselves.

AGRICULTURE'S CAPACITY TO RESPOND

When Secretary Freeman considered the capacity of agriculture to expand food aid, he had in mind the 60 million acres presently diverted from production. In Chapter Two, the forecast of agriculture's capacity to produce over the remainder of the century was limited to land currently used and the 60 million acres presently diverted from crop production. However, M. L. Upchurch has stated that possibly an additional 150 million acres of land could be developed for crop production (2). This land could be made available in the longer run by irrigation, drainage, and clearing at estimated total development costs ranging from $30 to $50 billion. R. F. Daly (Chapter Two) and Upchurch have included productivity increases as an important future source of agriculture capacity.

The approximately 60 million acres presently diverted from crop production may be thought of as land potentially available in the short run to meet expanded total agricultural demand. Reference to Table 14.3 indicates the magnitudes of acreages diverted from specified crop production purposes during the period 1956–66. From 1961–66, 54 to 65 million acres of cropland were idled under federal programs annually. In one sense, that is the acreage that society rented from farmers to reduce the magnitude of the surplus problem and to increase farm in-

TABLE 14.3. Cropland diversion: acreage diverted under specified programs annually, 1956–66*

Year	Acreage Reserve	Conservation Reserve	Feed Grain	Wheat	Cotton	Cropland Conversion	Cropland Adjustments	Total†
			(*million acres*)					
1956	12.2	1.4	. . .	. . .	. .	. .	. .	13.6
1957	21.4	6.4	. . .	. . .	. .	. .	. .	27.8
1958	17.2	9.9	. . .	. . .	. .	. .	. .	27.1
1959	. . .	22.5	. . .	. . .	. .	. .	. .	22.5
1960	. . .	28.7	. . .	. . .	. .	. .	. .	28.7
1961	. . .	28.5	25.2	. . .	. .	. .	. .	53.7
1962	. . .	25.8	28.2	10.7	. .	. .	. .	64.7
1963	. . .	24.3	24.5	7.2	. .	0.1	. .	56.1
1964	. . .	17.4	32.4	5.1	0.5‡	0.1	. .	55.5
1965	. . .	14.0	34.8	7.2	1.0‡	0.4	. .	57.4
1966§	. . .	13.3	32.0	8.2	4.7	0.4	2.0	60.6

* Source: USDA.
† Total diverted including acreage devoted to substitute crops.
‡ Not required to be put to conserving uses.
§ Except for conservation reserve, represents enrolled acreage Agr. Stab. and Conserv. Ser., USDA, *Agricultural Statistics 1966*, GPO, p. 541.

comes. The output mix from which this acreage was diverted will have significance when the composition of potential increases in export demand and related costs are discussed.

FOOD AID ALTERNATIVES

GENERAL IMPLICATIONS

A full analysis of the policy question of whether to increase or diminish the flow of our food aid to developing nations would consider the comparative value of food aid to recipients as well as the social costs or saving to ourselves from altering the level of this aid. Concern with the implications of this policy choice for American agriculture focuses attention upon the latter. A rough estimate will be made of the marginal treasury costs of maintaining the existing flow of food and fiber aid by examining the policy alternative of eliminating food aid sales for foreign currencies, barter, and long-term dollar credits. Following this will be an equally rough estimate of the marginal treasury costs of expanding and changing the mix of food aid to fill the free world's nutritional deficit forecasted for 1970.

In justifying this approach to the policy question of food aid, we might venture the opinion that much of the current debate about the value of food aid is motivated by cost considerations. The proponents of expanding food aid as an instrument of our foreign economic policy have been much persuaded by the apparent cost advantages of this aid form. Dollar for dollar an expansion of food aid may not yield as much value as other forms of economic assistance, but the additional taxpayer costs will be partially offset by the saving of diversion payments over the range of expansion until the 60 million diverted acres are brought back into production. Another possible offset against the cost of expanding food aid is the fact that food aid sales for foreign currency help support our diplomatic, military, and commercial activities in recipient nations. Moreover, since these activities are often larger than could be financed by our commercial exports to these nations, currency earned by food aid helps stem the drain upon our balance of payments.

Proponents of food aid expansion might also argue that the marginal social costs would be less than for assistance giving rise to claims against our industrial economy. The capacity of the latter has been strained by domestic and war demands while agriculture not only has excess land capacity but underutilized labor and equipment. Finally, food aid proponents might argue—albeit somewhat irrelevantly to the question of food aid's cost—that an expansion of food aid is politically more feasible than general economic assistance because the public is concerned with the world food problem and because farmers and subsidiary agricultural interests can be counted upon for support.

If these arguments are accepted without reservation, it goes without saying that one would be predisposed to argue that food aid has great value to the recipient nations as well. But, by the same token, some who would question the value of food aid are also motivated by consideration of the internal impacts of expansion. To be more specific, there are reasons for agriculture to be ambivalent about, if not in outright opposition to, expansion of food aid. For one thing, the current social equilibrium may not be so stable that agriculture can ignore the distinction between the costs of food aid and the domestic support programs. In the present land diversion program, agriculture now has an alternative to food aid that is acceptable to the farmers and far less costly for taxpayers: The taxpayer cost of paying the farmer as much for diverting acreage as he would net from the output of those acres is about one-third the cost of producing, processing, and shipping food aid. Notwithstanding the acreage diversion payment offset, therefore, expanded food aid will cost the taxpayers more money. We may call it foreign aid and, indeed, it may be foreign aid as well as aid to our merchant marine and other domestic businesses but in the public mind it may be simply farmer aid. Far from being the release valve for the public pressure to change farm programs—the charge of a few years ago—expanded food aid may be the agent that upsets the social equilibrium and embroils agriculture in further painful program experimentation.

Perhaps this fear is unwarranted, but there are other reasons for a lack of farmer enthusiasm about expanded food aid. In the context of the recent 5 to 6 percent annual growth of farm exports, virtually all of which has been commercial, many farmers—particularly those of the soybean and feed grain-producing areas—may well expect that many of their diverted acres will be called back into production by the growing commercial demand over the next few years. A comparatively modest 3 percent rate of export growth would require, even with continuation of the rapid trend of productivity growth, that most of the 60 million diverted acres be brought back into production by 1975 if prices are to be maintained at present levels. If these acres come back into production in response to the growth of commercial exports, at the very least farmers stand to gain increased freedom from government management and reduced dependence upon taxpayer support.

In contrast, if the diverted acreage is brought back into production sooner because of expanded food aid, farmers may gain little in the way of additional income, because of the loss of the diversion payment, and their dependence upon the taxpayer would be no less and, indeed, would appear to be larger in the eyes of the public. More than this, in a context of growing commercial exports, farmers may stand to lose some good-price years. The critical question involved, in terms of its short-run implications and possibly for its long-run implications as well, is whether expanded food aid would augment or diminish the stability of the nation's food and fiber prices.

Since the value of food aid to recipient nations depends upon its availability to them in times of food crises as well as upon its availability on more than a year-to-year basis for development purposes, it might be argued that expanded food aid commitments would increase the probability of high-price years. But this contingency would seem to be provided for by the present plan of maintaining an "ever normal granary." If in conjunction with the operation of this commodity reserve, the USDA retains some flexibility in meeting food aid commitments—and this flexibility might well be enhanced by a larger total flow of food aid—the result may be greater price stability than would have existed in the absence of expanded food aid. An unexpected burst of foreign commercial demand could be countered almost immediately by a reduction in government inventory and/or a reduced flow of food aid. In contrast, if the acres to be used for this expanded food aid remain out of production, the supply response to an unexpected increase in demand would be delayed and the magnitude of the response would be dependent upon farmers' price expectation that might be perverse.

If expanded food aid can, in fact, lead to greater price stability, there may be an opportunity cost for farmers but, at the same time, a benefit for consumers that would be an offset against the expanded social cost of food aid. However, at least part of the estimated $300 million annual taxpayer cost of the commodity reserve should be measured against this benefit and included in the marginal treasury costs of expanding food aid. Moreover, even if food aid is effective as a price stabilizer, this consumer benefit may be largely negated by the impact of food aid upon the level of food and fiber costs over the near term and possibly in the long run.

If we endeavor to gear the mix of food aid to the nutritional needs of developing nations—and it goes without saying that the value of food aid to their development importantly depends upon this—the marginal treasury costs may be significantly higher than if we return the land to producing its previous mix of goods. For one thing, the program costs status of the available increments of land may result in smaller diversion payment offsets against an altered mix of food aid. More than this, to obtain the proper food mix the prices of certain commodities may have to be bid up with a resulting greater cost to consumers.

Taking a longer view there is the question of how expanding food aid would impact upon the efficiency with which agricultural resources will be utilized over the remainder of the century. Would the trend toward larger and more efficient farms be slowed? Would food aid tend to accelerate or retard the bidding up of land prices to the detriment of investment in productivity-increasing inputs? At this point, it is problematical what, if any, impact food aid might have upon agricultural productivity.

In a content of rapid growth in commercial exports, food aid might act as a price stabilizer and, therefore, as a dampener to speculation in farm land. But even in this event, there remains the question of how price stability might affect the productivity trend.

MINIMAL OR PRESENT LEVEL OF FOOD AID

This section examines the treasury costs and other consequences of a policy choice to maintain the present level of food aid as opposed to the alternative of reducing the volume of food aid to the amounts presently provided for disaster relief and donations while at the same time maintaining the present levels of domestic prices and net farm income.

In 1965, total agricultural exports under specified government programs were $1.452 billion, about average for recent years. All but $280 million of these exports were sales for foreign currency, barter, and long-term dollar credits. This $1.172 billion is the component of programmed exports upon which much of the criticism of food aid has centered. We estimate that discontinuance of these "surplus" shipments would add 15 to 17 million acres to the 60 million acres now diverted from production. Most of these additional acres would be diverted from wheat production. The cost of this additional acreage diversion is roughly estimated to be $354 million. Thus, the resulting saving in the cost of domestic farm programs would be about $818 million if we were to discontinue these exports while maintaining the level of net farm income.

The impact of this $818 million reduction in the program would be felt immediately by shipping and storage businesses, industries processing outputs and supplying inputs to agriculture, and the local communities around which this production occurs. Moreover, the saving to the taxpayer would be less than this amount. About one-fourth ($293 million) of the $1.172 billion is used for U.S. purposes in recipient countries. If these expenses in recipient nations are maintained, the treasury saving would be in the magnitude of $525 million.

This $525 million saving might also be interpreted as the marginal treasury cost of maintaining the present level of concessional food shipments. Thus, total foreign and domestic benefits need only amount to 45 percent of the $1.172 billion to exceed the net treasury costs of providing present levels of food aid.

FILLING THE FREE WORLD NUTRITIONAL GAP

This section attempts to make a rough estimate of the marginal treasury costs of expanding and changing the mix of food aid to fill the free world nutritional gap forecast for 1970. Recalling Table 14.2, the F.O.B. export value of the required quantities of food was estimated to be $2.3 billion. However, this total does not include the treasury costs of ocean transportation and export subsidies. At the same time, it does not take account of the acreage diversion payment offsets. Table 14.4 indicates the additional production in terms of acres and dairy cows required to close the nutritional gap in the various food-deficit regions of the free world. The data were obtained by applying recent average yields and processing conversion rates to the tons of budgeted food requirements shown in Table 14.2.

In Table 14.4 defatted soygrits and soybean oil are joint products. The acreages required for production of the designated quantities of each are shown. The total required for the quantity of oil indicated would yield more than enough grits as a processed by-product. While this is true for the free world total, it isn't necessarily true for each region of the world as shown in Table 14.4. The region made up of India and other South Asia is the only one in which the acreage required to meet vegetable oil deficits through soybean oil production would exceed the acreage required to alleviate vegetable protein deficiencies with soygrits. Because the greater aggregate acreage is indicated to

TABLE 14.4.   Estimated acreages and cow numbers required to produce specified commodities to the free world food gap by regions of the world, 1970

Region	Wheat	Rice	Corn and Other Grains	Soybeans Gilts	Soybeans Oil	Total Acres* (by individual region)	Non-fat Dry Milk
	(1000 acres)					*(1000 cows)*	
Africa	497	11	252	1,228	811	1,571	1,723
India & other South Asia	8,422	180	819	1,321	11,805	21,226	3,890
West Asia	1,544	33	104	442	376	2,057	...
Other East Africa	5,165	110	303	5,447	...	5,578	2,701
Latin America	1,828	39	482	70	51	2,400	55
Free World	17,456	373	1,960	8,508	13,043	32,832	8,369

* Does not consider feed requirement acreages for dairy cows, and includes only the greater acreage requirement for bean oil.

meet oil deficiencies, these acreages are carried across to the compilation of total acres required.

The indicated quantities of nonfat dry milk were converted to thousands of dairy cows, but the conversion of dairy cows to acreage required for additional feed production was not made. Rations fed these cows could vary considerably. For example, tons of hay equivalents per cow in roughage could vary from 1.3 to 5.1, and pounds of grain and other concentrates fed per cow could vary from 1650 to 5290 based on 1965 data, depending upon averages for states of possible location of expanded cow numbers. On the national average, though, a little less than two acres would provide the roughage per cow and approximately five-sixths of an acre of feed grain would produce the concentrate as grain. Thus, for the indicated cow numbers, approximately 23 million more acres might be needed for dairy feed. Not all of this requirement would necessarily come from the same 60 million acres of cropland diverted under present programs. Even so, the total number of acres required for dairy feed and other food items falls short of the 60 million diverted acres.

While the total acreage requirement would seem to pose no problem, changing the mix of food aid is another matter. To fill the animal protein requirement with nonfat dry milk, currently the cheapest source in the customary pattern of American agriculture, our national dairy herd would have to be increased by 50 percent. Because of the sheer magnitude of this requirement and the implied costs to the taxpayer and consumer, it is no small wonder that much attention has been given to the possibility of fortifying grain products with synthesized proteins or substituting other protein sources such as fish concentrates.

A second pressure point concerns the vegetable protein and oil requirements, which is illustrated in Table 14.4 with soybeans. The 13 million acres required for oil implies a 38 percent increase from the present soybean acreage. Because of the rapidly increasing feed demand for soybeans at home and in developed countries abroad, the inducement of this increase could involve substantial increases in price or substantial time for farmers to complete adjustments at present price levels. But other products could be substituted for soybeans as a source of oil and protein in the meanwhile. Peanuts, pulses, cottonseed oil, safflower, lard, tallow, and corn oil are examples of products that might be substituted as market conditions warrant. Moreover, the gross availability of land for soybean production would appear to present no serious problem because of Conservation

Reserve acreage releases, diverted feed grain acreage, and diverted cotton acreage. Similarly, since about half the 60 million acres were diverted from feed grain production, there would be no problem meeting the 2 million acre requirement for corn and other rough grains.

Recalling Table 14.3, only 8.2 million acres are presently diverted from wheat production. Yet the 17.2 million additional acres required for filling the energy gap can probably be found within the 60 million diverted acres. Beyond this level, however, a substantial increase in wheat prices might be necessary to induce the substitution of this grain's production for that of higher value crops.

Because the existing pattern of American agricultural production is not wholly compatible with the needed nutritional mix for the total of the free world's food-deficit regions, foreign and domestic economic policy considerations will necessarily influence the volume and mix of food aid actually offered. For this reason, it is important to consider the nutritional deficiencies of the free world by region. For example, it will be noted in Table 14.4 that West Asia, i.e. the Middle East, and Latin America would require little animal protein but substantial amounts of grain. Other East Asia, i.e. Southeast Asia, shows no vegetable oil deficiency but a very large vegetable protein deficiency.

All of which is to say, if domestic economic considerations or treasury budget constraints lead us to modify our intention of gearing the mix of food aid to needs, the nutritional value of that aid to recipient nations will vary among the regions of the world. Alternatively, in the event it is U.S. policy to limit expanded food aid to particular regions of the free world, it can be seen readily how the mix of food aid would be affected, still assuming that we are governed by the particular nutritional needs of the recipients.

Estimated additional net treasury costs of closing the free world nutritional gap of 1970 are shown in Table 14.5, where costs are estimated roughly to be \$2.4 billion, approximately the same as the F.O.B. export value shown in Table 14.2. In other words, cost additions due to ocean transport charges approximately equal savings from land diversion payments. The marginal government costs of this expansion would approximate \$40 per acre of additional land required as compared to \$33 per acre for maintaining the existing level of food aid. One reason for the increase in per acre cost is that no offset was assumed for value received by the United States for use of counterpart funds.

TABLE 14.5. Cost components and net treasury cost of filling the free world nutritional gap

	Export Value	Ocean* Transportation	Land Diversion Offset	Net Treasury† Cost
	million dollars			
Wheat‡	$ 872.8	$ 94.3	$ 36.9	$ 930.2
Grain‡	209.7	34.5	57.1	187.1
Rice	67.3	8.1	...	74.0
Soybean Grits & Oil	795.2	95.4	205.8	684.8
Nonfat Dry Milk	463.5	55.6	...	519.1
Total	$2,408.5	$287.9	$299.8	$2,395.9

* The extra cost assumed by the Treasury for grain shipped on U.S. ships. The estimates for wheat and grain were taken for the Senate Hearings referred to in Table 14.1. In the remaining commodities it was assumed that ocean transportation costs were 12 percent of export value.

† Includes export subsidy.

‡ Export value for wheat and grain calculated from data provided on page 500 of the Food for Freedom Hearings before the U.S. Senate Committee on Agriculture and Forestry. The values of the remaining commodities are taken from Table 14.2.

The existing level of food aid generates more than enough funds to support diplomatic and other U.S. activities in recipient countries. Another reason for the higher per acre costs is that the diversion payment offsets would not be as large as would apply to acreage presently producing for foreign currency, barter, and long-term dollar credit sales.

In the first place, diversion payments for wheat would apply to only 2.4 million acres of the 17.2 million required. Secondly, relatively small amounts of feed grains are indicated in this mix. Thirdly, the saving in diversion payments for feed grain acreage devoted to additional soybean production is shown smaller by the amount of price support paid to farmers growing soybeans on acres diverted from feed grain acreage. This stems from the assumption that all the additional soybeans would be grown on land diverted from feed grains. Should this not be the case, the land diversion offsets for soybeans would be still smaller. Finally, no diversion offset is shown for nonfat dry milk because the export costs are probably understated and because much of the additional land required to feed the cows probably would not be presently diverted from crop production.

It should be pointed out that Table 14.5 does not include the cost of the existing level of food aid because the food deficit itself was estimated after taking account of existing concessional shipments. Thus, the total government cost of filling the free world food deficit would be in the neighborhood of $3.8 billion annually, or $3.5 billion if current U.S. uses of counterpart funds are taken into account. In passing the amended Food for Peace Bill in 1966, Congress authorized the expenditure of $3.3 billion for this purpose in each of the next two years. This is not to say, of course, that this much will be spent but it indicates the willingness of Congress at that time to consider the possibility of a vigorous expansion of food aid to about 2.5 times the recent level.

SUMMARY AND CONCLUSIONS

It is here reiterated that the authors of this chapter have not intended to make policy recommendations concerning the role and level of food aid. For one thing, it is taken for granted that it will be national policy to encourage commercial exports but the possible conflicts between this goal and that of expanding the concessional component of exports have not been considered. More importantly, the merits of alternative forms of economic assistance to developing nations have not been considered and the question of food aid's value to them has been more or less ignored. Instead, concentration has been upon food aid's impact upon the domestic economy. However, some of the cost estimates presented are appropriate for comparison with estimated benefits from maintaining, decreasing, or increasing levels of food aid. For example, it is significant that the total value of domestic and foreign benefits from the present shipments of commodities for foreign currency, barter, and long-term dollars credits need only exceed 45 percent of the $1.172 billion total taxpayer cost to be greater than their net federal cost.

It is also significant that farm program and other cost offsets tend to diminish with expansion of food aid. Indeed, the offset for U.S. uses of foreign currency does not apply to expansion and if we were to fill the free world food deficit, the per unit farm program offsets would diminish to the point where they would barely cover the additional transportation costs. More than this, while it appears as if the 60 million diverted acres gives the United States more than enough capacity to fill the existing food gap, stresses might appear in the short run if nutrient needs of recipient countries govern the mix of the additional production. In particular, the required amounts of wheat, soybeans, and animal protein may imply higher than estimated social expenditures and commodity prices. Thus, the per unit cost of extending food aid would doubtlessly rise with expansion and would require a higher rate of benefits than is needed to justify the present level of food aid.

At the same time, however, the benefits to recipients from expanded food aid would be higher if the commodity mix is geared to nutritional needs. And the expansion of food aid introduces the possibility of an additional domestic benefit. In context of rapidly growing commercial exports, farm program managers may have greater flexibility in stabilizing domestic prices with their year-to-year choices of the quantities and quality of food aid than they would with land diversion decisions alone. In turn, this could have a beneficial impact upon the long-term efficiency of agricultural production. At this point, these are merely possibilities and in the absence of careful study no judgment is made as to whether these domestic benefits would be an important offset against the additional cost of expanding food aid.

Beyond these cost implications, the authors believe that there are other ideas latent in the chapter that deserve consideration in policy-maker deliberations as to the proper level and role of food aid. It is submitted that past experience with the surplus disposal program may lead to misconceptions, both at home and abroad, about the nature of the choice before us. In the first place, unlike the situation just a few years ago, food aid is no longer needed, even indirectly, to support the level of farm income. Quite apart from the real prospect of continued rapid growth in commercial exports, this objective can be achieved at a small fraction of the cost of extending food aid. What the United States has to offer the world today is not an unwanted surplus that must be disposed of to preserve a political equilibrium at home, but rather a national asset with a *controllable* potential to produce valuable commodities beyond those needed for commercial purposes. In other words, with legislation now in existence. we may choose to conserve this valuable asset until it is fully called into production by commercial demand or we may choose to use the excess potential of this asset now to produce the kinds and quantities of agricultural commodities that developing nations need but cannot afford. If we choose to pursue vigorously the latter course, there should be no misunderstanding on the part of ourselves or the recipient nations that we have done so out of choice, at considerable cost, and for the benefit of the recipient nations.

Secondly, it is submitted that past experience with the P.L. 480 program is not sufficient evidence upon which to judge the impact expanded food aid might have upon recipient nations. If the limits of congressional authorization were reached, the flow of food aid would be more than double the annual shipments of the past. And even this may understate the comparative impact upon developing nations. In the past, shipments have been made to many nations that are no longer suffering from food deficits. Moreover, only a small share of past shipments—i.e. Title II and the donations component of Title III—were specifically administered with the development and nutritional needs of recipients as a governing factor. This is not to denigrate the benefits to recipient nations from the bulk of concessional food and fiber shipments that were disposed of through commercial channels, but an expanded budget devoted to the specific food needs of recipients might have 10 to 20 times the nutritional impact the past program has had in the world's emerging nations.

If benefits on such a scale were to materialize, however, far greater expense and administrative effort in recipient nations would be required than for the surplus disposal program of the past. Indeed, perhaps the most important factor limiting the value of food aid is the ability of recipient nations to distribute it to those who need it—particularly to their malnourished children. Were it not for this obstacle and the implied sacrifice of long-term development from use of their scarce resources to overcome it, the authors would venture the opinion that the United States could do nothing within the next five or six years on a comparable scale and at comparable cost to Americans that would contribute as much to the welfare and future development of these nations than this investment in the health of their human resources.

LITERATURE CITED

1. Menzie, E. L., *et al.* Policy for United States Agricultural Export Surplus Disposal. Tech. Bul. 150, Ariz. Agr. Exp. Sta., Tucson. 1962.
2. Upchurch, M. L. The Capacity of the United States To Supply Food for Developing Countries. In: Alternatives for Balancing World Food Production and Needs. Ames: Iowa State Univ. Press. 1967.

Index